How To
Go To War

Andrew Blick

in association with Democratic Audit

POLITICO'S

First published in Great Britain 2005 by
Politico's Publishing, an imprint of
Methuen Publishing Limited
215 Vauxhall Bridge Road
London SW1V 1EJ

10 9 8 7 6 5 4 3 2 1

A CIP catalogue record for this book is available from the British Library

ISBN 1 84275 131 X

Printed and bound in Great Britain by
Mackays of Chatham

Contents

For Nicola

Foreword

A few weeks before the opening attacks of the Iraq War of 2003, a senoir Cabinet Office official turned to the history books to see how Clement Attlee in 1950, Sir Anthony Eden in 1956, Margaret Thatcher in 1982 and John Major in 1991 had constructed and run a 'war cabinet' for the purposes of fighting the Korean, Suez, Falklands and Gulf wars.[1] For when the British Constitution goes to war, history and precedent *matter*. For this most chilling and serious of state activities relies on the mystery of the ancient royal prerogative of peace and war, unpublished legal opinions by attorneys general and the care and attention that due process – through the full and proper use of collective Cabinet government – brings to it.

Unless and until the UK Parliament passes a War Powers Act, this very British mixture of ancient practice, custom, precedent and Whitehall procedures will remain the pavers of the road to future wars. It was anxiety about the care and attention to due process and collective practice that so worried Lord Butler and his fellow privy counsellors as they inquired into the collection and use of intelligence on weapons of mass destruction in the run-up to the Iraq War.[2] It worries me still.[3]

Should the British state be cranked up for war once more, there is now no doubt about the book to which the top civil servants in the

Cabinet Office's Defence and Overseas Secretariat should turn first. It is Andrew Blick's *How To Go To War*.

Peter Hennessy, FBA
Attlee Professor of Contemporary British History
Queen Mary, University of London
March 2005

Prologue

What to do and what not to do

On 26 July 1956, the Egyptian President, Gamal Abdel Nasser, announced that he was nationalising the Suez Canal Company. In late October, with diplomatic talks still underway at the United Nations, Israel, France and Britain secretly arranged to prevent him through armed intervention. The British Prime Minister at the time was the Conservative, Sir Anthony Eden. His nerves, temper and health were poor, and he was using much medication. He developed an irrational, personal loathing of Nasser, whose regime he was determined to destroy. A domineering premier, Eden was prone to unwelcome intervention in the business of departments. Even though his speciality was foreign affairs, it did him little good over Suez.

Eden kept explicit knowledge of his agreement with France and Israel out of full Cabinet, which itself failed to act as an effective check upon him. Cabinet members may have known more than some of them later gave they impressions they did. The Civil Service was not fully informed of what was intended. After the fact, Eden lied about his plans to the House of Commons. His leadership style could be informal, even chaotic. At least one important meeting with the French was not minuted – on his instructions. The inner group of ministers around him did not have strong links with the full

Cabinet and its membership was fluid. Its objectives were split between political direction and military planning.

It has transpired that a supposedly well-placed secret source, whose information on Nasser's regime helped form Eden's policy, might not even have been based in Egypt. Eden may have failed to take proper account of intelligence assessments which did not fit his existing prejudices, as well as cautions from his senior official, Norman Brook, and from the US President, Dwight D. Eisenhower. Warnings about the economic impact of an action from the Treasury either did not reach him or were ignored. The top lawyer in the Foreign Office advised that an operation of the sort he contemplated had no legal basis. Advance planning did not extend beyond the immediate military action and into the projected period of occupation and reconstruction of a post-Nasser Egypt. Eden resisted a recall of Parliament over the summer of 1956 to discuss the crisis. Labour, the main opposition party, became vehement in its criticism of him. Amongst many others, both the queen and his immediate predecessor as premier, Winston Churchill, were concerned about Eden's actions.

Most importantly for him, Eden's policy failed, abandoned in the face of US opposition, which inspired a sterling crisis. He did not manage to remove Nasser from power or, as he hoped to do, check Soviet influence in the region. His policy was judged unfavourably internationally, damaged relations with the US, severely compromised Britain's status as a world power, and created divisions in the country, his party and the Cabinet. His health worsened further and he resigned as Prime Minister early in 1957, with a ruined reputation. Thereafter, in Whitehall and political folklore, Eden was represented as having conducted himself improperly, with a disastrous outcome. In the words of one author, describing his use of an inner team of ministers, 'Eden's conduct of the Suez crisis was, quite simply, an object lesson in how not to do it'.[1]

In the following work, I describe the domestic, political concerns of democratic war leaders, and how they can deal with them. It takes the form of a manual for the senior figure in a government who seeks personal success and the retention of office, and is willing to manipulate, bend, alter or ignore existing rules and procedures – but wishes to avoid Eden's fate.

In my analysis across different historical periods and varied types of conflict, the countries I have concentrated on are, first, Britain, and second, the United States (US). They are the two great democracies which have waged war the most and the longest in modern times. I give some attention to other nations, too. Comparisons are made between leaders, constitutions, the internal measures taken, and ideological and party political developments. The problems and solutions common to all times and places are ascertained. To conclude, I propose what a Prime Minister in Britain today, faced with the particular form of military alert associated with international terrorism, should do.

All the case studies I have used contain within them, in varying proportions, examples of good and bad practice. It is possible, for instance, that Eden did not get everything wrong and a self-preserving war leader can draw positive lessons from his story. Though not approving of their surreptitious nature, Tony Shaw has found Eden's methods of media management effective on their own terms. Shaw writes,

> *By using the well-established system of unattributable news dissemination heavily loaded in favour of the provider; by capitalizing on the unhealthy intimacy between the press and government in Britain; and by exploiting the British press's overwillingness to censor itself, supported by an arsenal of powerful legal weapons, Anthony Eden's attempts to fashion the press to his liking proved to be remarkably successful.*

Moreover, Shaw argues, 'It is indisputable that during the Suez crisis the BBC's editorial independence was subjected to a most severe test. Bar invoking the reserve powers...which enabled the government to "take over" the corporation in certain circumstances, Eden did everything possible to turn it into his official mouthpiece'.[2]

I have deliberately drawn heavily on the premiership of Tony Blair, for a number of reasons. He is the most controversial British war leader since Eden – indeed, many of the criticisms levelled at the two are similar. His handling of the Iraq War and the War on Terror has made a very special impact on political actors and observers, likely to shape future perceptions and conduct, as Suez did. He has demonstrated an abundance of the techniques available to someone in his position, with a more even balance between successes and self-generated difficulties than Eden. I seek to help make good the frequent lack of historical or international comparison in analysis of Blair's leadership. The deficiency is illustrated by the following example.

Recently, plans to apply 'control orders' – stopping short of imprisonment – to terrorist suspects have attracted much attention and denunciation. But little reference has been made to the mass, full internment programmes, applying variously to foreign nationals and British subjects, of earlier periods, including in both world wars and in Ireland. More recently, executive detention was used under the Conservative Prime Minister, John Major. In 1991, Britain was a member of the international coalition which expelled Iraq from Kuwait. At the time, Nick Cohen has noted, fifty Palestinians present in Britain were detained pending deportation because of suspected 'links to terrorism', and thirty-five Iraqis captured in Britain – supposedly soldiers – were held as prisoners of war in a camp on Salisbury Plain. Decisions were made on a basis of intelligence information which was not publicly revealed, on the grounds that to do so would compromise methods and sources – an argument still employed at present. Normal judicial procedures were not used, with appeals to be made to a security panel of 'three wise men'. For deportees, there was a possibility of torture or execution at the country of destination. Amongst the critics of the practice the Labour MP, David Blunkett, was quoted in the press in January 1991 as saying 'There has got to be a balance between protecting us from terrorist acts and denying human rights in a way that contradicts everything we say as a democratic nation'. Ten years later, as Home Secretary, he faced the dilemma he had described.

The alleged terrorists – who were not all even released immediately after the war – included Abbas Cheblak, 'an advocate of Arab-Israeli rapprochement who had written a sympathetic study of the Jews of Iraq and criticised the invasion of Kuwait'. The campaign to release him was 'organised by the [guest] editor of the *Jewish Quarterly*'. Another internee, Ali el-Saleh, 'a computer salesman from Bedford', seemed to have been detained because 'his wife's sister had married a man whose uncle was [the Palestinian terrorist] Abu Nidal'. Those deemed soldiers were in fact 'engineering and physics students whose scholarships came from the Iraqi military'. Taking into account such evidence, reflecting on the episode a decade later, Cohen concluded, 'the arrests were a PR operation designed to gull a mulish press and public into thinking all was well.'

Here is another illustration of a lesson war leaders can draw from studying the experiences of their counterparts and predecessors. Presentation is important to the maintenance of public support, but servicing its requirements can lead to policies which not only negate other government objectives, such as security, but produce bad publicity in the longer-run. In Cohen's words

A few people did wonder what would have happened if Iraqi hit squads had been in Britain. The legal maxim that it is better for 99 guilty men to go free than for an innocent man to be convicted has its converse: when the forces of law and order waste their time pursuing the innocent, the guilty are free to do what damage they can.

If the use of detention in 1991 was a mere publicity stunt, then it was, as Cohen suggested, a dangerous one. It may have produced pleasing headlines for the Major government, but an attack by genuine terrorists who had been neglected by security agencies certainly would not.[3]

War leaders can learn from their own experiences as well as others'. Eden, since he left office so soon after Suez, had little chance to correct faults, even had he wished to do so. It has been different for Blair. For instance, one recent well-informed article has shown how, taking into account British intelligence failures in Iraq, the secret community has adjusted its approach. In future, findings will be 'tested and re-tested in a more rigorous way ... At every level of the intelligence system ... scepticism will be encouraged'. A number of structural reforms will facilitate the agenda. The Intelligence and Security Committee (ISC), a group of parliamentarians, formally appointed by and reporting to the Prime Minister, will chase its implementation. For the reforms to work, it has been suggested, a number of other changes are necessary, including protection for heads of agencies and chairs of the ISC against 'the difficulties that can arise when ministers are confronted by what they need to know, rather than what they wish to hear'.[4] Partly because of recent wide and intense discussion of how to go to war, Blair's administration has been presented with the opportunity to learn and adapt. To some extent, he has utilised it. He and whoever succeeds him should continue to do so.

This work has only been possible thanks to the help and support of a number of people. I would like to thank Sean Magee and Emma Musgrave of Politico's Publishing for commissioning and producing my second book so soon after publishing my first.

Invaluable advice on content and drafts came at various stages from Robin Blick, Professor Stephen Graubard, Professor Peter Hennessy (who first suggested I write about the Iraq War and the British constitution), Professor George Jones, and Professor Stuart Weir. All interpretations and errors of fact or omission are my own.

While writing this book, I was employed by Democratic Audit, Graham Allen MP, Professor Stephen Graubard, Lord Radice, and writing articles for Craig Hoy at *Whitehall and Westminster World*. All of these experiences helped me learn more about the subject. Sarah Lawrence shared an office with me in the House of Commons.

Finally, I would like to thank my family including Karen Blick, Harry and Kathleen Hitchings, and Nicola Brookbanks.

1   Introduction

War and democracy do not fit together comfortably. The former is associated with centralised leadership, arbitrary executive activity, an enlarged state intervening in society and a need for national consensus. All of these can be anathema to the latter. That is why, for the senior government figure in a country such as Britain, engaging in armed conflict brings with it many complications. A leader seeking out a manual for guidance may require more than is available in official documents. Fortunately, a number of prime ministers and presidents have left on record their accounts of the tasks they undertook, the problems they encountered, and their means of overcoming them. Combined with the views of other observers and commentators they describe how to go to war.

While war and democracy may not appear the most likely partnership, the two are often obliged to coexist, providing ample material for study. An examination of Tony Blair's Labour administration as it participated in the War on Terror and the invasion of Iraq provides a useful starting point. Blair's status as a seasoned war leader has been widely remarked upon. In the words of John Kampfner, 'It is some feat to go to war five times in six years.' The conflicts used to make up the statistic were the air strikes against Iraq of 1998, the Kosovo (1999) and Sierra Leone (2000) conflicts, and the invasions of Afghanistan (2001) and then Iraq (2003).[1] The domestic response to the threat of international terrorism since 11 September 2001 (as distinct from its external manifestations, including the Afghanistan action) has been of even greater long-term internal significance. There have been revealing developments in the way government operates. They include measures introduced in the name of national security, which potentially conflict with liberal values. At the same time, the War on Terror has been presented as being conducted in defence of democracy.

Britain's participation in the invasion of Iraq produced political and constitutional strain of a sort meriting investigation. The policy was challenged in a variety of ways, over its legality, wisdom, whether the government was deceiving the public and if constitutional propriety was being followed. The same controversy led to much material being brought into the public domain, thereby making a thorough examination of events surrounding the war possible. Disagreement over the conflict extended as far as a split in the Labour Party, with two dissenting Cabinet ministers subsequently providing their accounts of events. A number of parliamentary and other investigations took place. The suicide of David Kelly, the Ministry of Defence scientist who was the source for allegations reported by the BBC about the role of No. 10 in the production of a published intelligence-based dossier, led to the Hutton Inquiry. There were many public hearings and submissions involving senior government figures. Before the invasion, Blair referred to strong evidence for the existence of weapons of mass destruction in Iraq, but none were found there. Consequently, intelligence and the way it had been presented were subject to intense scrutiny, prompting the Butler Review. Though – of necessity – not carried out as openly as the Hutton Inquiry, it brought significant revelations into public view. The variety of investigations that occurred additionally cast light upon the conduct of the War on Terror. As Peter Hennessy puts it, 'the Hutton hearings' transcripts and the Butler report are sans pareil. Taken together, they represent a lightning flash of a kind that no historians of government or historians of intelligence have seen before in the UK.'[2]

Observations of recent occurrences in Britain can be tested and enhanced through comparisons with war leaders in other democratic (or semi-democratic) historical periods and countries. They include David Lloyd George, the British Prime Minister in the First World War and Winston Churchill, who held the same post in the Second World War. Premiers in more limited conflicts were Clement Attlee in Korea, Anthony Eden in Suez, Margaret Thatcher in the Falklands and John Major in Kuwait. Since the US has been the scene of a Civil War and participated for sustained periods in both world wars, Abraham Lincoln, Woodrow Wilson and Franklin D. Roosevelt, presidents in the respective conflicts, have been considered.

As well as the total, limited and civil varieties referred to above, war can take other forms. Formal or legal definitions are misleadingly narrow, as demonstrated by the fact that one insurance case held that there was no 'war' in Vietnam. From the perspective of the senior politician, there are common features to a variety of different types of combat and military campaign, regardless of their official categorisation. For that reason attention should be given to approaches taken by government towards terrorism in earlier periods, including the anarchist attacks which occurred internationally from the late nineteenth century, and Irish campaigns. Another form of conflict was the Cold War between the Western and Eastern blocs. The modern state of Israel provides an example of a country subject to constant military alert and the French Fifth Republic was founded out of a crisis triggered by colonialist rebellion.

A consideration of the subjects described above will assist a democratic war leader in approaching the following:

- How to manage government at the highest level and deal with senior members of the administration; and what the functions and powers of a war leader are (Chapter 2)
- How to exercise executive discretion in the face of domestic constitutional restraints and scrutiny, international regulation and the law (Chapter 3)
- How to intervene in society to bring about an effective war effort, ensuring the required machinery of government exists to do so (Chapter 4)
- How to justify a conflict and present it to the public and ruling party; and what the political repercussions can be (Chapter 5)

Military matters and international relations are not the concern of the present work. Neither are the practicalities of intelligence gathering, nor judgements over whether engagement in a war is wise or just. The focus is upon leaders who have already embarked upon a campaign, had one thrust upon them, or have determined to do so in the near future, rather than how to decide whether or not to take such action.

2   War Leaders, Ministers and Courtiers

War is very much the concern of the senior figure in a government
Leaders will have a number of functions and responsibilities in
armed combat; they will be expected to take a close interest in it;
and they will probably wish to

Streamlined, centralised decision-making by small groups of
individuals may be deemed necessary

The powers of prime ministers and presidents can significantly
expand at times of conflict – but the demands upon them are
immense and they may neglect other activities or become
embroiled in political difficulties

There are a variety of means by which British war prime ministers
can exercise control over their administrations, such as manipulation of the Cabinet agenda and the use of patronage. Yet in
Britain, unlike the US, a tradition of collective decision-making
exists. To ignore it entirely may lead to disputes, criticism and
weakened decision-making

War leaders may wish to establish inner 'war cabinets', as well as
advisory units working directly to them; they may rely on small
groups of allies, or even individual aides

Blair, a dynamic leader, pursued an informal, centralised style,
which enabled him to secure his desired policy in Iraq. But

subsequent changes to methods of operation suggest he has accepted some criticisms that official procedures were neglected to an inappropriate extent

'The Position of Number One'

During the First World War, Winston Churchill was demoted from the post of First Lord of the Admiralty, becoming Chancellor of the Duchy of Lancaster, after the military disaster at Gallipoli in 1915, for which he was blamed. Subsequently he left the government altogether, volunteering for military service himself. He later wrote, 'I was ruined for the time being . . . and a supreme enterprise was cast away, through my trying to carry out a major and cardinal operation of war from a subordinate position.' On the other hand, commenting on the job he enjoyed the most, that of Prime Minister, which he came to in the Second World War, Churchill stated, 'In any sphere of action there can be no comparison between the positions of number one and numbers two, three, or four.'[1]

As Churchill's observation suggests, war tends to be very much the concern of the senior figure in any government. Such individuals are likely to exercise tight control over its management. Indeed, there will probably be an expectation that they do so, both from within the administration and in the outside world, including the media. One reason for the tendency is that, since armed combat implies critical consequences for human life, international relations and internal affairs, it ought to be attended to at the highest level. Prime ministers and presidents endeavour to oversee official decision-making and implementation, where once kings rode into battle at the head of their armies. Churchill's personal involvement with the Second World War was such that in 1944 he even sought to observe the

Normandy landings from a navy vessel and then tour the beaches, but was dissuaded.

In a conflict, rapid, purposeful action is required; the dispersal of authority across large groups may waste time on discussions and result in a lack of coordinated action. After becoming Prime Minister late in 1916, David Lloyd George established a small War Cabinet. He noted in his *War Memoirs* that his reason for setting up a group of a lesser size than full Cabinet was 'because with a larger number of people it meant so many men, so many minds; so many minds, so many tongues; so many tongues, so much confusion; so much confusion, so much delay'.[2]

Other motives for the concentration of power include the fact that secrecy is vital; the fewer people made party to plans, the more secure they are. The 1945–51 Labour Prime Minister, Clement Attlee, initially confined knowledge of the British atomic bomb programme to a special committee, since, in his view, certain Cabinet members were untrustworthy. Later in the century, following the invasion of Kuwait, Operation Desert Storm was scheduled to begin against Iraq just before midnight on 16 January 1991. John Major, the British Prime Minister at the time, notes, 'So tight was the security that not even the War Cabinet or close ministerial colleagues were told of the action until the last hours before it began.' Even the Foreign Secretary, Douglas Hurd, 'was informed about an hour before the first bombs fell'.[3]

War leaders may often have to develop new methods to achieve their objectives. The quest for effective central direction of government has involved innovation and reinterpretation of existing rules and arrangements. John Grigg describes the foremost characteristics of Lloyd George, when he was Prime Minister in the First World War, as 'vitality, urgency, improvisation, ideas ranging from the inspired to the foolhardy, ruthlessness, resourcefulness, and an astonishing disregard for convention'.[4] Lloyd George contrasted with the Liberal Prime Minister he supplanted, Herbert Asquith. According to George Cassar, Asquith

> *lacked a sense of adventure and was attracted more by established practice than by innovation. As long as Cabinet business proceeded along lines which he set, he was content to regulate input and, if necessary, to arbitrate between members . . . Asquith did not regard it as part of his duty to resolve issues under discussion or suggest new directions in policy. He relied upon others in the cabinet to provide the dynamism and creative spark.[5]*

War leaders can be in possession of one particular power that, though immense, they will probably never wish to use. The French and US presidents and the British prime minister have personal responsibility for launching nuclear attacks. (Though it has been suggested that a British premier is not able to order but authorise such a strike, providing a safeguard against an unhinged incumbent.) A full-scale conflict of that sort would leave very little for the senior politician concerned to preside over. In the aftermath, an inevitable breakdown of communications would lead to an indefinite period of decentralised government – if any meaningful official authority existed at all. (A similar, though less severe, devolution to regional seats of administration could be expected after a major terrorist attack.)

The enhanced responsibilities associated with conflict mean that the job of leader in such circumstances can be a massively demanding one. Delegation of certain tasks may be required. To concentrate on securing victory and not be distracted by parliamentary duties, under Lloyd George, the Prime Minister's normal function as Leader of the House of Commons was passed to the Conservative War Cabinet member, Andrew Bonar Law, with whom the premier formed an effective partnership. Churchill arrived at a similar arrangement.

Military conflict can distract from other issues. Churchill's overwhelming interest in defence and foreign affairs left less room for domestic matters. As will be shown later, developments at home during the Second World War may have led to his enormous election defeat of 1945. The American Civil War leader, Abraham Lincoln, has been described by Edward S. Corwin as – understandably – devoting 'great attention . . . to the war front' and possessing a 'temperamental indifference to problems of administration'. Consequently, he 'left the leaders of Congress to take counsel respecting needed legislation from the individual members of his Cabinet whose departments were the most immediately concerned', leading to 'unprecedented measures' in the Legal Tender Act of 1862 and the Draft Act of 1863. Corwin concludes, 'The war was fought, in short, by a kind of diarchy.'[6]

If a campaign goes badly, the person at the top is likely to be undermined, or even supplanted. British prime ministers are vulnerable because they are dependent upon a majority in the legislature and mass resignations by Cabinet members would make their positions untenable. In the words of G. W. Jones, 'It might be expected that war raises up prime ministers, like Lloyd George and Churchill, but it has destroyed the careers of as many as it has elevated.'[7] Both Asquith (in 1916) and Neville Chamberlain (in 1940) were forced out during a war. Similarly, on 16 June 1940, the French Prime Minister, Paul Reynaud, attempted to persuade his Cabinet to accept a British proposal for merged sovereignty between the two countries. It was a final attempt on the part of Churchill to ensure continued French belligerency and keep the French navy out of German hands. Reynaud was unsuccessful and resigned, to be replaced by Marshal Philippe Pétain, who arranged surrender to the Germans.

A US president, on the other hand, will normally only have to remain alive to retain office for a full term. Yet of the major war leaders neither Lincoln, who was assassinated, nor Franklin D. Roosevelt, who suffered a long illness during the Second World War, managed that. Woodrow Wilson did not die, but was nevertheless weakened both by poor health (he suffered two strokes) and the failure to implement his plan for a peace settlement following the First World War. Towards the end of his presidency he was virtually inactive.

In addition to the notion of the heroic individual at the head of an administration, the idea of teamwork as essential to success is a potent one. The existence of a powerful leader implies the exclusion of others who might, in more peaceful times, have a larger role. One author, describing Lincoln as 'a solitary genius', writes that he 'came to regard Congress as a more or less necessary nuisance and Cabinet as a usually unnecessary one'.[8] But taken to an extreme, unwillingness to delegate, trust juniors, or tolerate dissent, are weaknesses. Wilson has frequently been portrayed as flawed in such respect. According to Lloyd George, Wilson suffered from 'personal hatreds . . . suspiciousness . . . intolerance of criticism and [a] complete lack of generosity towards men who dared to differ from him'. Associated with his traits, Lloyd George wrote, Wilson was 'vigilantly jealous of all who seemed to dispute or even impinge upon his authority. He would not share or delegate the minutest particle of power.'[9] (There was an exception to the rule, described later.) Harry Truman, who was Franklin D. Roosevelt's final Vice-President and successor, expressed the view in his memoir that 'Roosevelt . . . spent too much time doing the work that should have been delegated to the Cabinet. He was his own Secretary of State nearly all the time he was President. He was his own Secretary of the Treasury. And when it came to the operation of military affairs, he was his own Secretary of War and Secretary of the Navy.'[10]

Where actual or possible armed combat is concerned, there is ample scope and precedent for a British prime minister to – in an administrative sense – lead from the front. The office has never been formally defined and therefore provides its holder with much discretion. Peter Hennessy, in his study of the premiership,[11] has noted how, from the earliest emergence of the role, those who occupied it have been entrusted with functions key to the conduct of war. Robert Walpole, often regarded as the first Prime Minister, was responsible for disposing of the 'secret vote', that is, funds used for espionage purposes (though at the time its main application was for political bribery). Enhancements to the office were partly prompted by the emergence of modern combat. Devolution of monarchical responsibilities to the premier was encouraged by the administrative strains which the Napoleonic wars placed upon George III. It was in the unusual set of circumstances which prevailed immediately after the First World War that the prime minister acquired the power to decide when to request a dissolution. Previously, it had belonged to Cabinet as a whole. From the early stages of their development in the Second World War, atomic weapons were within the prime ministerial, as opposed to Cabinet, ambit.

Conflict, then, has encouraged and permitted augmentations in the roles of premiers. It has had a similar effect upon French and US presidents. Charles de Gaulle's establishment of the French Fifth Republic in 1958 was triggered by a military crisis in the French colony, Algeria. Fearing a putsch in mainland France, the President of the Fourth Republic, René Coty, requested that de Gaulle, then in supposed retirement, form a government. On 28 September, a referendum endorsed the new constitution de Gaulle sought. An alteration to it was similarly approved in 1962. Since then, French presidents, before 1958 invested by parliamentary ballot, have been directly elected by universal suffrage. They are not politically responsible to the legislature. Terms are long – seven years in duration – and sitting presidents can run for office again. Only if convicted of high treason can they be removed. Presidents appoint prime ministers and can dissolve the National Assembly. They are able to take on special powers at times of national emergency.[12]

The description of the president in Article II of the US Constitution, which opens 'The executive power shall be vested in a President of the United States of America', has left much room for interpretation, not least in times of combat. In order to win the Civil War, Lincoln expanded his powers and those of the presidency in general. Presidents take an oath to 'faithfully execute the Office of President of the United States and . . . to the best of my ability preserve, protect and defend the Constitution of the United States'. Lincoln argued that such a duty was a source of power, using it to introduce a variety of emergency measures, considered in Chapter 4. It has been argued that 'in proceeding as he did Lincoln permanently recruited power for the President'.[13]

Another Lincoln innovation was to conflate the part of the US Constitution installing the President as 'Commander in Chief of the Army and Navy of the United States, and of the Militia of the several States, when called into the actual Service of the United States' with that stipulating that he 'shall take Care that the Laws be faithfully executed.' By combining the two, Lincoln created what he termed the 'war power.' He engaged in considerable exercises of presidential authority. They included calling up militia, blockading Southern ports, closing the mail to disloyal publications, and detention without trial. In Lincoln's Constitution, Daniel Farber argues of such 'decisive action' that 'most of his acts were not explicitly authorized by any specific statute. Indeed, a few of his actions were apparently contrary to express statutory language or appeared to violate explicit constitutional commands. Yet charges of a presidential dictatorship were overblown. Lincoln remained very much a democratic leader throughout the war. But he was a democratic leader who often operated without explicit legal sanction.'[14]

Armed conflict continued to enhance the authority of US presidents in the twentieth century. Stephen Graubard writes that the period 'saw the White House become incontestably the most powerful organ of government'. The tendency, he argues, was in large part 'made necessary by the demands of modern war and the security hazards posed by atomic and thermonuclear weapons'.[15]

While British prime ministers have oversight of major appointments within them, the armed forces are formally answerable to the Sovereign. By contrast, the US Constitution makes the President the Commander-in-Chief. But does that stipulation lead to greater direct influence? The US tradition of closer association between politics and the military increases the likelihood of intrigue on the part of senior staff. During the Korean War, the US General Douglas MacArthur developed his own ideas over how the conflict should be fought, which diverged from those of the Democratic President Truman. A fellow leader of the time, Attlee, noted that, as the Korean war escalated,

> There was considerable support in America for an extension of the war. Some people were anxious for a show-down with Russia. MacArthur was a Republican and a possible future candidate for the Presidency, and this, I think, led to insufficient control of his activities. It always seemed strange to me that he had never been called back to America for discussions with the Administration. He had not been in America since before the War. The only time that he met the President was when Mr. Truman himself went to meet him in the East. This appeared to us a curious relationship between Government and a General.[16]

In the spring of 1951, when Truman announced that a ceasefire proposal should be prepared, MacArthur issued an aggressive proclamation of his own. At that point Truman decided to recall MacArthur, despite prescient warnings from his advisers that there would be popular outcry in support of the general.

Individuals and collectives

Of the present functions performed by British prime ministers, a number are particularly relevant to conflict and afford them authority over their administrations. Only premiers can call Cabinet meetings, which ministers are almost invariably obliged to attend. Prime ministers chair Cabinet and are responsible for its agenda. All of these powers are significant, but are subject to constraining political realities. As is shown below, Blair was (in one account) able to resist a discussion of Iraq at one Cabinet (in 2002), but could not possibly expect to avoid it being talked about at all prior to the invasion. There is in Britain a convention of collective government, which a war leader must take into account. According to the doctrine, Cabinet must be given a chance to address major issues. The *Ministerial Code*[17] states that:

> The business of the Cabinet and Ministerial Committees consists in the main of:
>
> a. questions which significantly engage the collective responsibility of the Government because they raise major issues of policy or because they are of critical importance to the public;
>
> b. questions on which there is an unresolved argument between Departments.

War certainly fits into category *a*, and could well be included in *b*. In other words, in theory at least, subjects must be engaged with by Cabinet as a group, whatever the centralising urges of a war leader. But the section of the *Ministerial Code* quoted above simply describes what the main 'business' of Cabinet or its committees is. It does not explain what, precisely, is meant by 'business.' Something could be talked about in Cabinet or a committee, but that does not necessarily mean that the relevant decision need be made there. The Prime Minister does not have to take or abide by a vote when there is disagreement. But the *Ministerial Code* additionally states:

> *The Cabinet is supported by Ministerial Committees . . . [which] support the principle of collective responsibility by ensuring that, even though an important question may never reach the Cabinet itself, the decision will be fully considered and the final judgement will be sufficiently authoritative to ensure that the Government as a whole can be properly expected to accept responsibility for it.*

According to the passage above, then, a 'decision' has to be 'fully considered', in order for any 'final judgement' to become 'sufficiently authoritative' for 'the Government as a whole . . . to accept responsibility for it'. That would seem to imply the same rules apply if an issue reaches the full Cabinet.

There is also a stated expectation that ministers are to be circulated with papers in advance:

> *In all cases the Secretary should be given at least seven days' notice of any business likely to require substantive policy discussion (including business to be raised orally) which a Minister wishes to bring before the Cabinet or a Committee. Memoranda should be circulated in sufficient time to enable Ministers to read and digest them, and to be*

properly briefed. Memoranda for Cabinet and Ministerial Committees should be circulated at least two full working days and a weekend in advance of the meeting at which they are to be discussed.

The *Ministerial Code* cannot practically be strictly adhered to at all times. In the words of Lord (Robin) Butler, talking to the House of Commons Public Administration Select Committee (PASC):

events move much more quickly than they did in the past and the procedures for Cabinet which are in the Ministerial Code, which says that papers should be circulated at least 48 hours before a Cabinet meeting and preferably the weekend before so that Cabinet Ministers can read and absorb them and get briefed on them, becomes increasingly difficult to fulfil.[18]

The tendency referred to by Butler could provide an excuse for a prime minister wishing to exclude the wider Cabinet from deliberation.

As will be shown, it seems such rules were not followed in advance of the Iraq War of 2003. But drawing up and interpreting the *Ministerial Code* is the responsibility of premiers themselves. There is, therefore, neither collective ownership nor independent enforcement of the principle of Cabinet government. In that sense, premiers are participants in a game, but for which they devise the rules and act as umpires. The flexibility thereby afforded to a premier is a great potential source of authority that a war leader can exploit. Yet a prime minister at a time of conflict ought to consider the fact that if ministers feel the convention of Cabinet discussion is not being adhered to, disgruntlement may arise. It is additionally possible that fuller discussion can lead to better decision-making.

A potential political advantage provided to a prime minister by the principle of collective government is that it spreads responsibility for the public advocacy of decisions. It entails, in the words of the *Ministerial Code*, the maintenance of 'a united front when decisions have been reached'. Using their particular advantages vis-à-vis Cabinet, premiers may be able to secure the adoption of a policy – perhaps of a highly controversial nature – but present it as a team effort, even if that is not the reality. The idea of a group of senior politicians purposefully deliberating together over important matters could be considered useful for presentational purposes at times of emergency. Different ministers – who may not even agree with the decision and possibly argued against it in private – can command the support of varied constituencies in Parliament, party and the country at large, broadening the appeal of the action being carried out and making the position of the administration and the premier more secure.

Arguably, collective responsibility should, to some extent, remain a two-sided arrangement, placing requirements on the Prime Minister to engage Cabinet, rather than simply obliging its members to publicly profess agreement with policy. If attention is given only to the 'outward loyalty' aspects, strains can result. In March 2003, an event of constitutional irregularity occurred when Clare Short, the Secretary of State for International Development, appeared openly to criticise the Prime Minister in a BBC interview shortly before the attack on Iraq. In a work published in 2004, Short notes the constitutional theory 'that leading figures in Parliament come together in Cabinet, discuss all contentious issues, thrash out agreement and then are all collectively loyal to the conclusions reached'. But, Short goes on, 'in the Blair government, there is no discussion of this nature ... The term collective responsibility is now being used to demand loyalty to decisions on which Cabinet members were not consulted, let alone that were reached collectively.'[19]

It seems that, in Short's opinion, a decision was taken by Blair in his *coterie* over Iraq which had not been shared with Cabinet. Talks which took place, supposedly carried out on a basis that war was not inevitable, were merely a pretence, she informed the BBC. She complained, 'we have detailed discussions either personally or in the Cabinet and then the spin the next day is: "we're ready for war" . . . I'm worried now that people like me are being told "yes, all this is under consideration", but we're on a different path . . . it looks very worryingly as though we're on a timetable set by the US for their . . . military deadlines.' At one point, responding to a question about Blair's actions, she stated, 'I'm afraid that I think the whole atmosphere of the current situation is deeply reckless; reckless for the world, reckless for the undermining of the UN in this disorderly world . . . reckless with our government, reckless with his own future, position and place in history.' She stated further, 'If there is not UN authority for military action . . . I will not uphold a breach of international law or this undermining of the UN and I will resign from the government.' In fact, she did not leave until 12 May, after the invasion was completed, even though it had no fresh UN authorisation. With some persuasion, she stayed on.

A war leader in the US will not be subject to the same tradition of collective government. Presidents are understood to be more powerful relative to their cabinets. Nevertheless, challenges to their authority, even at times of conflict, have occurred. Truman once wrote, 'Lincoln had a great deal of trouble with his Cabinet because some of them got it into their heads that they, and not the President, were the policy-makers.'[20] Among the prominent characters Lincoln recruited was, in the words of Burton J. Hendrick, his 'most powerful rival for the [Republican Presidential] nomination', William H. Seward. Seward seemed to contemplate the establishment of 'a kind of British cabinet system in place of the one handed down by the fathers'.

In that structure, 'Lincoln was to be sovereign on the British model, while [Seward] was destined Prime Minister. Just as the

British Prime Minister had almost autocratic power in naming the members of the cabinet, so Seward believed that . . . he should select the men who were to form the presidential council.' The new regime 'was to be a Seward administration and . . . the supreme task of saving the Union rested on his shoulders' . In April 1861 Seward wrote to Lincoln stating, 'We are at the end of a month's administration, and yet without a policy, domestic or foreign.' After making a number of proposals, he argued 'whatever policy we adopt there must be an energetic prosecution of it. For this purpose it must be somebody's business to pursue it and direct it incessantly. Either the President must do it himself, and be all the while active in it, or Devolve it on some member of the cabinet. Once adopted, debates on it must end, and all agree and abide. It is not my especial province. But I neither seek to evade nor assume responsibility.' Through the communication, Hendrick suggests, 'Seward in fact demanded . . . that he be made dictator and that the administration elected the previous November be abrogated.' Lincoln was unimpressed.[21]

Franklin D. Roosevelt, as a war leader, had little regard for collective deliberation, favouring bilateral dealings. Truman notes, 'In my eighty-two days as [Roosevelt's] Vice President, only a few Cabinet meetings were held . . . I soon learned that little of real importance was discussed, for Franklin Roosevelt usually had conferences before with individual members of the Cabinet and after the meetings, and it was then that detailed discussions usually took place.'[22] Frances Perkins, who held executive office throughout Roosevelt's presidency, records that 'in the early days, there [were] many cabinet meetings with [a] flavour of full cabinet discussion and expression on matters of policy. But as the years went on, Roosevelt's cabinet administration' came to be characterised by 'a direct relationship between a particular cabinet officer and the President in regard to his special field, with little or no participation or even information from other cabinet members. Certainly almost no "cabinet agreements" were reached.' The tendency was balanced by other characteristics. She goes on, Roosevelt 'administered by the technique of friendship, encouragement, and trust. This method of not giving direct and specific orders to his subordinates released the creative energy of many men. They looked to him for courage, for strength, for mobility of purpose, for the leadership that a democracy must have for its full effectiveness.'[23]

Patronage and Power

Another function of a British prime minister is the selection and removal of ministers and the allocation of their portfolios. While US presidents, given the prevailing separation of powers, do not recruit from the legislature, in Britain, cabinets almost always comprise individuals sitting in one of the two Houses and there is an expectation that the large majority will be from the Commons. That represents a limit on the choice available. In exercising the power of appointment, one objective of a war leader should be to select individuals on a basis of meritocratic, as opposed to political, criteria. During times of conflict, premiers have enjoyed, in some ways, greater leeway in this respect than at other times. In the Second World War, individuals from beyond party politics – such as businessmen – were recruited for their personal credentials. There are various practical factors that must be afforded importance, including the need to sustain support for the administration, possibly on a multi-partisan basis. Potentially effective candidates might have to be passed over. Others who are troublesome, or rivals of the leader, may, out of necessity, be included. Indeed, those who are able are also likely to be ambitious, with their own leadership aspirations. Lloyd George, central to Asquith's government during the First

World War, eventually took over as premier. Similarly, Churchill was made First Lord of the Admiralty in 1939 under Neville Chamberlain, whom he replaced the following year.

The political considerations that must be taken into account where personnel decisions are concerned are indicated by the fact that, in 2003, Blair removed neither Robin Cook, Leader of the House of Commons, nor Short from his Cabinet (indeed, he did his utmost to retain them, short of abandoning the war). Yet both opposed the invasion of Iraq without another UN resolution, indicating such in discussion when the opportunity arose. While Cook resigned of his own volition, Short was kept on, even after publicly criticising the Prime Minister and his policy. Presumably, they were regarded as valuable because of their credentials as representatives, to some extent, of the Labour Left, certainly not Blair's constituency. Departures from Cabinet shortly before the conflict began were probably regarded as undesirable, since they would heighten the controversy surrounding it and be seen as weakening the government. In the summer of 1914, Asquith fought to persuade four individuals unhappy with the war from resigning and was successful in the case of two.

Lloyd George provided a vivid description of the complexities that attended responsibility for the appointment of ministers. He noted that, when forming his administration at the end of 1916, 'Had my hands been free, the men I thought best fitted to assist me in counsel and in the effective organisation of the Nation for war would have been chosen without reference to Party politics', including back-benchers and selections from outside Parliament. Yet, since his base of support in the Commons was uncertain, with many Liberals and Irish Nationalists continuing to favour Asquith, he was forced to balance various cross-party interests as best he could. As well as Conservatives, 'it was a matter of the first national importance to bring the Labour Party into active co-operation with the new Government', in order to ensure the support of workers for the total war effort (though Labour already had a representative in the previous Coalition administration). One Liberal he would have liked to have recruited, he wrote, was 'Mr. Winston Churchill – one of the most remarkable and puzzling enigmas of his time . . . His fertile mind, his undoubted courage, his untiring industry, and his thorough study of the art of war, would have made him a useful member of a War Cabinet.' Unfortunately, nearly all the Conservative ministers 'were unanimous in their resolve that he should not be a member of the Ministry, and most of them made it a condition precedent to their entry into the Government that he should be excluded'. They felt he was indiscreet and unreliable.[24]

Churchill experienced difficulties not dissimilar to Lloyd George's when he became Prime Minister in 1940. The make-up of his first War Cabinet, set up on 11 May 1940, was determined to a large extent by political contingency, rather than the choices he would have made given a blank sheet. It included his predecessor as premier and political opponent for a number of years, Chamberlain. Though he built up a team he was probably happier with over time, Churchill was subject to strong political considerations, such as the need for goodwill from the labour movement, a factor in the presence of Ernest Bevin, the trades union leader, in the government (though Bevin was not without ability).

A war leader may lose one or more ministers at inconvenient times, and they may prove difficult to replace satisfactorily. In late 2004 Blair's Home Secretary, David Blunkett, responsible for coordinating security against terrorism and implementing a large legislative programme partly to that end, left office over a personal scandal. Following the Argentinian invasion of the Falkland Islands in April 1982, Lord (Peter) Carrington, Margaret Thatcher's Foreign Secretary, was, she writes, 'talking about resigning'. She attempted to 'persuade him to stay. I felt that the country needed a Foreign Secretary of his experience and international standing to see us through the crisis.' Yet, she notes, 'there seems always to be a visceral desire that a disaster should be paid for by a scapegoat. There is no doubt that Peter's resignation ultimately made it easier to unite the Party and concentrate on recovering the Falklands.' Along with Carrington, two other senior Foreign Office ministers left. Thatcher records having to convince her Defence Secretary, John Nott, not to go too. She alighted upon Francis Pym as Carrington's successor. Pym, Thatcher writes, was

> *in many ways the quintessential old style Tory: a country gentleman and a soldier, a good tactician, but no strategist. He is a proud pragmatist and an enemy of ideology; the sort of man of whom people used to say that he would be 'just right in a crisis'. I was to have reason to question that judgement. Francis's appointment undoubtedly united the Party. But it heralded serious difficulties for the conduct of the campaign itself.* [25]

There may be a temptation for war leaders to allot additional portfolios to themselves. Churchill's private secretary, John Colville, wrote, 'He mistrusted the Foreign Office whose members he regarded as defeatist and prone to socialism. It was, however, a source of regret to him that he had held every great office except that of Foreign Secretary.' Indeed, 'There were even occasions on which he said to me that he would take over the Foreign Office and run it from 10 Downing Street. No word of this ever reached the corridors across the way, but I think that he seriously considered it.'[26] Though never becoming his own Foreign Secretary, Churchill concentrated much power in his hands, especially over the armed forces, through his taking on the post of Minister of Defence. As he later wrote, 'It was

. . . understood and accepted that I should assume the general direction of the war . . . The key-change which occurred on my taking over was of course the supervision and direction of the Chiefs of Staff Committee by a Minister of Defence with undefined powers. As this Minister was also the Prime Minister, he had all the rights inherent in that office . . . the actual war direction soon settled into a very few hands.'[27]

Cabinet ministers are likely to seek the favour of the person who possesses considerable influence over their prospects. Here is a potential source of authority of which a war leader must be aware. A foreign secretary pleased to have been given that post and happy to remain in it may consequently be more amenable to prime ministerial policy proposals. Yet, as the behaviour of Cook and Short indicates, the power is finite. That is particularly the case when the careers of the individuals concerned are in the descendent. Premiers have to take into account the fact that resentment is likely on the part of someone who has been demoted within Cabinet. Blair cannot have ingratiated himself with Cook when moving him from the post of Foreign Secretary to that of Leader of the House of Commons after the June 2001 General Election.

At least one US war leader has been forced to balance a number of considerations when appointing his Cabinet. Hendrick writes that, at the time of Lincoln's assumption of the presidency, the Republican Party 'was something new – only four years old; and had never before won a national election. Moreover, it was by no means united or composed of sympathetic elements. In fact, hardly any such unit as a Republican Party existed on the day of Lincoln's election.' The position was precarious, then, the ruling party, such as it was, diffuse. Consequently, there was a need to build the best possible government team from all available talent, regardless of particular orientation. Lincoln placed a number of powerful competitors in high office. As Hendrick writes,

> *For a President to appoint a rival for nomination to his cabinet was not unprecedented, but to collect under his wing nearly all the disappointed men whom he had defeated in the [Republican] convention [of 1860] represented a new experiment in party conciliation . . . Lincoln was not one of those Presidents who hesitate to surround themselves with men as strong or stronger than themselves. He deliberately sought the most commanding associates he could find, not at all fearful that they would gain the upper hand, entirely confident of his own ability to control and direct and to retain complete authority in his own hands.*[28]

The British premier's influence over appointments extends to senior positions beyond the Cabinet, taking in the intelligence agencies, the armed forces, the Civil Service, other parts of the public sector, the judiciary, the Anglican Church, and even Regius professorships at Cambridge and Oxford. Prime ministers have oversight of the award of honours, which are distributed extensively for war service, military or civilian. Such authority can, in theory, be used to neutralise opponents (by bringing them 'within the camp'), as well as reward supporters, and establish allies in positions of influence. But it has limitations and brings with it dangers.

In 2004 the Archbishop of Canterbury, Rowan Williams, regardless of the role of No. 10 in his appointment, publicly criticised Blair's approach over the invasion of Iraq, especially the use and presentation of intelligence. Delivering a sermon at St Benet's Church, Cambridge, Williams, who, according to *The Times*, had already 'often made clear that, along with nearly all religious leaders in Britain, he was opposed to the war in Iraq', stated, 'There were things government believed it knew and claimed to know on a privileged basis which, it emerged, were anything but certain. There were things which regional experts and others knew which seemed not to have received attention.' He went on, 'the evidence suggests to many that obedience to a complex truth suffered from a sense of urgency that made attention harder.' *The Times* interpreted him as indicating 'that the Government had, by its behaviour over Iraq, lost its right to obedience from its citizens'.[29]

In another exercise of his influence over personnel, Blair must have had a role in the appointment of the heads of two major inquiries into events associated with the Iraq War. The first, the Hutton Inquiry, was favourable in its findings from the point of view of the government. Next, the Butler Review, though it contained statements which could be construed as portraying the administration in a poor light, was not as direct in its criticisms as Hutton had been towards those it deemed culpable. However, the credibility of both was publicly challenged, with some sections of the media portraying them as serving the purposes of those who had appointed them. In that sense, prime ministerial involvement in the establishment of inquiries, while it might seem useful, can also prove counterproductive.

The Butler Review contained an important warning regarding the dangers to a war leader of the deployment of prime ministerial patronage. When referring to the Joint Intelligence Committee (JIC), the body responsible for producing intelligence assessments for ministers on a basis of the work of the various agencies, it stated, 'We see a strong case for the post of Chairman of the JIC being held by someone with experience of dealing with Ministers in a very senior role, and who is demonstrably beyond influence, and thus probably in his last post.' While being the source of favour can be extremely useful for inducing compliance from ambitious individuals, there is a role for independent counsel. An area where it is particularly necessary is that of intelligence. It is important to prevent, in the words of Butler 'policy imperatives from dominating objective assessment'.[30]

Another prime ministerial authority is over the regulation of and recruitment to the Civil Service. Here lies more potential leverage which can be used effectively by a war leader. It provided Blair, during the various conflicts he engaged in (and throughout his premiership), with a means of exerting greater influence over government. He was served by a large number of special advisers (more than twenty-five), where other Cabinet members were mainly limited to two each. Such aides are appointed on temporary contracts, subject to individual ministerial or prime ministerial patronage. Hence their loyalty is primarily owed to the person they serve, rather than the government as a whole, or indeed the bureaucratic machine. Blair, therefore, had at his disposal a contingent of staff concerned with securing his particular policy objectives and political interests. In addition, he increased the number of permanent civil servants working for him, especially in the field of foreign affairs. But in total, the number of staff working in the departments far exceeds those employed in No. 10.

The Prime Minister often acts as the senior national representative at international summits and engages in bilateral discussions with other world leaders. Such a role can provide a certain freedom of action, with the participant in the negotiation afforded some discretion, able to return with a *fait accompli*. A premier enjoys greater flexibility in circumstances of that sort than, say, a foreign secretary. (Though, given Britain's reduced international circumstances, as compared with its past status as a great imperial power, a prime minister's bargaining position in relation to a country such as the US may not be a strong one.) A prime minister might even enter into an agreement with other parties which – perhaps because it would be likely to provoke dissent – is not fully, explicitly revealed to Cabinet. The premier can honour the commitment through using the other tools of manipulation described in the present chapter. That probably happened when Anthony Eden arranged, with France and Israel, to retake the Suez Canal, which had been nationalised by the Egyptian government, in 1956. Short seems to be of the view that Blair had committed Britain to the US schedule for the invasion of Iraq, without admitting such to Cabinet. The approach can be an effective means of avoiding arguments, damaging resignations and other problems. However, it is hazardous. The action in question might not be a success and the subterfuge can become apparent at an inconvenient moment.

While US presidents are their own heads of state, a wartime prime minister will need to give attention to relations with the monarch. It is understood that the occupant of the throne enjoys, with regard to government, the rights to be consulted, to advise and to warn. Opportunity to exercise them arises at weekly meetings with the premier. Queen Elizabeth II receives the relevant papers (as her successor will), which she reads thoroughly. Prime ministers can, therefore, expect to be examined on detailed aspects of war policy by someone who has dealt with leaders dating back to Churchill; a daunting prospect. Indeed, the Queen possesses more substantial access to sensitive official information and the most senior government member than the chair of a parliamentary select committee would dare to dream of.

In the past, monarchs in the democratic era may have had limited influence (in the form of effectively vetoing a plan) on war leaders. It seems that in 1918, Lloyd George considered the possibility of assuming personal control of the War Office, but was put off the idea by the King, George V, who disliked it. In October 1943 George VI wrote to Churchill expressing extreme reservations about 'Operation Overlord', the plan already agreed between the Allies to land in France. That was not sufficient to stop them. However, as discussed above, when Overlord began, Churchill sought to witness the operation first hand. It was only an intervention from George VI that finally stopped him.

Of the royal prerogatives, most of which have passed in practical terms to ministers, some remain personal to the monarch. First, there is the granting of dissolutions. A war leader seeking an early general election, perhaps to resolve a political crisis, obtain a mandate for an action, or exploit popularity gained from a victory, cannot necessarily assume that one will automatically be granted. The most relevant example of a request for a dissolution being refused comes not from Britain, but South Africa. In 1939 General Hertzog, the Prime Minister, who opposed participation in the Second World War, asked for a dissolution after a parliamentary vote went against him. It was not granted and Hertzog was replaced by General Smuts. Formal South African belligerency against the Axis powers was thereby secured.

The second remaining personal prerogative is to appoint prime ministers. Normally, there will be no doubt as to who should occupy the post, namely the leader of the majority party in the House of Commons. Yet neither Lloyd George nor Churchill fitted that description at the point when they first came to the premiership. The process that resulted in Churchill's selection in 1940 was particularly complicated, in part since there was more than one feasible candidate to succeed Neville Chamberlain. Whether a prime minister might in future be removed on monarchical initiative, perhaps for pursuing a war (or a peace settlement) to the grave detriment of the national interest is a matter for speculation. As discussed, Hertzog was forced out of office.

Since many prime ministerial and other government powers are exercised in the name of the monarch, it is necessary to ensure that plans are in place for the eventuality of the incumbent being killed, incapacitated, or detained. Other countries have detailed stipulations for such an outcome. The Swedish 'Instrument of Government' states that 'If the Realm is at war, the Head of State should accompany the Government. Should he find himself in occupied territory or separated from the Government, he shall be deemed to be precluded from carrying out his duties as Head of State.' In Britain, similar concerns influenced the drafting of the Civil Contingencies Act 2004. It makes provision for central government to issue immediate legislation in an emergency. Regulations are to be formally introduced – in the form of orders in council – by the monarch, but if that is difficult a senior minister or the Prime Minister can do so.

In fact, whatever else happens, it is extremely unlikely that a vacation of the post of formal head of state, from which other authority flows, will come about. The succession takes place instantly. It follows primarily an hereditary course, though a Sovereign may not be and cannot marry a Roman Catholic and must be in communion with the Church of England. There are 37 immediate candidates in line and more could be found if necessary. Where the individual concerned is a minor, infirm of body or mind, or is unavailable (perhaps held prisoner), the Regency Act 1937 comes into play. At least three of the Sovereign's spouse, the Lord Chancellor, the Speaker of the House of Commons, the Lord Chief Justice and the Master of the Rolls can make a declaration of incapacity. If unwell or intending to be absent from the realm, the Sovereign can, by Letters Patent under the Great Seal, appoint Councillors of State (who will be the monarch's husband or wife, if there is one; and the four individuals next in line for the succession, or if there are less than that number, as many as there are) to exercise royal functions, excluding dissolving Parliament or bestowing honours. It should therefore be possible even in extreme circumstances to arrange for orders in council, since there are around four hundred members of the Privy Council and the only clear quorum is that the monarch (or proxy) is present to preside.

War Cabinets, Advisory Units and Aides

Armed combat has encouraged the streamlining of government, with the formation of smaller 'War Cabinets', which in Britain can arguably be traced to a 'Standing Council for War' set up in the 1620s. In 1889 the Hartington Commission recommended structural changes to be implemented for times of combat. It was only after poor administrative performance in the Boer War at the turn of the twentieth century that the Committee of Imperial Defence was formed in 1904. Lloyd George established a War Cabinet, charged with oversight of the conduct of the conflict. A small body, of the War Cabinet's five initial members Lloyd George was the only Liberal, with three Conservatives and one Labour representative. When asked by a delegation of Labour leaders if they would be 'dictators', he records replying, 'What is a Government for except to dictate?'

The War Cabinet was serviced by a newly established secretariat. Previously, the directing committee of British government had not been served by such a body. The first secretary to the War Cabinet was Sir Maurice Hankey. He took on the task of recording decisions and then communicating them to the government departments concerned. The development amounted to bureaucratic revolution. Before then, the only account of Cabinet discussions was contained in the letter the Prime Minister wrote to the King. Lloyd George noted, 'I have no recollection of Sir Henry Campbell Bannerman or Mr. Asquith ever making a note of the conclusions arrived at, except in very exceptional cases.' As a result, 'now and again there was a good deal of doubt as to what the Cabinet had actually determined on some particular issue.'[31]

The exact make-up of a War Cabinet requires particular attention. Both Lloyd George and Churchill balanced different parties within them. It may be necessary to exclude certain individuals, even if they are senior in the government or allies of the leader. On 6 April 1982, with Argentina occupying the Falkland Islands, Thatcher told her Cabinet that she was setting up OD (SA) [South Atlantic], a sub-body of the Cabinet Overseas and Defence Committee, 'which became known to the outside world as "the War Cabinet"'. In constructing it, she was influenced by an audience with Harold Macmillan, the former Conservative premier. Thatcher records

> *His main recommendation was to keep the Treasury – that is, Geoffrey Howe [an ally of the Prime Minister] – off the main committee in charge of the campaign, the diplomacy and the aftermath. This was a wise course, but understandably Geoffrey was upset. Even so I never regretted following Harold Macmillan's advice. We were never tempted to compromise the security of our forces for financial reasons. Everything we did was governed by military necessity.*[32]

As Thatcher's remark suggests, whether or not an inner group is officially called a 'War Cabinet', it is likely to become labelled as such, not only in Britain but elsewhere. Truman once described how, during the Korean War, he convened a body 'they called the war cabinet; I never called it that, but that's what the papers called it'.[33]

Colin Seymour-Ure, in his study of the subject, provides further counsel to a war leader, writing

> *two dangers facing a War Cabinet are those of tunnel vision and of the undue influence of military or technical considerations. The full Cabinet, best suited in principle to relate the problems of the war to the Government's other problems and goals, risks finding itself flanked by a War Cabinet to close to the war and by a Parliament which is too far way and too excitable.*

Seymour-Ure concludes that, of the bodies set up for the Korean, Suez and Falklands conflicts, the most effective was the first of the three. It was 'the Committee which was already an established part of the machinery of government, with a fixed membership.'[34]

In a sense, Lloyd George's innovation, which developed into the Cabinet Office, though it helped him coordinate his administration, may have entrenched the principle of collective decision-making, through creating the machinery to put it into practice. The creation of new structures working directly to a war leader, rather than a Cabinet body, may be helpful. They can be deployed for a variety of purposes, including policy development, administrative organisation and furthering the political interests of the war leader. In addition to the Cabinet secretariat, Lloyd George established a team attached individually to him, comprising his personal appointees. The Prime Minister's Secretariat, formed at the end of 1916, soon became known as the 'Garden Suburb' because it was housed in huts on the lawn in the Downing Street garden. The initial complement of staff was five, with members given particular policy areas to cover. John Turner argues that the Garden Suburb was believed necessary because 'The political debate of the first two years of the war, stimulated by Lloyd George and his political allies of the moment, had thrown up a Platonic ideal of the wartime Prime Minister as omniscient dictator. Since this had been accompanied by the demand, met in abundance, for more government exercised through bevies of sub-dictators, it was especially necessary to provide the means of omniscience.' Yet, Turner goes on, 'The Garden Suburb, consisting of five junior men without executive responsibility and with only clerks and typists to assist them, could do little to maintain the comprehensive and continuous oversight of government demanded by this presidential concept of war-leadership.' In fact, 'The real task, as seen from Lloyd George's point of view, was to strengthen the Prime Minister's position in an environment which . . . was . . . subject to the risks of parliamentary politics.'[35]

The Second World War, too, saw the establishment in Britain of a body exclusive to the premier. In October 1939, as First Lord of the Admiralty, Churchill asked his friend, the physicist Professor Frederick Lindemann (known as 'the Prof'), to set up a staff for the collection and coordination of statistics as well as providing broader counsel. When Churchill became Prime Minister, he took it with him and the Prime Minister's Statistical Section was formed. In total, the team numbered around twenty, roughly six economists, one scientific officer, a career official with economic training, six 'computers', two or three clerical workers and four chartists employed drawing diagrams. Contact was maintained with nearly every government department. The section's submissions, on Churchill's insistence, were kept as short as possible, so that he had time to read them. Donald MacDougall, a member, noted, 'The Section was . . . much more than a purely statistical one. It was concerned not merely with the collection and presentation of statistics but with the conclusions to be drawn from them, and it also made frequent recommendations on general economic policy.' As MacDougall states, 'it was essentially personal to the Prime Minister;

it worked continuously for him; it had some idea of what was in his mind; it knew the sort of thing he wanted to know and how he liked to have it presented; its loyalty was to him and to no one else.'[36]

Similar parallel developments occurred in the US. Franklin D. Roosevelt was the originator of the large presidential staff and support structure which exists today. Initially, a US head of state wishing to obtain assistance funded it personally (George Washington paid his nephew $300 a year to help with correspondence). The first appropriation – for one private secretary – was not made until 1857. In 1929 two more were added, along with an administrative assistant. Then, in 1936, Roosevelt charged Louis Brownlow, chair of the Public Administration Committee of the Social Science Research Council, with examining possible means of improving the effectiveness of the presidency. According to one author, 'Brownlow wanted to go significantly beyond the concept of the president as a business manager to the doctrine of administrative leadership. That is, the president's role should become a creative one in which he would be responsible for the ends of administration as well as the means . . . The intent was to establish institutional staff agencies to handle the routine of day-to-day operations so the president would be free to devote his major attention to the future direction of government programs.'[37]

Brownlow's committee reported the following year. Concluding that 'the president needs help' it argued that 'His immediate staff assistance is entirely inadequate.' There was a need to recruit individuals who, Brownlow argued, 'should be men in whom the president has personal confidence'. Roosevelt signed Executive Order 8248 on 8 September 1939, activating the Executive Office of the President (EOP). More substantial than the body the Brownlow report seemed to propose, initially it comprised five units, including the Bureau of the Budget, previously part of the Treasury

Department, and the White House Office (WHO). The order stated, 'There should be in that Office in the event of a national emergency or threat of a national emergency such an office for emergency management as the President shall determine.' In 1940, the Office for Emergency Management was set up, providing the President with the counsel of a wide variety of experts for the organisation of rearmament. Roosevelt's innovation, then, occurred with the threat of war and the need for national mobilisation in mind, and was used extensively to that end. The EOP – retained by Roosevelt's successor, Truman – still exists today. The number of *de facto* EOP staff rose considerably over time, even to exceed five thousand.[38]

Prime ministers may wish to keep around them informal collections of allies, whether officially employed or otherwise. It means that they can have individuals they trust close at hand, to provide the counsel and support that may not be available through the more regular channels. As is discussed below, Blair seemed to find such an entity useful in 2003. Throughout his ministerial career, Lloyd George was disposed towards operating within a coterie which he took with him to Downing Street. Once installed at the White House, in addition to his Cabinet, Roosevelt surrounded himself with a variety of counsellors including experts, financiers, trades unionists and academics, which the press came to label his 'brains trust'. Churchill, too, drew upon the support of a variety of allies, including the aforementioned Lindemann. However, it is advisable consciously to avoid overdependence on such groups. It is likely to attract criticism for 'cronyism' and may lead to policy formation based on too narrow an outlook. While Churchill had a personal court, 'He always retained unswerving independence of thought' and resisted being 'swayed by the views of even his most intimate counsellors. Many people made the mistake of thinking that somebody . . . for whom the Prime Minister had the utmost respect and affection, would be able to "get something through".'[39]

A leader may find one individual aide particularly useful. But there is a danger of excessive reliance on a single assistant. It may lead to poor decision-making, cause resentment among those who feel excluded and attract unwanted media interest. For nearly all of his presidency, Wilson was served by 'Colonel' Edward Mandell House, once described as 'Woodrow Wilson's other self'. For six years House had the use of two rooms in the White House. His status was achieved without holding formal office. It has been written that 'The history of America between 1912–1920 is the history of their friendship . . . never before in the history of our country [the US] were there two men holding in their hands simultaneously the reins of government.'[40]

Philip Bobbitt describes House as becoming

> *the most famous American in the world . . . excepting only his ally and friend Woodrow Wilson. This fame was the result of a friendship unique in twentieth century American political history, for Wilson had devolved on the silent and mysterious Colonel the extensive powers of the U.S. presidency . . . House was often sent on missions to foreign governments though he was given no precise instructions save the president's assurance that he knew House would 'do the right thing'. House bypassed the Department of State entirely and communicated directly with Wilson by a private secret code. Indeed the two men seemed always to communicate with one another in a kind of mutual but exclusive sympathy.*[41]

Lloyd George, who observed the two during the Versailles Treaty negotiations, writes that 'House was about the only man that Wilson really trusted amongst his associates and counsellors. He gave him that abnormal measure of confidence because House very adroitly gave Wilson the impression that the advice he gave was not his own but Wilson's idea.'[42] He appears to have been instrumental in bringing about US belligerence on the British and French side in the First World War.

House did not seek public attention, but it found him. According to one study of his relationship with the President, 'He studiously avoided newspaper interviews . . . House was promptly dubbed a silent man of mystery. Scores of articles speculated about his activities. His avoidance of the press resulted, if anything, in even more publicity than he would have got had he deliberately courted it. The brashest press agent would shrink from ascribing to any client the pervasive powers which the puzzled journalists ascribed to the modest Colonel.'[43]

The ultimate failure of Wilson's First World War policy was associated with his dependence upon House and the development of a certain autonomy on the part of the latter. Wilson took no member of the Senate with him to the peace conference at Paris in 1919. Given, in the words of John Cooper, 'The Senate's role in treaty-making – particularly the requirement of consent by a two-thirds majority in order to complete the process of ratification' that may have been a mistake. Further, he brought no Republicans, but was accompanied by House. As Cooper puts it, Wilson 'may have missed a bet. During the Civil War, Abraham Lincoln had preferred to have his main rivals and critics in his cabinet where he could keep an eye on them. Wilson might have done well to follow that example.'[44] During the peace negotiations, there was a dramatic and final break between President and aide. It seems that Wilson felt House to have in some way exceeded his remit when acting on the President's behalf. In Bobbitt's words, Wilson had 'lost the one political adviser capable of steering him through the system' and 'Without his benign Mephistopheles, Wilson was returned to his Faustian study.'[45]

Wilson suffered a stroke during his campaign for public acceptance of the treaty. Increasingly, in place of House, he came under the influence of his second wife. His health never recovered and Senate ratification was not secured, meaning that the US did not join the League of Nations, the very organisation that Wilson had fought to establish.

Perhaps a model for the more effective use of a single aide is provided by Harry Hopkins, who was a favourite of Franklin D. Roosevelt, serving in various capacities through the latter's presidency. During the war, Hopkins lived in the White House and acted as 'a channel of communication between the President and various agencies of the Administration, notably the War Department, and the ready means of informal contact with foreign dignitaries'. He performed many other very personal functions for Roosevelt and represented him on crucial foreign missions, including meetings with Churchill and Joseph Stalin. Alluding approvingly to his eagerness to proceed with business, Churchill once joked that Hopkins would be granted a peerage in Britain, with the title 'Lord Root of the Matter'. In the war, Hopkins achieved significance – arguably, in some cases, usurping Cabinet members – despite having no legally legitimate authority (though he was brought on to the White House payroll as 'special assistant to the President' in 1942), or even his own desk. Understandably, jealousy and suspicion were provoked. Robert E. Sherwood, Hopkins's biographer, notes

> he was generally regarded as a sinister figure, a backstairs intriguer, an Iowan combination of Machiavelli, Svengali and Rasputin. Hostility toward him was by no means limited to those who hated Franklin Delano Roosevelt. There were many of Roosevelt's most loyal friends and associates, in and out of the Cabinet, who disliked Hopkins intensely and resented the extraordinary position of

*influence and authority which he held. He was unquestionably a
political liability to Roosevelt, a convenient target for all manner of
attacks directed at the President himself, and many people wondered
why Roosevelt kept him around.*

But, Sherwood argues, 'Hopkins never made the mistake of Colonel
Edward M. House, which caused the fatal breach with Wilson, of
assuming he knew the President's mind better than the President
did.'[46]

Blair's Leadership and the Iraq War

Tony Blair became Britain's most experienced war Prime Minister
since Churchill, engaging variously in air strikes, interventions,
invasions and the War on Terror. His style was that of dynamic
leader even when he was in opposition. Making use of a relatively
large team of aides, he played an extensive role in the cross-
departmental business of government. In relation to Iraq, Blair's
technique for managing Cabinet seems to have entailed permitting
its members to talk about what was surely a potentially controversial
issue – although in one account preventing them from doing so at an
important point – also breaking it into small groups for security
briefings and utilising bilateral discussions. There were not, however,
papers provided for Cabinet gatherings, which were, under Blair,
historically short, with the circulated minutes brief. The formal sub-
committee machinery was not used. One minister claims to have
encountered attempts to prevent her from talking to an intelligence
agency. Through machinery of government changes, Blair shifted
oversight of information provided by the 'secret' community – the
contribution of which is vital to any military action – away from the
Cabinet collective and towards a smaller inner group.

Blair was a clear advocate of a powerful premiership, especially where international conflict was concerned. He told the House of Commons Liaison Committee in July 2002 that

> *I make no apology for having a strong centre. I think you need a strong centre particularly . . . in relation to foreign policy and security issues [as well as public service reform], I think . . . that the simple fact of the matter is that in today's world there is a lot more that needs to be done at prime ministerial level. You need . . . a stronger centre.*

In opposition Blair used a team of personal aides who accompanied him into office. Once he was installed at No. 10, a growth in the staff attached to the Prime Minister's Office, as compared with previous administrations, occurred. The most rapid expansion was in politically appointed special advisers (from a figure of around six or seven under Major, to more than twenty-five). Further, there were extra seconded permanent civil servants, working in the Private Office, concerned with foreign affairs. As Blair put it to the Liaison Committee:

> *in relation to foreign policy . . . we have changed and brought in, for example, Sir Stephen Wall, and Sir David Manning who are now my advisers there. That has expanded from where we were before. When I first came to office John Holmes . . . was literally handling all foreign policy matters, all European matters, all defence and security matters and Northern Ireland. It just is not possible to do the job effectively with that much pressure being placed on one person.*[47]

His approach had implications for his dealings with Cabinet ministers and the extent to which he engaged them in the decision to invade Iraq. Robin Cook, Foreign Secretary from 1997–2001,

41

thereafter Leader of the House of Commons and Lord President of the Council, resigned from the Cabinet before it began, since an additional UN Resolution authorising action had not been obtained. Cook wrote in a 2003 book, 'Tony does not regard the Cabinet as a place for decisions.' In March 2002, when reservations were expressed over Iraq at a Cabinet meeting, 'Rather than attempt to sum up the discussion of this supreme body of collective government, he responded as if he was replying to a question and answer session from a party branch.'[48]

But, in a June 2003 appearance before the Commons Foreign Affairs Committee (FAC), Cook said that 'members of the Cabinet did not express anxiety about the drift to military action. I would regularly comment on it. Clare [Short, the Secretary of State for International Development] would sometimes join in those discussions. I would quite often join the discussions. Other than that I do not recall anybody consistently questioning the drift to military action.' He was of the view that

> on the question of Iraq you could not have hoped for fuller opportunities to discuss in Cabinet the matter. We discussed it in Cabinet more than any other issues, probably more than the other issues added together in the six months between September 2002 and March 2003 . . . it would be perfectly reasonable for the Prime Minister to conclude that . . . the Cabinet was with him.[49]

Yet Short felt that the discussions which took place were unsatisfactory. Her view of Cabinet meetings under Blair, which lasted, on average 'something under an hour' with 'lean' minutes produced, was unfavourable. She told FAC that, on occasion, before the Cabinet, members were 'asked if you want to raise anything'. She requested a discussion of Iraq in September 2002, but the Prime

Minister 'said that he did not want it raised in the Cabinet and he would see me personally'. What she described as 'The first proper open discussion' took place in October, 'when members of the Cabinet just gave their opinions about the whole situation in the Middle East'. (Though, in her book, she referred to a 'long and full discussion on Iraq at Cabinet' in September, and a refusal in July.)[50] From then on, debate took place most weeks, often instigated by Short, but, she said, 'it was what I call "guided discussion". It was, "So what's the latest?"' By that time, there was a 'compliant atmosphere in the Cabinet and it was clearer and clearer where things were going and there was a kind of loyalty'.

At the meetings, Short recounted, 'there were no papers'. Therefore, rather than 'a thorough investigation of an options-type discussion' there were merely 'kind of updates, "Where is everything?", and then often a, "Yes, I'm very hopeful we will get a second Resolution" type of assurance'. In place of 'a thorough kind of collective decision-making' there was a 'kind of giving consent . . . by not objecting. The Prime Minister would ask the Foreign Secretary and others to update on what is going on and then he gives his own conclusion as to where things are.' As war began to appear inevitable, Short noted, 'it was arranged at one point that small groupings of the Cabinet would go for briefings with the Chair of the Joint Intelligence Committee, and we went in groups of two or three.'

As the invasion drew closer, Short said, 'the Defence and Overseas Policy Committee never met. There was never a paper . . . before any Cabinet committee or any meeting and it was all done . . . verbally.' The tendency signified, in her view, 'a collapse of normal British procedures for decision-making'. Short was of the opinion that, consequently, the government made mistakes. 'I think some of the poor quality goes with the collapse in the proper decision-making processes . . . these are extremely serious matters for our government

43

system.' She claimed, 'after September/October' 2002, there was an attempt by No. 10 to block her from discussing Iraq with the Secret Intelligence Service (SIS, commonly known as MI6), whom she often dealt with. When she protested directly to the Prime Minister, she was allowed to see them.[51] In 2004, Short wrote, 'I ask myself now, why the attempt to restrict access? I think it reflects the fact that Tony Blair and his entourage were running the policy in a very informal and personal way and wanted to keep knowledge to themselves in order to keep control.'[52]

The Butler Review of intelligence on weapons of mass destruction presented a picture similar to Short's. (Butler, as a former Cabinet Secretary under three premiers, was well qualified to comment on prime ministerial management methods.)

> *In the year before the war, the Cabinet discussed policy towards Iraq as a specific agenda item 24 times. It also arose in the course of discussions on other business. Cabinet members were offered and many received briefings on the intelligence picture on Iraq. There was therefore no lack of discussion on Iraq; and we have been informed that it was substantive.*

But, 'The Ministerial Committee on Defence and Overseas Policy did not meet.'

A smaller entity, including Short in its number, was set up, but only, it seems, when the war had already begun – in other words, when the decision had been made and implemented. In July 2003 Blair told the Commons of the existence, 'during the course of the conflict, [of] an ad hoc group of Ministers, which I chaired'. The group 'met 28 times'. Its members were 'the Deputy Prime Minister, the Chancellor of the Exchequer, the Secretary of State for Foreign and Commonwealth Affairs, the Home Secretary, the Secretary of

State for Environment, Food and Rural Affairs, the Secretary of State for International Development, the Leader of the House of Commons, the Secretary of State for Defence, and the Attorney General'.[53]

Under Blair, Butler found, there were structural developments to the intelligence machinery which served to favour prime ministerial rule as opposed to Cabinet deliberation. The Review referred to 'Two changes' with 'implications for the application of intelligence to collective ministerial decision-making'. First, there was 'the splitting of the Cabinet Secretary's responsibilities through the creation of the post of Security and Intelligence Coordinator'. The arrangement enabled the latter 'to devote the majority of his time to security and intelligence issues in a way that the Cabinet Secretary . . . could not'. The change was prompted in particular by the 11 September 2001 attacks. Butler observed that, as a consequence,

> *the Cabinet Secretary is no longer so directly involved in the chain through which intelligence reaches the Prime Minister. It follows that the Cabinet Secretary, who attends the Cabinet and maintains the machinery to support their decision-making, is less directly involved . . . in advising the Prime Minister on security and intelligence issues. By the same token, the Security and Intelligence Co-ordinator does not attend Cabinet and is not part of the Cabinet Secretariat supporting Cabinet Ministers in discharging their collective responsibilities in defence and overseas policy matters.*

Second, 'two key posts at the top of the Cabinet Secretariat, those of the Head of the Defence and Overseas Secretariat and Head of the European Affairs Secretariat, were combined with the posts of the Prime Minister's advisers on Foreign Affairs and on European Affairs respectively.' The effect was to 'weight their responsibility to the

Prime Minister more heavily than their responsibility through the Cabinet Secretary to the Cabinet as a whole'. Butler described this as 'a shift which acts to concentrate detailed knowledge and effective decision-making in fewer minds at the top'.

If not with Cabinet, where did power reside? Butler referred to the fact that 'over the period from April 2002 to the start of military action, some 25 meetings attended by the small number of key Ministers, officials and military officers most closely involved provided the framework of discussion and decision-making within Government'. This group seems to have been Blair's inner team for the Iraq War. When asked whether the body described was a 'proper Cabinet committee', a well-placed source told Peter Hennessy, 'It's pretty damn close to it. It met pretty well daily at 8:30 with a fixed membership and prepared papers. If it had been called a Cabinet committee it would not have been any different.'[54]

Short, more dramatically, told FAC of a 'close entourage' around Blair, comprising three special advisers: Alastair Campbell, Jonathan Powell and Baroness (Sally) Morgan, and a career official, Sir David Manning. In Short's words, 'That was the team, they were the ones who moved together all the time. They attended the daily "War Cabinet". That was the in group, that was the group that was in charge of policy.' Short felt that the Foreign Secretary, Jack Straw, who might be expected to have a considerable interest in the matters under consideration, was compliant in government by clique. As she put it, Straw 'would have a close relationship with the Prime Minister and the entourage, but I think the decisions were being made by the Prime Minister and the entourage and the Foreign Secretary was helpful. He went along with those decisions.'

Regarding Short's suggestion that there was an 'in group' surrounding the Prime Minister, excluding Cabinet members, of which he was a part, Campbell told the FAC, 'I was at a huge number of meetings with the Prime Minister during the Iraq conflict, and before and since.' As to whether decisions were taken when ministers were not present, Campbell said, 'It depends what sort of decisions you mean.' Were it to relate to which television programme Blair should appear on, or which day of the week he would meet President Bush, 'that is the sort of decision we might take in that group'. But, 'If you are talking about a decision about whether the Prime Minister was going to commit British forces into action, the idea something like that is going to be taken without full consultation of his ministerial colleagues in the Cabinet is nonsense.'[55]

Blair's team of aides seems to have used particularly informal working methods. When appearing before the Hutton Inquiry, Powell referred to the occurrence on 7 July 2003 at No. 10 of

> *a sort of running meeting . . . the Prime Minister popped into a working breakfast that morning. He then came down to his office about 9 o'clock and asked to see David Omand and Kevin Tebbit and John Scarlett. They were not immediately available and a separate meeting was going on in Alastair Campbell's office . . . including the Foreign Secretary and a number of officials . . . So there was a meeting going on there with them, John Scarlett came from that meeting to see the Prime Minister briefly, then went back. David Omand then arrived, then Kevin Tebbit arrived . . . So it is a sort of running meeting with people coming and later the Foreign Secretary and the rest of the people from the meeting with Alastair Campbell came along as well.*

Asked, 'So the meeting gets bigger as time goes on?', Powell replied, 'It gets smaller and bigger and bigger and smaller, yes.' Could he tell the inquiry what was said? 'As far as my memory allows me to do so, yes . . . No minutes were kept of this meeting or subsequent meetings we are probably going to discuss.' 'Is that the normal course, that they are just discussions and no one is bothering to write them down because they are free flowing, as it were?' Powell said, 'the usual pattern is about three written records for seventeen meetings a day . . . because there is no purpose served by minutes unless they are either recording people visiting from outside . . . or if they are action points that need to be taken forward.'[56]

Blair's approach enabled rapid decision-making in small groups consisting of individuals whom he felt he could trust and rely upon. To hold more formal discussions based on papers in full Cabinet or to convene the Defence and Overseas Affairs Sub-Committee might have slowed processes down, or encouraged more dissent. Perhaps, if presented with memoranda, Cabinet would have subjected policy to greater scrutiny. It might have encouraged more assertiveness on their parts. In attempting to formulate ideas in written form, perhaps the discretion afforded the Prime Minister by more nebulous conversations would have been lost. Advance submissions, describing a selection of options, would encourage discussions in which participants put forward a variety of contrasting ideas. While they might not have approved of the lack of papers, senior ministers could not claim that they had not been given a chance to express views. When telling the Commons in July 2003 that 'There was no meeting of the Cabinet Defence and Overseas Policy Committee' from September 2002 to March 2003, Blair went on to say that 'the reason why this was not necessary was that Iraq appeared on the agenda of Cabinet as early as March 2002. From 23 September 2002 until after the conflict, Iraq was discussed at every regular Cabinet meeting.' Blair referred additionally to the ad hoc body that met during the war.[57] In Short's view, he 'was managing us, reassuring us and keeping us on side whilst he and his entourage decided what to do. No decisions were made in Cabinet.'

Blair used his prime ministerial licence to skew policy oversight towards him and away from the collective. He was able to ensure British participation in the invasion of Iraq without a major Cabinet rebellion taking place. Dissent was voiced, according to a Short diary entry, at a September 2002 Cabinet, where Short 'did teaching on the just war etc. Alan Milburn and Estelle Morris and others then spoke v openly re why now? Why him? What about the Palestinians? Palenstinians came up repeatedly and UN.'[58] But reservations which may have existed were not driven home. As war began to look increasingly likely, if a sufficient number of senior ministers threatened to quit, the policy (and perhaps the holder of the premiership) would probably have had to change. In that sense power still resided with Cabinet, though it remained latent in form. Commenting on Blair and Iraq, Lord (Richard) Wilson, Butler's successor as Cabinet Secretary, quoted G. W. Jones's statement, 'Prime Ministers are only as powerful as their colleagues allow them to be.'[59]

There were drawbacks to the leadership method Blair used over Iraq. Collective discussion can enhance the quality of decisions taken. Moreover, the neglect of Cabinet or its subcommittees, though it may be effective in securing potentially controversial policy options with the minimum disruption, can be a source of public criticism of a Prime Minister. Short has made comprehensive condemnations of Blair's approach to leadership in war and peace, as well as what she described to the FAC as 'the collapse in the decision-making process . . . I think is very, very poor and shoddy work and is a deterioration in the quality of British administration which is shocking . . . this is our political system, this is our country's decision-making system and it is not good enough.' She argued that 'the decision-making was sucked out of the Foreign Office which I think is a great pity because there is enormous expertise about the Middle East in the Foreign Office and certainly the Foreign Office

[had] the expertise to understand what [was] necessary to achieve the second Resolution.'

Butler noted receiving 'evidence from two former Cabinet members, one of the present and one of a previous administration, who expressed concern about the informal nature of much of the Government's decision-making process, and the relative lack of use of established Cabinet Committee machinery'. The report further argued that a consequence of Blair's style was to 'limit wider collective discussion and consideration by the Cabinet to the frequent but unscripted occasions when the Prime Minister, Foreign Secretary and Defence Secretary briefed the Cabinet orally'. While 'Excellent quality papers were written by officials' they 'were not discussed in Cabinet or in Cabinet Committee'. The lack of 'papers circulated in advance' made it 'much more difficult for members of the Cabinet outside the small circle directly involved to bring their political judgement and experience to bear on the major decisions for which the Cabinet as a whole must carry responsibility'.

The combination of changes in the 'key posts at the head of the Cabinet Secretariat' and 'The absence of papers on the Cabinet agenda' lessened 'the support of the machinery of government for the collective responsibility of the Cabinet in the vital matter of war and peace'.

Butler concluded,

We do not suggest that there is or should be an ideal or unchangeable system of collective Government, still less that procedures are in aggregate any less effective now than in earlier times. However, we are concerned that the informality and circumscribed character of the Government's procedures which we saw in the context of policy-making towards Iraq risks reducing the scope for informed collective political judgement.

Later in the year, appearing in front of PASC, Butler referred to the value of collective responsibility again. He explained, 'the way in which the Cabinet is designed to operate, where ministers representing all the interests in Government can contribute, is important to good decision making.' The value was that 'you sometimes find that a quite surprising department that you think has got no real interest in an issue has got a crucial point that they want to make.' Therefore, 'it is important that information should be given to the Cabinet in a form in which members of the Cabinet can get briefed on, can think about and then contribute to the discussion, particularly on very important issues like peace and war.' But he conceded, 'I do not think that during my time as Cabinet Secretary we had cracked the problem of adapting these procedures to a faster moving world . . . there is more work to be done on that.'

In a *Spectator* interview in December 2004, Butler was more overtly critical, arguing that Blair should

> restore open debate in government at all levels up to the Cabinet. *The Cabinet now and I don't think there is any secret about this doesn't make decisions . . . the government reaches conclusions in rather small groups of people who are not necessarily representative of all the groups of interests in government, and there is insufficient opportunity for other people to debate, dissent and modify.*[60]

Wilson, who was of a similar mind to Butler, made comments suggesting that Blair's informality, rather than expanding prime ministerial authority, might have made it less likely that decisions would be implemented properly – a problem that Lloyd George identified ninety years previously. Wilson has said

Formal meetings and minute-taking . . . may seem bureaucratic and not 'modern'; but good minutes make sure that everyone knows what has been decided. The official machine responds well to a decision which is properly recorded by a No. 10 private secretary or the Cabinet Office. I believe there is a connection between proper processes and good government.

Wilson went on,

Different Prime Ministers have different ways of doing business and there is no 'right' way of running a Government. It is quite possible to reconcile due process with an informal style. But the risk is that informality can slide into something more fluid and unstructured, where advice and dissent may either not always be offered or else not be heard.[61]

Blair and others within the administration seemed to take note of some of the problems identified above. Upon the publication of the Butler Review, he announced that any future inner groups for war would be formally convened ad hoc Cabinet committees. And, prompted by Hutton, 'The Cabinet Secretary, Sir Andrew Turnbull, instructed that there should be a return to a very old technology. Minutes are back.'[62]

3 Restraint and Scrutiny

- In Britain, governments can conduct war under the royal prerogative, without formal dependence upon Parliament
- There is an expectation of informal consultation, and the executive is subject to political realities – but nevertheless enjoys considerable influence over the legislature
- Often, in foreign countries, responsibility for armed conflict is shared between branches of state, an arrangement stipulated in codified constitutions. Yet, under such circumstances, war leaders remain able to provide themselves with room for manoeuvre
- War leaders have ample opportunity to evade thorough scrutiny by select committees and are able to prevent confidential information from becoming public. But they may wish to be seen to submit themselves to examination, through establishing inquiries themselves
- British governments are not obliged to publish the legal advice they receive on war, nor is there a tradition of intervention in the prerogative war powers by the courts
- In the US, where judicial review is more developed, executives have still proved able to avoid restriction of their actions
- Though in theory it could be, an action such as the invasion of Iraq is unlikely to be tested under international law

- Nevertheless, governments are likely to seek to present their actions as legal
- A war leader may attempt to work through international organisations, or justify their interventions on humanitarian or self-defence grounds

The Prerogative

A British government making war will not be troubled by formal domestic constitutional constraints. Much of the activity involved can be carried out under the royal prerogative, that is executive authority, comprising the remnants of pre-democratic, monarchical rule. While, as the constitution has developed, powers previously possessed by the head of state have become subject to Parliament and the courts, some have not. Of them, many are effectively exercised by (though officially only on the advice of) ministers.

No record is kept of the use of prerogative powers. Nobody knows for certain what they all are. Here, then, is an area of constitutional fog, of which an executive is well placed to take advantage, in order to maximise its room for manoeuvre. If seeking to retain the advantages it brings, it may be advisable for a war government to follow a long-standing tradition and maintain the existing uncertainty. It has been possible to refuse to provide information about one aspect of the prerogative to MPs (the award of honours), on the grounds that it is a concern of the monarch, about whom Parliamentary Questions are improper. It is believed that these authorities cannot be extended. Therefore, attempting to publish an exhaustive list of them is unwise. It would be unfortunate to leave something off it that might be needed subsequently.

According to possibly the first ever full official statement on the subject, provided by the government to PASC, the prerogative includes the appointment and regulation of the Civil Service, the commissioning of officers in the armed forces, directing the disposition of the armed forces in the UK, the granting of honours, the making of treaties, the declaration of war, the deployment of the armed forces on operations overseas, and the recognition of foreign states. The submission noted, 'The conduct of foreign affairs remains very reliant on the exercise of prerogative powers. Parliament and the courts have perhaps tended to accept that this is an area where the Crown needs flexibility in order to act effectively and handle novel situations.'[1] The legislature and the judiciary, then, have lacked the statute, the precedent and – it would seem – the will to interfere directly in certain activities of government, one of which is the conduct of warfare.

Though in possession of the prerogative, a war prime minister in Britain will have to pay heed to certain non-statutory arrangements for involving the legislature. One relates to the forging of military alliances. After the First World War, there was criticism of the diplomacy which had preceded it and a view that secret agreements had led to the conflict. In 1924 Arthur Ponsonby, Under-Secretary of State for Foreign Affairs in the first Labour administration, undertook to lay any treaty subject to ratification before the House for 21 days and to inform the House of all other 'agreements, commitments and understandings which may in any way bind the nation to specific action in certain circumstances'. Ponsonby stated, 'if there is a formal demand for discussion forwarded through the usual channels from the Opposition or any other party, time will be found for the discussion of the Treaty in question.' When Stanley Baldwin took office as Conservative Prime Minister in 1924, the 'Ponsonby Rule' was dropped, but it was revived by Labour in 1929 and has become a constitutional convention. The understanding now (excepting in times of emergency) is that it applies not only to ratification but additionally to accession (when Britain joins a treaty of which it is not an original signatory), approval and acceptance. There is no guarantee that every treaty will be discussed. Part of the Mutual Defence Agreement, allowing for cooperation over nuclear weapons technology between Britain and the US, was renewed in 2004, without a debate occurring, despite its controversial nature.

There is an expectation that, during potential or actual hostilities, Parliament will be kept informed of developments through regular ministerial statements. Governments hold debates (as well as their being triggered by opposition parties or individuals MPs). They may be held on two types of motion; for the adjournment of the House, or of the substantive variety. The former permits a vote on the procedural matter 'that this House do now adjourn', while the latter entails the government seeking support for a motion specifically endorsing its policy.

Two votes of the latter sort were held in February and March 2003 (and were the occasions for enormous Commons rebellions). Robin Cook records pressing for this at the time, using to support his view the fact of more formal procedures for involving the US Congress in such decisions. 'I found that Number 10 was stumped for a reply when I innocently asked whether as a good ally we really could do any less than the US in consulting the legislature.' Jack Straw, too, writes Cook, 'was just as robust on insisting on the right of Parliament to decide'. Consequently, a prime minister involved in a conflict in the future may be called upon to consult with MPs in a similar manner. It may be argued that a standard has been set which must be followed. Cook writes, 'I may not have succeeded in halting the war, but I did secure the right of Parliament to decide on war.'[2] However, one precedent does not necessarily make a convention, the term for a firm constitutional understanding. A war leader not wishing to hold a vote on a substantive motion can deny the existence of any such rule. Being expected to ask Parliament to approve a statement supporting the policy is not the same thing as a statutory requirement, within a specific framework, for its consent. Even if one is held, war leaders in Britain will still be able to exercise influence over the timing of a vote, as well as the wording of the motion, to their advantage.

Of late, some parliamentarians have become more assertive in their demands for reform of the prerogative, or at least greater oversight of its exercise. In 2004, PASC argued that

> *any decision to engage in armed conflict should be approved by Parliament, if not before military action then as soon as possible afterwards. In these most serious of cases, the decision whether or not to consult Parliament should never be dependent on the generosity or good will of government. A mere convention is not enough when lives are at stake. The increasing frequency of conflict in recent years is proof of the importance of ensuring that, when the country takes military action, Parliament supports the government in its decision.*[3]

Critics of the prerogative are likely to be drawn from one or more of a number of groups. They may disagree with a particular use it is being put to at a given time. Some simply seek a stick with which to beat the government, perhaps with a view to joining the executive at some point in the future and acquiring the use of the prerogative for themselves. Others have no hope of ever gaining access to it and seek to deny it to others. There may even be objections to it on genuine grounds of constitutional principle. But the prerogative is safe-guarded by the fact that its abolition would require the cooperation of those who have it at their disposal and have come to find it very useful. Senior politicians who oppose such executive authority do so when the possibility of their wielding it lies in the future or the past, not the present. As PASC noted, Jack Straw, the Foreign Secretary at the time of the invasion of Iraq, had been a vehement critic of the prerogative in opposition. Lord (Douglas) Hurd, who held Straw's post at the time of Iraq's expulsion from Kuwait in 1991, called for a stronger parliamentary role in 2004.

In defending the existence of the prerogative, it will be useful for a war leader to stress its practical limitations. Blair told the Liaison Committee in January 2003, 'I cannot think of a set of circumstances in which a Government can go to war without the support of Parliament . . . you can get into a great constitutional argument about this, but the reality is that Governments are in the end accountable to Parliament . . . for any war that they engage in.' Blair argued that it was not necessary to 'take that one step further and get rid of the royal prerogative . . . even though it may be strictly true to say that . . . Parliament is not the authority . . . can you honestly imagine a set of circumstances in which the Government is defeated by Parliament over a conflict and says, "Well I'm just ignoring that"?'[4] British war leaders can claim democratic legitimacy for their actions, then, even if carried out using the prerogative. At the same time, the chances of a government actually being defeated in the way referred to by Blair are slight.

Managing the Legislature

Despite recent stirrings on the part of the legislature in Britain, there is a strong tradition for it to lack autonomy as a branch of state in its own right. Its timetable is largely controlled by the executive which initiates most laws. Because of the first-past-the-post electoral system, governments in Britain are very likely to be formed by a single party with a majority of seats in the House of Commons. Such is not the case in a number of other states. In Germany, smaller groups can hold the balance of power. The US President is elected separately from Congress, often facing majorities in the House of Representatives or Senate of a rival party. The French President may be forced to cohabit with a prime minister of another complexion, though he does have the option of dissolving the National Assembly.

The tendency towards majority government in Britain helps avoid parliamentary disruption to the conduct of a conflict. Again, unlike in the US, ministers are drawn mainly from the Commons, with a leavening of peers. There is a 'payroll vote' – that is, members who, as part of the government, cannot oppose official policy in the House. Prime ministers, who make the appointments, possess leverage over the legislature. Backbenchers voting against a war could thereby harm their career prospects. But possession of the power of patronage creates not only allies (among the potential or actual beneficiaries) but enemies (in those from whom it has been withdrawn or withheld). Some are immune to it, perhaps because their careers are in the descendent, although they can be tempted by honours or peerages. The highly developed system of whips, responsible for party discipline, can be used to deliver the required result. But they are not omnipotent, as the rebellions of early 2003 demonstrate. Premiers faced with unease over a military action can appeal to MPs to place partisan loyalties ahead of the particular issue, or claim that they will resign if defeated, as Blair did over Iraq.

Despite all the leverage available, revolts still occur. And if an administration has truly lost the support of Parliament (a scenario alluded to by Blair above), then whether it held a vote or not, it could be subject to a 'No Confidence' motion. A rebellion that does not actually amount to a defeat can still be large enough to force a prime minister to resign. In 1940 Neville Chamberlain fell, following a large number of Conservative defections in a vote over the military disaster which occurred in Norway. In the lead-up to the Iraq War in 2003 it was not, in fact, Parliament as such which caused Blair the most difficulties so much as that section of it which comprised the Parliamentary Labour Party. In that sense it is possible that he could have won a vote, but reached a tipping point in terms of the number of Labour MPs opposed to his policy, making his pursuit of it as party leader practically unsustainable. The House of Lords, which has had a built-in Conservative majority, can make the rapid introduction of legislation difficult as it did with the Prevention of Terrorism Bill in 2005.

One source of room for manoeuvre on the part of the executive is the fact that, if a war incident occurs while the House is in recess, emergency recalls are within the gift of the executive, not parliamentarians, who could therefore theoretically be denied the chance even to voice their opinions. But political pressures find ways of coming to bear, even when denied formal outlets. In September 2002 Blair gave a press conference from his Sedgefield constituency indicating that Britain and the US were becoming less tolerant of Saddam Hussein. War seemed increasingly likely. Parliamentarians from all parties were concerned about Britain's possible involvement in a US-led Middle East venture but, since the House was on its summer break, did not have the opportunity to express their views. The Prime Minister was reluctant to bring about an emergency recall. A number of MPs, coordinated by Graham Allen, a Labour member who had been a whip from 1997 to 2001, threatened to organise their own 'Rebel Parliament'. A venue in Westminster was booked. At that point, Blair backed down and permitted them to reconvene officially.

Certain ancient parliamentary powers and procedures are now defunct. The Commons could once obstruct an action of which it disapproved by denying supply, that is refusing to provide funds to pay for it. Such an option was considered within the anti-war camp in 2003, but not taken up. How exactly it could have been pursued is unclear and the government majority which existed would have prevented it anyway. Once, Parliament's sanction against one of its own was impeachment. There have been less than seventy cases of such a practice, a large portion of which took place from 1640 to 1642. The most recent dates from 1806. Two hundred years later, with questions of the legality of the Iraq War receiving much attention, there was renewed interest in impeachment, to be used against Blair. Such a process would certainly be dramatic, but was implausible. If it had the support of a majority in the Commons, a government could prevent it from occurring, while if it did not, it would fall anyway, without any need for impeachment proceedings. Nevertheless, a call for them to be instigated appeared on the Commons Order Paper

War and the Formal Constitution

Executive leaders in a number of other democracies who wish to make war will be obliged to contend with more codified limitations.

The constitution of the French Fifth Republic states:

Article 35

A declaration of war shall be authorised by Parliament.

Similar rules apply elsewhere. However, it should be noted that, nowadays, formal declarations of war are passé (none has been made by Britain since 1942, against Siam). Conflicts are conducted without them being made, perhaps leaving open the possibility of bypassing the legislature, even where it has a formal role in official proclamations. Sweden's 'Instrument of Government', part of its constitution, is more broadly drawn, covering all troop deployments, and requiring compliance with domestic statute and international agreements. While a leader of such a country is subject to a higher level of regulation, it remains possible to respond autonomously to attacks on home territory:

Chapter 10, Article 9

The Government may commit the armed forces of the Realm, or any part of them, to battle in order to repel an armed attack upon the Realm. Swedish armed forces may otherwise be committed to battle or dispatched abroad only provided

1. the Riksdag consents thereto;

2. the action is permitted under an act of law which sets out the prerequisites for such action;

3. a duty to take such action follows from an international agreement or obligation which has been approved by the Riksdag.

A state of war may not be declared without the consent of the Riksdag, except in the event of an armed attack upon the Realm.

The Government may authorise the armed forces to use force in accordance with international law and custom to prevent violation of Swedish territory in time of peace or during a war between foreign states.

Restrictions elsewhere are, on the surface, even greater, particularly among countries whose constitutions were drawn up after defeat in the Second World War, such as Japan:

CHAPTER II: RENUNCIATION OF WAR

Article 9

Aspiring sincerely to an international peace based on justice and order, the Japanese people forever renounce war as a sovereign right of the nation and the threat or use of force as means of settling international disputes.

2) In order to accomplish the aim of the preceding paragraph, land, sea, and air forces, as well as other war potential, will never be maintained. The right of belligerency of the state will not be recognised.

Italy, too, is restricted, though not as strongly:

Article 11 (Repudiation of War)

Italy repudiates war as an instrument offending the liberty of the peoples and as a means for settling international disputes; it agrees to limitations of sovereignty where they are necessary to allow for a legal system of peace and justice between nations, provided the principle of reciprocity is guaranteed; it promotes and encourages international organisations furthering such ends.

Yet, both Italy and Japan managed to participate in the allied operation in Iraq from 2003.

Circumvention of potential domestic obstacles, even if they are formalised, remains possible. Uncertainties as to the meaning of wording may exist, or, indeed, can be developed. The US Constitution states that 'The Congress shall have Power . . . To declare War'. However, the President is described as 'Commander in Chief of the Army and Navy of the United States'. In fact, presidents have been able to dominate war making. Lincoln carried out frequent initiatives during the American Civil War that were not validated by the explicit prior consent of Congress. An outstanding example was the Emancipation Proclamation which was, in the words of one writer, 'a great victory for human liberty. It was also an extraordinary use of executive power.'

Issued in preliminary form by Lincoln on 22 September 1862, it stated that 'all persons held as slaves within any state, or designated part of a state, the people whereof shall then be in rebellion against the United States shall be then, thenceforward, and forever free'. Constitutionally, the President's recourse to such unilateral action has been defended on the grounds that the proclamation was 'effectively an order to military commanders in the field [of whom he was commander-in-chief], directing them to liberate slaves in conquered territory'.[5]

Other moves by Lincoln which lacked congressional approval at the time included calling for volunteers to join the army and transferring federal funds. His blockade of Southern ports implied a state of war, though, as discussed, the formal power to declare that resided with the legislature, not the executive. As the case of Lincoln demonstrates, a public emergency, or an overwhelming moral imperative, can be used as justification for autonomous action. In the First World War Wilson reduced the need for reference to the legislature by other means. Though the extraordinary measures taken had a basis in primary legislation, they were brought about through a huge bulk of administrative directives. In the 1930s, Congress tried to ensure US neutrality through passing legislation. Franklin D. Roosevelt arguably violated its constitutional authority and statute when he arranged for fifty destroyers to be given to Britain following the fall of France in 1940.

In the face of the executive conduct of war, legislatures may attempt to tip the balance of power back towards them. That could be a threat to an administration jealous of its independence. Even if such efforts are given statutory expression, they require sustained, concerted action, which may prove lacking at the critical moment. In 1964, following a supposed attack on US vessels in the Gulf of Tonkin, off the Vietnam coast, President Lyndon Johnson received almost unanimous support from Congress for a statement approving that he be able to 'take all necessary measures to repel any armed attack against the forces of the United States and to prevent further aggression.' It became became known as the 'Tonkin Gulf resolution' (though its real name was the 'Southeast Asia Resolution'). Johnson records that he was of the view that 'President Truman's one mistake in courageously going to the defense of South Korea in 1950 had been his failure to ask Congress for an expression of its backing.'[6] But, having obtained that support, he claimed it as *carte blanche* for the escalation of US involvement in the Vietnamese civil war, which came to be regarded as disastrous.

In response, to safeguard against further such exercises of authority, the 1973 War Powers Resolution (which came to be known as the War Powers Act) was adopted. The text describes its purpose to ensure 'that the collective judgement of both the Congress and the President will apply to the introduction of United States Armed Forces into hostilities, or into situations where imminent involvement in hostilities' is clear 'and to the continued use of such forces'. To that end, the President is obliged 'in every possible instance' to 'consult with Congress before introducing United States Armed Forces'. The 'every possible instance' proviso allows for responses to emergencies. In addition, consultation is required 'after every such introduction'. A written report to Congress is due within 48 hours of any action. Unless Congress authorises otherwise, the commitment has to be ended within 60 days (with the possibility of a further 30 days, if the safety of the troops so requires). Concurrent resolutions by Congress can force the withdrawal of the troops at any time, not subject to presidential veto. Some deployment as part of UN actions is allowed for without congressional involvement, under the War Powers Resolution and the UN Participation Act.

Successive presidents have denied the constitutionality of the War Powers Resolution, which has yet to be directly tested in court.

Moreover, according to one author, 'The 60-day clock has never been tested, and many members seem almost pained by the fact that the resolution exists.' When President Ronald Reagan sent marines to Lebanon in September 1982, acting as peacekeepers, 'nine months elapsed before Congress went so far as to direct the president to "obtain statutory authorization from Congress with respect to any substantial expansion in the number or role in Lebanon of United States Armed Forces".' Congress did not invoke the War Powers Resolution until late in September 1983, after several marines were killed and US forces began intervening in support of the Lebanese government. Yet, Congress then 'gave Reagan authority to act under the resolution for eighteen months and to use "such protective measures as may be necessary to secure the safety of the Multinational Force in Lebanon"'.[7]

Inquiry

Aside from the constitutional apportionment of powers, a war leader must give consideration to the possibility of being scrutinised by the legislature and other agencies. British ministers have to answer often hostile oral questions in the House on a regular basis (as well as written ones). But the occasions can be used as an opportunity for promoting policy. Responses can be particularly evasive if deemed necessary, though if ministers can be shown to have deliberately misled the House, they will be forced to resign. Cases of MPs causing extreme discomfort to an administration over a conflict through tabling questions are few. The Labour MP Tam Dalyell was persistent in his pursuit of the Thatcher administration over the sinking of the Argentinian warship, the *General Belgrano*, during the Falklands War. In addition to answering questions, ministers respond to points made in debates, as well as appearing before committees, discussed below. Whether the course of a discussion in

Parliament could actually convince substantial numbers of MPs to vote against the whip is doubtful.

Many British military campaigns and engagements have been subject to subsequent inquiry, of parliamentary and other varieties. Often, it was conducted to examine defeat or disaster and associated with political controversy. Britain entered the Crimean War in 1854, an involvement characterised by a series of failures, including the famous 'Charge of the Light Brigade' (in the wrong direction, with hundreds of casualties) and problems with the supply system. A motion to set up a select committee was passed in 1855 and the resulting report (published in two parts in 1855 and 1856) led to the establishment of a Board of General Officers, to investigate allegations against certain officers. It became known as the 'Whitewash Board' because it transferred culpability to Treasury officials.

When British ships attacked Turkish bases along the Dardanelles straits in 1915, as part of a plan to take the Gallipoli peninsula, six vessels were sunk or damaged. Landings were then attempted, but proved unsuccessful, with around twenty-six thousand British casualties (and a further twenty thousand allied troops of other nationalities dead). One source of weakness was a dispute between military and political leadership. Initially, the attempted invasion of Mesopotamia (in the area now called Iraq) during the First World War was similarly inept. Major-General Sir Charles Townshend was ordered to move on to Baghdad, became overstretched and was defeated by the Turks. The city was eventually taken in March 1917, but around twenty-seven thousand British deaths were incurred. A Bill was introduced into Parliament by the government establishing commissions to examine the Dardanelles and Mesopotamia. At first, the government had agreed to publish all the relevant documents. On official advice, the commitment was then withdrawn. In a private letter at the time, the premier, Asquith, noted that 'It is infinitely better to have a couple of secret inquiries, which will do no harm & may even do some good . . . than the publication of papers which, however edited, would have been in the last degree mischievous.' Cassar judges that Asquith, 'Had he analyzed the long-range consequences carefully . . . would have seen the obvious inherent dangers in submitting his government's performance to critical scrutiny. Asquith, in the eyes of the world, was not only acknowledging that grave mistakes had been committed but impugning his own leadership as well.'[8]

Sometimes, inquiries have been avoided. Singapore fell rapidly to a relatively small number of Japanese troops in 1942, with many prisoners taken. Despite demands from Parliament, no investigation was ever conducted; presumably it was considered undesirable to do so during the Second World War and the idea was never returned to. Despite the efforts of Labour MPs including George Wigg and Michael Foot, a committee of inquiry was never set up into the Suez affair.

Since 1979, a system of parliamentary select committees, monitoring individual departments and areas, has operated in Britain. (There are a variety of other parliamentary bodies, such as House of Lords committees and joint committees of both houses.) Select committees differ from many of their foreign equivalents in that they are concerned primarily with policy, administration and expenditure, not legislation (though an increasing amount of work is carried out here in the pre-legislative phase). That might lead them to be interested in military action. There are eighteen such bodies in the House of Commons. Ones with significance to a conflict may include Foreign Affairs, Defence, International Development, Home Affairs, Trade and Industry or even Science and Technology. There is no committee for examining the work of the Attorney General's department, however. Their existence is permanent. They may represent a threat to government, developing strong agendas of their own and engaging in undesirable scrutiny. Possibly, they might aspire to the role of primary medium for the examination of the executive conduct of war.

But there are ways in which parliamentary investigations can be obstructed or softened.[9] There are inbuilt advantages for the war leader when faced with a potentially damaging inquiry. The party balance of committees is proportionate to representation in the Commons. Consequently the government will have a majority, rendering the body less likely to attack executive activity and damage the administration. The whips decide who the members will be. Those sitting on committees are therefore recipients of patronage. Having been chosen by the executive, they are to some extent beholden to it. In theory, they can be removed. But in 2001, when the government tried to displace the chairs of two committees (including Foreign Affairs), it suffered a defeat in the House. It should be noted that opposition members are selected on the same partisan basis. They may be disposed towards inflicting harm. Individual members may value the pursuance of personal publicity above teamwork, reducing the likelihood of a concerted critique of policy being carried out. They do not have specific forensic training and are not assisted by counsel, benefits available to bodies such as the Hutton Inquiry. There is a tendency for committees concerned with 'national interest' issues, of which war is presumably one, to be as consensual as possible.

Other factors mitigate the potential of select committees to damage a war government. The resources at their disposal are limited. Total expenditure on select committees in the House of Commons for 2002–3 was £10.6 million, compared with £430 billion for government. The number of staff attached to each committee has been increased recently, but is a fraction of that available to those in the US.

Select committee work is focused to a considerable extent upon producing reports. While not being obliged to act upon any recommendations they make, the government is expected to respond to them. In theory, departments have to do so within two months. However, if they deem it beneficial, an arbitrary decision to procrastinate can be made. That may buy time to devise a reaction to a challenging set of conclusions, or to release them at a time when public interest will be lower, or distracted, or political momentum has been lost. An example of an accidental snub to a select committee in another policy area could provide the model for a method to be applied deliberately, when seeking to evade scrutiny of a military campaign. In July 2002 the Environmental Audit Committee published a report on claims that timber used in the refurbishment of the Cabinet Office had not come from legal and sustainable sources. No reply appeared until 1 July 2003. In September 2003 the Minister of State apologised, explaining that there had been a need for detailed consultation and that, further, an administrative error had 'led to the draft response being buried for three months.' There is little committees could do if such an approach were taken as a conscious delaying tactic, other than complain. They do have the power to embarrass ministers appearing before them, with respect to such grievances. It is possible for the government to issue extremely terse responses, if there is a desire to avoid engaging in the substance of an issue. In 2003 the Health Committee's annual report complained of 'shoddy treatment by the Department which we regard as wholly unacceptable'. The Department of Health had issued a single reply to three interlinked reports, seven months after the first was published. Indeed, the alternative to delaying a follow-up to an awkward report is to issue it as quickly as possible, for rebuttal purposes. It need not be particularly substantial. The use of surreptitious methods must be sparing, or they are likely to generate bad will to an extent that will be counterproductive.

A war leader may be concerned about the access to evidence possessed by select committees. They possess formal powers of summons, under *Standing Order No. 152 (4a)*, which states that they may send for 'persons, papers and records'. Yet there are two major exceptions: civil servants and members of either House. Recently, it was reported that Home Office ministers resisted requests to give evidence to the Science and Technology Committee when it was investigating the scientific response to terrorism. When David Kelly appeared before the FAC on 15 July 2003, Geoff Hoon, the Secretary of State for Defence, had stipulated that it would be on the condition that he was asked only questions relevant to the evidence given by Andrew Gilligan to the committee and not weapons of mass destruction in Iraq or the preparation of a government dossier in September 2002. But, in the event, they were touched upon and Hoon was unable to stop it. PASC has failed to secure the attendance of Jonathan Powell, the Prime Minister's Chief of Staff. Yet Blair's other senior special adviser, Alastair Campbell, appeared before it (in 1998, as Chief Press Secretary) and the FAC (in 2003, as Director of Communications and Strategy). Since leaving his post, he has had another session with PASC.

A British government engaged in conflict can utilise constitutional understandings to protect itself from invasive scrutiny. The principle of collective responsibility, discussed in the previous chapter, can provide a justification for secrecy. First, it is argued that for it to work, Cabinet must be able to engage in frank discussion, with participants confident that their views will not be publicly aired. Second, according to the doctrine of ministerial accountability, civil servants answer to their political heads of departments and their individual views and advice remain confidential. Both the above concepts can shield the executive from examination by the legislature.

Select committees enquiring into the conduct of a military conflict may attempt to extract information from officials. The *Ministerial*

Code stipulates, 'Ministers should . . . require civil servants who give evidence before Parliamentary Committees on their behalf and under their direction to be as helpful as possible in providing accurate, truthful and full information.' But there are careful restrictions on the type of information they may provide. Evidence giving to select committees by civil servants is regulated by the so-called 'Osmotherly Rules'. An internal government document, never formally approved by Parliament, they state that officials should 'confine their evidence to questions of fact and explanation relating to government policy and actions [and] . . . avoid being drawn into discussion of the merits of alternative policies where this is politically contentious . . . They should not therefore go beyond explaining the reasoning which, in the Government's judgement, supports its policy.' Osmotherly could provide for the executive to avoid supplying inconvenient information with respect to a war, explaining, 'The Government's commitment to provide as much information as possible to Select Committees . . . does not amount to a commitment to provide access to internal files, private correspondence, including advice given on a confidential basis or working papers.' Ministers have the final veto on everything. Even under the Freedom of Information Act 2000, aspects of which did not come into force until 2005, it is retained. In the words of Osmotherly, 'Because Officials appear on behalf of their Ministers, written evidence and briefing material should be cleared with them as necessary . . . Ministers are ultimately accountable for deciding what information is to be given.'[10] The government has recently proposed revisions to the rules, which introduce a presumption that the government will grant access to officials, special advisers and documents.

The types of information select committees would like, but cannot get, have recently been described by the Commons Liaison Committee. It referred to 'full records of past events and decisions, including those of the Cabinet and its sub-committees; internal reports, detailed options papers, documents passed between departments (including HM Treasury); and departmental work programmes and agendas such as are available at divisional or central level to management of a department and to Ministers'.

The Blair administration has used its power to withold co-operation from war-related inquiries. In September 2003 the Defence Committee complained at being refused copies of 'Lessons learnt' reports from Commanding Operations in Operation Telic (the name for the British action in Iraq), prepared as part of the MoD's assessment of it. The FAC experienced difficulty in obtaining actual Foreign Office telegrams as part of its Sierra Leone inquiry and more recently official papers on the Bali bombing, on the grounds that they were being supplied to the Intelligence and Security Committee (ISC).

The Defence Committee has recently noted

> *We have had some difficulty in encouraging openness and transparency within the MOD. We have on several occasions encountered refusals to provide documents that we have requested to see in confidence . . . MOD witnesses are not always as forthcoming as they might be: the MOD's advice to witnesses, published on the Hutton Inquiry website, appears to encourage reticence rather than the helpfulness which elected representatives might expect to receive.*

Since the executive has substantial control over the business of the House, it can prevent committees from asserting themselves when they feel they are being abused. In 2004 the FAC noted that, when meeting with obstruction to its Iraq inquiry,

> *The only way in which the Committee could have sought to insist on the attendance of official witnesses or the production of official papers*

would have been to make a Special Report to the House, or to table an appropriate Motion. Either course of action would have required the Government's agreement for a debate to be held in government time.[11]

Beyond what it may provide to select committees, a war government possesses broader controls over information that may be made public. The Freedom of Information Act, though providing for statutory access, contains numerous exemptions, and releases can be blocked by Cabinet ministers. Using their control over information, war leaders in Britain, if they wish, can make major decisions while revealing little of the basis on which they are formed. By such means, ends including the safeguarding of security and prevention of political embarrassment can be served. It is possible to make it harder for a challenge to a policy to be mounted, since arguments involve competing interpretations of commonly known facts.

There exist, then, a variety of means by which a British government minded to do so can thwart parliamentary investigation of a war. But it may be judged politically expedient to be seen to facilitate a full public inquiry. A means of doing so, but retaining influence over the process, is for the government to appoint one directly. It can be justified on the basis that such has been the practice in the past. Involving individuals of high standing can create the impression that the utmost importance has been attached to the matter. Using labels, such as 'a committee of Privy Counsellors' can serve similar ends. That was the approach taken by the Thatcher government after the Falklands War of 1982, establishing a body under Lord Franks, and by Blair in 2004 with the Butler Review.

The executive possesses influence over the scope of an inquiry it has convened itself that it would not with respect to one carried out by the legislature. One way in which a degree of control can be exercised is through the terms of reference. As far as possible, they must be devised to prevent investigations or conclusions damaging to the government. At the same time, if they appear overly restrictive, they will undermine the credibility of the exercise. After the Falklands War of 1982, the government formed a group of Privy Counsellors, chaired by Lord Franks, 'To review the way in which the responsibilities of Government in relation to the Falkland Islands and their dependencies were discharged in the period leading up to the Argentine invasion of the Falkland Islands on 2 April 1982, taking account of all such factors in previous years as are relevant'. The form of the Butler Review was modelled on Franks. Butler remarked to PASC that 'it was the complaint of some people . . . that [Butler's] terms of reference did not cover the case for or against war . . . Lord Franks' inquiry similarly did not cover that, he was not asked and did not cover whether the invasion of the Falklands was justified.'

If discretion is granted over the interpretation of terms of reference, a government-convened inquiry may well exercise it with moderation. On 21 July 2003, following the apparent suicide of the Ministry of Defence scientist, Dr David Kelly, Lord Hutton announced his appointment by the government to investigate it. His brief was 'urgently to conduct an investigation into the circumstances surrounding the death'. He stated at the time, 'I make it clear that it will be for me to decide as I think right within my terms of reference the matters which will be subject of my investigation.' At the launch of his report on 28 January 2004 and in its text he iterated that,

> *My terms of reference were: 'urgently to conduct an investigation into the circumstances surrounding the death of Dr Kelly.' . . . There has been a great deal of controversy and debate whether the intelligence in relation to weapons of mass destruction . . . was of sufficient strength*

and reliability to justify the Government in deciding that . . . military action should be taken against [Iraq] . . . I concluded that a question of such wide import . . . is not one which falls within my terms of reference.[12]

Hutton's, then, was not an investigation of policy decisions over Iraq.

The extent to which war leaders and their allies can determine the latitude of an inquiry even in advance of it being properly published was suggested during Hutton's appearance before PASC. He informed them that, on 18 July 2003,

[the Secretary of State for Constitutional Affairs] Lord Falconer telephoned me . . . He asked me to go to see him . . . and he then told me of the discovery of the body of a person who it was believed was Dr Kelly; and he said that the Government had decided to hold an inquiry into the circumstances of the death . . . He asked me to be the Chairman, and I thought it was my duty to agree to that request. So it all happened in a very short space of time.

Later, Hutton said that

I think when I saw the Lord Chancellor the terms of reference had not been precisely defined . . . the Lord Chancellor, in the course of the day, formulated them and told me that was what he was proposing and I agreed to that . . . The request was made quickly. My decision to accept was made quickly . . . If I had gone back and said, 'I consider these terms of reference are inappropriate or inadequate, I think they should be amended', I am quite sure . . . [Falconer] would in all probability, have agreed.[13]

On 3 February 2004, shortly after Hutton reported, Straw announced Blair's decision to form a Committee to Review Intelligence on Weapons of Mass Destruction (WMD), comprising Privy Counsellors, chaired by Butler and meeting in private. Its terms of reference were:

> to investigate the accuracy of intelligence on Iraqi WMD . . . and to make recommendations to the Prime Minister for the future on the gathering, evaluation and use of intelligence on WMD

The method of determining the form of the Review was similar to that taken for Hutton. Once again, the government used the intitiative, presenting the person it wished to head the body with arrangements virtually fully formed. Like Hutton (and other public servants) Butler was unlikely to refuse to undertake such a task. Butler told PASC that he was 'on the outskirts of Mexico City . . . and my guide's mobile phone rang'. It was the Prime Minister's Chief of Staff, Jonathan Powell, who told Butler

> 'Robin your country needs you again' and we went between two hills and transmission was cut off . . . At the time I was first rung, the Government had already decided that it was going to use the model of the Franks Inquiry in that it was to be an inquiry of Privy Counsellors. The Government had very strong ideas about the membership. The terms of reference were already being discussed with the Leader of the Opposition and the Leader of the Liberal Democrats. They were a long way down the track . . . I had the terms of reference faxed through to me . . . I was able to look at them but . . . it would not have been easy to discuss them with anybody . . . I was rather puzzled about the grammar of them, but I did not think it was worth waking anybody up to make a point about that.[14]

Cross-party participation was sought in the Butler Review, but not obtained. The Liberal Democrats declined from the outset. According to Menzies Campbell, their Shadow Foreign Secretary, the reason was that 'the remit is confined to intelligence and weapons of mass destruction. It deals neither with the workings of government, nor with political decision making based on intelligence.' He asked, 'should not the Prime Minister and others . . . be willing to submit to scrutiny of their competence and judgment in the discharge of their responsibilities?'[15]

Initially, the Conservative Party proposed to participate in Butler with the Shadow Foreign Secretary, Michael Ancram MP, lamenting that such a body had not been convened sooner. However, the official opposition soon joined the Liberal Democrats in arguing that the committee was inadequate, on the grounds that Butler was interpreting his terms of reference too narrowly. (Michael Mates, the Conservative member, carried on in a personal capacity.)

There will be a tendency for the opposition to see such reviews as a point-scoring opportunity. In Butler's terms of reference, the Liberal Democrats and Conservatives sensed a trap. They feared that, if ensnared, they would be participating in and thereby enhancing the credibility of a review which, because of restrictions on its scope, could not be used as an effective weapon. That hindered the government in its attempt to obtain cross-party legitimacy for a report, while limiting in advance its potential to harm.

A war leader may find it helpful if inquiries are made up of and staffed by individuals closely associated with the executive. Butler's operation was an 'in-house' Whitehall one. He has noted 'that the members of the staff of the review were all civil servants, predominantly drawn from the departments and agencies which were the subject of the review and where their futures lie. Yet there was never any question in the mind of the committee – nor has any question been raised outside – about their objectivity and commitment.'[16] Counting Butler himself, his review team included two retired civil servants and a field marshal. Of the two MPs on the Butler inquiry, one, Ann Taylor, was the Chief Whip from 1998 to 2001. Between them, the five members were in possession of thirteen honours.[17]

There are drawbacks to exercising influence in the ways described above. If an inquiry is perceived as lacking in independence, too close to or limited by the executive in such terms as its personnel, scope or conclusions, its legitimacy may be publicly questioned, defeating the purpose of holding it in the first place. The public reaction to the Franks, Hutton and Butler reports is evidence of the fact. As Tony Wright, the Chairman of PASC, put it to Hutton (who agreed it was an accurate characterisation of his rise and fall in media estimation), 'when you were sitting you were sainted: you were this fearless forensic investigator . . . The moment you reported, you were an establishment lackey.' But such condemnation of an investigation as pandering to the requirements of the executive will be beneficial to a war leader if it serves to distract attention from criticisms that are included in its findings. Butler referred to reservations regarding Blair's neglect of Cabinet government. Yet they did not receive the attention they might have from sections of the media opposed to the Prime Minister, which concentrated on portraying Butler as an executive stooge.

Governments are likely to view specially convened investigations as safer vehicles for public investigation than select committees. War leaders may therefore wish to ensure that inquiries established directly by the executive are accorded more significance than their parliamentary equivalents. They can do so by extending more co-operation to the former than they do to the latter, in terms of the provision of documents and witnesses, and not applying regulations such as the Osmotherly Rules. Anyway, were the executive not to furnish bodies it had convened itself with ample evidence, that would be to negate the purpose of their establishment: to submit publicly to a form of scrutiny.

Hutton's was an administrative rather than a judicial inquiry; it possessed only moral authority. Nevertheless, it was given extensive access to evidence from official and other sources. At the outset Hutton announced, 'The Government has . . . stated that it will provide me with the fullest cooperation and that it expects all other authorities and parties to do the same . . . It is . . . my intention to conduct the inquiry mostly in public.' Around three pages of evidence were withheld from publication for reasons of national security, as well as some personal information and police witness statements. Hearings were protected from libel proceedings. Civil servants were provided with assurances that evidence they gave would not be held against them. The Butler Review, it was announced at the time of its formation, was to be granted 'access to all intelligence reports and assessments and other relevant Government papers, and will be able to call witnesses to give oral evidence in private'.

The inequality of the treatment accorded Hutton and Butler, and that which could be expected by a parliamentary select committee, was plain. In the wake of Hutton, the House of Commons Liaison Committee issued a note[18] stating that, although it was not a statutory inquiry under the Tribunals of Inquiry (Evidence) Act 1921 and could not therefore compel attendance of witnesses, 'the absence of formal powers does not seem to have limited its access to those from whom it wished to take evidence. The Prime Minister, the Chairman of the Joint Intelligence Committee, and even the Chief of the Secret Intelligence Service gave evidence on the record.' Another contrast with parliamentary inquiries can be found in the Scott inquiry on Arms to Iraq in the mid 1990s, which was guaranteed access to any civil servant, and that they could give evidence on their own behalf. Aside from witnesses, the Liaison

Committee complained of another disparity between the treatment of select committees and the Hutton Inquiry. The latter had access to a wide range of written material from government departments and agencies. It was posted on the website, scanned in its original form (with some parts blanked out). A select committee, the Liaison Committee argued 'would not be given the form of documentary evidence supplied to Hutton . . . [such as] the correspondence or loose minutes between senior officials and the mass of e-mails.' Further, it 'would not be given the nature of documentary evidence supplied to Hutton, much of which would fall into the categories of advice to Ministers or paper [*sic*] whose release would adversely affect the candour of internal discussions'. Finally, 'a select committee would not be given (and might not ask for) documentary evidence as opposed to information.' It was noted that speed of provision was far better for Hutton than was often the case for select committees.

Butler offered a possible motive for the inequality of treatment, telling PASC that

> *select committees inevitably bring in the party political aspect and governments are less confident about revealing very sensitive papers to select committees that contain members of other political parties. Select committees, I believe, go out of their way to behave very responsibly and honourably about this but it is a factor one just cannot ignore and I think that is what makes it more difficult for select committees to get access to the most sensitive papers.*

Another body, the Intelligence and Security Committee (ISC), may seek to investigate aspects of the conduct of a war. It is closer to the executive – in terms of the way it is staffed and its membership is determined – than a select committee and it is less prone to partisan divisions. A government may therefore regard it as another safer agency of scrutiny than a parliamentary body. Blair told Hutton that, when allegations emerged about Downing Street's role in the production of the *Iraq's Weapons of Mass Destruction* dossier,

> *There was a raging storm going on. And it was clear, because there were a lot of calls for inquiries, there was going to have to be some sort of inquiry into it. I thought that the Intelligence and Security Committee were the right people to deal with this . . . I thought they would deal with it in a sensible way.*[19]

Under the Intelligence Services Act 1994, the ISC is responsible for examining the three Intelligence Agencies. Though composed entirely of peers and MPs, the ISC is not a parliamentary committee. It is appointed by the Prime Minister (in consultation with the Leader of the Opposition). The nine members act within the so-called 'ring of secrecy'. Annual reports to the Prime Minister are published, with some deletions. It also provides ad hoc papers. Its clerk and secretarial support are supplied by the Cabinet Office.

The ISC can request information from the heads of agencies, which must be supplied, provided it is not 'sensitive' and unsafe to disclose. A secretary of state can veto disclosure on the grounds that 'the information appears to him to be of such a nature that, if he were requested to produce it before a Departmental Select Committee of the House of Commons, he would think it proper not to do so.' In fact, though a 'Departmental Select Committee of the House of Commons' is used as a yardstick for disclosure, the FAC has complained that the ISC receives better treatment than the FAC does from the government. A war leader might use the ISC as an alibi for non-cooperation with parliamentary investigations. The FAC has noted that 'since the ISC was set up, successive Secretaries of State have on more than one occasion refused to allow FAC access to the agencies, on the grounds that Parliamentary scrutiny of those agencies is carried out by the ISC.'

The chances of the ISC engaging in scrutiny of a sort unwelcome to the government have been reduced by the fact that, although it receives privileged official access, in other respects its evidence-gathering potential has been limited. In 1999, the Home Affairs Committee, in its report *The Accountability of the Security Services,*[20] noted that

> there are no express powers in the [Intelligence Services] Act for the Committee to obtain information from anyone other than the heads of the Agencies, whereas a select committee's powers to summon witnesses or demand information from the public at large are almost – theoretically at least – unlimited; additionally . . . the ISC . . . depend to a significant extent on the quality of the relationship with the Agency heads.

Though it has, since 1999, secured better access, government cooperation with the ISC does not have to be absolute. In its *Annual Report 2003–2004*[21] the Committee noted there was no official response to its own report on weapons of mass destruction, which appeared in September 2003, until February 2004. The government's stated reason for the delay was that it was waiting until Hutton's findings were published. However, the ISC stated that, when it finally received it, it was 'not satisfied with the Government's Response. It emphasised only four key conclusions while either rejecting or failing to address fully many of our other conclusions and recommendations. We regard this as extremely unsatisfactory.' The committee further noted that 'in May of this year [2004] we were given a further eight JIC [Joint Intelligence Committee] papers relating to Iraqi WMD and UN inspections . . . which a subsequent check had revealed had not been given to us last year. This causes us considerable concern.' The ISC had 'received an apology and we accept that there was no deliberate attempt to withhold information from us. However, we are concerned that some internal systems and record-keeping within the Cabinet Office's Intelligence and Security Secretariat are defective.'

Even in countries such as the US, where the legislature is stronger, its efforts at inquiry can be resisted. Presidents have denied congressional committees the ability to question officials. In the mid-twentieth century, Corwin wrote 'I know of no instance in which a head of department has testified before a congressional committee in response to a subpoena or been held for contempt for refusal to testify. All appearances by these high officials seem to have been voluntary.'[22] The National Commission on Terrorist Attacks Upon the United States was created by congressional legislation in late 2002. President George W. Bush, when signing the law establishing it, emphasised 'the President's constitutional authority to withhold information the disclosure of which could impair foreign relations, the national security, the deliberative processes of the Executive, or the performance of the Executive's constitutional duties.' He and his Vice President Dick Cheney offered to meet only with the commission's chair and vice chair, not the full membership.

Legality and War

As well as the role of the legislature, senior politicians participating in combat must be aware of legal considerations, internal and external. The *Ministerial Code* refers to the 'overarching duty on Ministers to comply with the law, including international law and treaty obligations'. It states, 'The Law Officers must be consulted in good time before the Government is committed to critical decisions involving legal considerations.' As discussed in the previous chapter, the *Ministerial Code* is not independently owned or enforced, and prime ministers are responsible for drafting and interpreting it. They can, therefore, influence the manner of consultation with law officers.

In the circumstances of a controversial war, as was the case with the invasion of Iraq in 2003, the government may come under pressure to make legal advice it has received public. If it wishes to, it can avoid doing so. The *Ministerial Code* iterates, 'The fact and content of opinions or advice given by the Law Officers . . . must not be disclosed outside Government without their authority.'[23] On 14 March 2003 Blair informed the House that 'There is a longstanding convention, followed by successive Governments and reflected in the ministerial code, that legal advice to the Government remains confidential. This enables Government to obtain frank and full legal advice in confidence, as everyone else can.'[24] But Parliament was about to vote on the coming military action, without knowing the official view of its basis in law. There was some speculation as to whether the Attorney General, Lord Goldsmith, had told the government that the invasion would be illegal. If faced with such suspicions, a government which has claimed a convention for not revealing advice will, nevertheless, be able to make the gist of it public, if it wishes. It may be judged wise to go as far as to issue an account of the view, but not the actual text. That was done on 17 March 2003, when the Attorney General, Lord Goldsmith, published a version of his advice, which is discussed below. But that led some to wonder whether anything significant was omitted in the drafting process. It is probably advisable, if at all possible, when revealing the views of the Attorney General on a war, to do so in their original form, unless there is an aspect of them which it is considered prudent to suppress, or if there is a desire to create the impression that the actual text is more persuasive than it is.

British war leaders can utilise tradition and precedent in order to afford themselves freedom of action in other ways, including resisting judicial interference in the royal prerogative. There is an official view that 'the King (and Queen) can do no wrong (for example the Queen cannot be prosecuted in her own courts)'. That serves to illustrate the impunity with which Prerogative powers can be exercised. In addition, as noted above, 'the courts have perhaps tended to accept that [foreign policy] is an area where the Crown needs flexibility in order to act effectively and handle novel situations.'[25] There has been some judicial creep into areas of executive action. The courts seem to have jurisdiction to enquire into the way in which the prerogative is used, provided the power in question is itself justiceable. Aspects of the prerogative are subject to judicial review, but to be decided on a case-by-case basis.[26]

A government wishing to preserve its capacity for independent action would be well advised to press for the maintenance of the tradition of judicial non-interference. The Blair administration was determined that a court would not rule on the legality of the Iraq War. In the summer of 2004 the Head of the Diplomatic Service, Sir Michael Jay, submitted a statement to a hearing at the Court of Appeal at the Royal Courts of Justice (it was not ultimately cited in evidence). The case was that of the 'Fairford Five', peace protesters charged with conspiracy and criminal damage at a Gloucestershire airbase the previous year. They believed the Iraq war was unlawful and were acting to prevent it. It had been ruled in May that the question of the legality of the Iraq War, which they sought to use in their defence, was not justiceable.

Jay stated that

> it would be prejudicial to the national interest and to the conduct of
> the Government's foreign policy if the English courts were to express
> opinions on questions of international law concerning the use of force
> by the United Kingdom and the United States which might differ

from those expressed by the Government and advanced by it in the conduct of international relations.

Circumstances 'in and relating to' Iraq were 'most sensitive in international relations at the present time'. Jay went on, 'If the opinion of an English court, expressed in a formal judgment, differed from that of the Government, this would inevitably weaken the Government's hand in its negotiations with other States.' Allies 'which have agreed with and supported the United Kingdom's views on the legality of the use of force, could regard such a step as tending to undermine their own position'. Less friendly powers 'could seize upon such a judgment and use it to question the Government's position in the course of diplomatic negotiations concerning Iraq and more widely'. 'Serious risks' might be entailed. 'It is likely that such a decision would provide encouragement to those in Iraq who are using violence to destabilise the situation, including insurgents, terrorists, former regime loyalists and those in Middle Eastern Countries who are supporting them.' A critical ruling could 'undermine the Government's standing with Arab and Islamic countries, and could give comfort and encouragement to terrorist organisations'. Attempts by Britain 'to negotiate and secure effective measures against proliferation of weapons of mass destruction (and in particular to prevent them becoming available to terrorist organisations) could be hampered' along with 'efforts to secure co-operation of States in measures against terrorists based in other countries, and measures to secure cooperation in the exchange of information vital to security matters'.

The more developed judicial review which exists in other countries, especially the US, need not constrain a war leader excessively. Describing the Supreme Court assessment of Woodrow Wilson's emergency programme of the First World War, Corwin notes, 'The fact is that the Court had the opportunity to pass upon very little of it . . . during the period of the war; the legislation had accomplished its purpose before the formalities could be got through – something that with a little contriving would happen in any war.' The Court upheld, after the fact, Lincoln's blockade of Southern ports. It did not support the measures including the trial of civilians by military commissions carried out in the Civil War. Wilson's restrictions on freedom of speech and the press, his implementation of conscription and various economic interventions, were subsequently cleared by the judiciary. Under Franklin D. Roosevelt, policies such as the imposition of sanctions by executive agencies in support of rationing were upheld. The declaration of martial law in Hawaii in 1941, following the Japanese attack on Pearl Harbor, was ruled 'illegal' and 'unconstitutional', but as late as 1946.[27]

In addition to domestic legal considerations conditioning how a government may act, there are external regulations which a war leader must take into account. Arguments over whether a particular action is in compliance with such standards are difficult to resolve, since it is unlikely that they will be heard by a court. In that sense, a war leader in a democratic society is not likely to be formally found personally in breach of international law, or penalised as such; nor is a state. Despite that, it is important for presentational and political purposes to be able to argue that an action is legal. As well as a constraint, international organisations and standards can be used by a senior national politician in pursuit of a particular campaign. It is possible to construct a case for engaging in combat without prior UN consent.

Leaders must be aware of the official etiquette for commencing armed conflict, which changes over time. Observing it need not alter the substance of a particular action. Hostilities may occur without an official state of war existing; indeed, that has become a commonplace. Equally, states may declare war on others for political purposes with no intention of fighting. Such was the case with some Latin American countries during the Second World War which wished to indicate their support for the Allied cause against the Axis powers. In some cases, historically, a declaration has been used as a final threat, actually helping to avoid hostilities.

Traditionally, lawyers did not believe formal statements to be necessary to an action, especially if demands of some sort had already been issued. But around the turn of the nineteenth–twentieth centuries, in the words of Ingrid Detter, 'since an attack with modern weapons could be executed with greater speed than before . . . there was a body of opinion that declarations of war should be made obligatory, as swift attacks were almost synonymous with treacherous attacks.' In 1907, the idea was included as a stipulation of the third Hague Convention, prompted in part by the controversy surrounding surprise attacks upon Russian warships by Japanese torpedo boats in 1904. States were now required to issue either a declaration of war or an ultimatum, according to an agreed form. Following the formation of the League of Nations and the Kellogg-Briand Pact of 1928, both of which sought to prevent war (the latter attempting to outlaw it altogether), nations, while still engaging in military conflict, returned to doing so without formal statements. At present, 'The position . . . appears to be that war may well exist although there has been no declaration of war.' Article 2 (4) of the United Nations (UN) Charter, discussed below, forbids use of armed force if directed against the territorial integrity of any state or if it is inconsistent with the purposes of the UN. But as Detter writes, 'War may be technically outlawed; but wars still occur.'[28]

International law is not yet fully codified, though bringing this about is the objective of the UN International Law Commission. What are the means by which it might be ruled upon? The

International Court of Justice (ICJ) is the principal judicial organ of the UN. The ICJ's judgements are binding under the UN Charter, but it lacks a direct enforcement mechanism. A war leader cannot be held personally culpable by the ICJ, which is a civil court and handles cases between states. A country has to bring a case for it to be heard. If a military action causes the removal of a regime, as with the invasion of Iraq in 2003, then the new government would be unlikely to seek redress through the ICJ. If a case is brought to the ICJ, as it was over US intervention in Nicuragua in the 1980s, a war leader may follow the example of the US at the time and deny the right of the court to consider the matter, pulling out of proceedings part of the way through.

The International Criminal Court (ICC), unlike the ICJ, deals with individuals and their responsibilities, and is a body for criminal prosecutions. It had a prolonged gestation period, underlining the fact that international action on such matters is difficult to generate and sustain. As long ago as 1948, clearly influenced by then recent events, the UN General Assembly, in Resolution 260, called for the International Law Commission 'to study the desirability and possibility of establishing an international judicial organ for the trial of persons charged with genocide'. Finally, the jurisdiction of the ICC came into force in 2002. It is independent of, but has an agreement with, the UN. The ICC can prosecute for genocide, crimes against humanity and war crimes. There were difficulties in agreeing on a definition of crimes of aggression. While Britain is signed up to the ICC, along with other democratic countries, the US is not. Leaders not participating in schemes designed to ensure certain standards of conduct are adhered to may be reluctant to engage in joint missions with those who are. In 2002 the US opposed renewing the mandate of the UN peacekeeping mission in Bosnia and Herzegovina: it was concerned that its personnel might be exposed to prosecution by the ICC. It is theoretically possible that the leader of a democratic country could fall foul of the ICC, though perhaps far-fetched.

There are a number of international declarations and conventions with possible or clear relevance to war. As a Council of Europe member state, the UK is party to the European Convention on Human Rights (ECHR), which was incorporated into domestic law by the Human Rights Act 1998. Adherence to it can restrict the actions of a war leader in a number of ways, discussed here and in the next chapter. Few countries have taken the option to derogate from parts of the ECHR. Britain did so in the late 1980s, with respect to anti-terrorist legislation – and again in 2001, as will be shown. The ECHR requires states to act against terrorism, though not to be too heavy-handed in so doing. In July 2002, the Council of Europe adopted its 'Guidelines on human rights and the fight against terrorism'. It stated that the attacks of 11 September 2001 'have been perceived as a direct assault on the fundamental values of human rights, democracy and the rule of law which are our shared heritage'. The Council was concerned that

> *The temptation for governments and parliaments in countries suffering from terrorist action is to fight fire with fire, setting aside the legal safeguards that exist in a democratic state. But let us be clear about this: while the State has the right to employ to the full its arsenal of legal weapons to repress and prevent terrorist activities, it may not use indiscriminate measures which would only undermine the fundamental values they seek to protect. For a State to react in such a way would be to fall into the trap set by terrorism for democracy and the rule of law . . . It is precisely in situations of crisis, such as those brought about by terrorism, that respect for human rights is even more important, and that even greater vigilance is called for.*

The guidelines began by noting the existence of 'States' obligation to protect everyone against terrorism'. In other words, safety from attacks of the sort perpetrated on 11 September 2001 was in itself a fundamental individual right. Yet, in pursuance of that end, governments had to be sure to prohibit 'arbitrariness' and ensure compliance with the law. In addition, 'The use of torture or of inhuman or degrading treatment or punishment is absolutely prohibited, in all circumstances.' Information gathering by the authorities should be conducted within the bounds of domestic legality and proportionality with the aims towards which it was directed. It had to be subject to supervision by an independent authority. Intrusions into privacy (body and house searches, bugging, telephone tapping, surveillance of correspondence, the use of undercover agents) were to be within a statutory framework. Counter-terrorist activity had to be designed in such a way as to minimise the deployment of lethal force.

Arrests could be carried out only on a basis of reasonable suspicion. The individuals concerned had to be informed of the reasons for the detention and brought before a judge rapidly. Police custody ought to be of a 'reasonable' period of time. There had to be a possibility for formal challenge to such processes, as well as to pre-trial confinement. Anyone accused of terrorist activities had 'the right to a fair hearing, within a reasonable time, by an independent, impartial tribunal established by law'. There was to be a 'presumption of innocence'. Penalties imposed could not be heavier 'than the one that was applicable at the time when the criminal offence was committed'. Further, 'Under no circumstances may a person convicted of terrorist activities be sentenced to the death penalty; in the event of such a sentence being imposed, it may not be carried out.' Detention had to be carried out 'with due respect for human dignity'. States were required to ensure that, when asylum status was refused, the applicant was not sent somewhere where they would be exposed 'to the death penalty, to torture or to inhuman or degrading treatment or punishment'. The same applied to expulsion. Furthermore, 'Collective expulsion of aliens is prohibited.' While the US used capital punishment, 'The extradition of a person to a country where he/she risks being sentenced to the death penalty may not be granted.' No one could be sent where they were likely to be subject to 'torture or other degrading treatment'.

Importantly for Britain, the guidance stated that

> When the fight against terrorism takes place in a situation of war or public emergency which threatens the life of the nation, a State may adopt measures temporarily derogating from certain obligations ensuing from the international instrument of protection of human rights, to the extent strictly required by the exigencies of the situation, as well as within the limits and under the conditions fixed by international law . . . States may never, however, and whatever the acts of the person suspected of terrorism, or convicted of such activities, derogate from the right to life as guaranteed by these international instruments, from the prohibition against torture or inhuman or degrading treatment or punishment, from the principle of legality of sentences and of measures, nor from the ban on the retrospective effect of criminal law . . . The circumstances which led to the adoption of such derogations need to be reassessed on a regular basis with the purpose of lifting these derogations as soon as these circumstances no longer exist.

In addition to the ECHR, numerous UN documents exist: the 'Universal Declaration of Human Rights', the 'Convention against Torture and Other Cruel, Inhuman or Degrading Treatment or Punishment', and the 'Convention on the Prevention and Punishment of the Crime of Genocide'. They, along with the 'Geneva

Conventions', prescribe forms of conduct during a war (and some of them could possibly be cited as justifying an action).

The UN Charter is relevant to the question of whether or not a war can legitimately be fought in the first place. Article 2 (4) of the Charter states that

> *all Members shall refrain in their international relations from the threat or use of force against the territorial integrity or political independence of any state, or in any other manner inconsistent with the Purposes of the United Nations.*

The UN Security Council (UNSC) has primary responsibility within the UN for matters of security and peace. Even it may be subject to the UN Charter, in which case it could theoretically exceed its own authority – not something which has been tested directly. No provision exists for judicial review of Security Council decisions. There are five permanent members: China, France, Russia, the UK and the US; as well as ten which are elected by the General Assembly for two year terms. The UNSC can make recommendations, call for actions, or impose obligations upon members. Its substantive decisions need nine votes, with any of the five permanent members able to block them.

Chapter VII of the UN Charter describes circumstances in which the UNSC may intervene. 'Intervention' is not synonymous with military action in legal terms. The former may involve sanctions or the violation of airspace to supply aid. According to Article 39, 'The Security Council shall determine the existence of any threat to the peace, breach of the peace, or act of aggression and shall make recommendations, or decide what measures shall be taken . . . to maintain or restore international peace and security.' The Security Council can then (as stated in Article 41) *decide what measures not involving the use of armed force are to be employed to give effect to its decisions, and it may call upon the Members of the United Nations to apply such measures. These may include complete or partial interruption of economic relations and of rail, sea, air, postal, telegraphic, radio, and other means of communication, and the severance of diplomatic relations.*

If such sanctions (in the words of Article 42)

would be inadequate or have proved to be inadequate, [the UNSC] may take such action by air, sea, or land forces as may be necessary to maintain or restore international peace and security. Such action may include demonstrations, blockade, and other operations by air, sea, or land forces of Members of the United Nations.

In these circumstances it may call upon 'All Members of the United Nations . . . to make available . . . in accordance with a special agreement or agreements, armed forces, assistance, and facilities, including rights of passage, necessary for the purpose of maintaining international peace and security'.

As has been shown, a country which enjoys permanent membership of the UNSC is therefore able to veto its resolutions. War leaders can thereby prevent the UNSC from acting in ways which they regard as undesirable. Alterations to the balance of power on the UNSC may make increased rejections necessary. In 1966 the UNSC was expanded from eleven to fifteen members. Up to 1968 the then Soviet Union had exercised 103 vetoes, France four, Britain three, China (Taiwan took its seat) one and the US none at all. Thereafter, the US in particular utilised them increasingly, becoming the primary blocking country by the 1980s, for such objectives as supporting its ally, Israel.

As well as preventing them, the UNSC can legitimise and concert actions for war leaders. Resolution 83, dated 27 June 1950, determined 'that the armed attack upon the Republic of Korea by forces from North Korea constitutes a breach of the peace'. It recommended that 'Members of the United Nations furnish such assistance to the Republic of Korea as may be necessary to repel the armed attack and to restore international peace and security in the area'. A US-led action followed. Similarly, forty years later, Resolution 678 of 29 November 1990 noted that 'despite all efforts by the United Nations, Iraq refuses to comply with its obligations . . . [to obey the UNSC and withdraw from Kuwait] in flagrant contempt of the Security Council.' The UNSC demanded 'that Iraq comply fully . . . and decides . . . to allow Iraq one final opportunity, as a pause of goodwill to do so'. It authorised 'Member states cooperating with the Government of Kuwait, unless Iraq on or before 15 January 1991 fully implements . . . the above mentioned resolutions, to use all necessary means . . . to restore international peace and security in the area'. It requested 'all States to provide appropriate support for the actions undertaken'. Iraq did not comply and was ejected from Kuwait in another operation in which the US was foremost.

A war leader may use the UN for coordinating anti-terrorist activity. On 28 September 2001 the UNSC issued Resolution 1373, stating that it was *Deeply concerned* [italics in original] by the increase, in various regions of the world, of acts of terrorism motivated by intolerance or extremism.' It called upon 'States to work together urgently to prevent and suppress terrorist acts, including through increased cooperation and full implementation of the relevant international conventions relating to terrorism'. There followed a detailed list of areas in which they were to act. Resolution 1373 established the Counter-Terrorism Committee (CTC), which comprised the fifteen Security Council members. The CTC was charged with monitoring the implementation of Resolution 1373. Its method of working was to analyse reports submitted by countries relating to their compliance with 1373 and ask follow-up questions. The first priority from the point of view of the CTC was that the necessary legislation was in place, then that it was properly enforced by the government concerned and that there was in existence appropriate executive machinery to do so.

There are limitations to the use of UN resolutions such as 1373. The CTC was not a body for bringing about sanctions, nor did it hold a list of dangerous organisations or people. Getting states to co-operate even to the extent of producing written submissions was not always easy. In January 2003, the UNSC noted that '13 States . . . have not yet submitted a first report [they were supposed to do so within 90 days of the adoption of 1373] and . . . 56 States . . . are late in submitting further reports.' The idea of international cooperation, of which Resolution 1373 was an expression, certainly made some progress. Many countries introduced new statute following 11 September 2001, enabling action along the lines advocated in Resolution 1373.

A war leader may not find it appropriate or possible to obtain explicit UN authorisation before moving against a military enemy. In invading Iraq in 2003, the US referred to Article 51 of the UN Charter, which states, 'Nothing in the present Charter shall impair the inherent right of individual or collective self-defence if an armed attack occurs against a Member of the United Nations.' But the Charter does not provide a detailed account of the 'inherent right of . . . self-defence'. It exists in customary international law and enables the use of military action to defend against attack, repel and expel hostile forces, and infringe upon the territory of another state if hostilities are emanating from there, if enemy bases are located there, or if it is providing refuge for aggressors. There are limits to such responses. They should be both necessary (that is, there should be no other realistic and non-violent course of action) and proportionate to the degree of action required to fend off the incursion. Usual rules of war apply, too.

The right of self-defence is open to widely differing interpretation. Consequently, war leaders may both utilise it to justify their own actions and criticise its supposed exercise on the part of other states. The US, as is discussed below, has lately developed a doctrine of pre-emptive action. Yet, in the past it has objected to similar activity on the part of others. In 1837 a ship, the *Caroline*, was sunk in a US port by British subjects who believed it was supplying rebels in Canada. Two American citizens were killed, prompting a challenge by the US Secretary of State. The Israelis bombed a nuclear reactor in Iraq in 1981. A UN Security Council Resolution condemning the attack was supported by the US (and was passed unanimously).

It is possible to argue that a defence can be initiated before an attack has occurred. Interception, such as stopping a missile launch in progress, is generally accepted as legitimate. But if troops are being massed on a border, but have not yet been given the order to move, there is a question as to whether it should be permissible to take measures against them. The right to anticipate has been asserted. It was the claimed basis of Israel's actions against Egypt and other Arab countries in 1956 and 1967. Some argue that it is applicable not only to hostile states, but terrorist groups. Israel attacked the Palestinian Liberation Organisation (PLO) headquarters in Tunisia in 1985 using this justification, as did the US in bombing Libya the following year.

The US now explicitly portrays terrorism as a continuous campaign made up of individual strikes, against which it can protect itself by pre-emptive action, the so-called 'Bush Doctrine'. It rests on the argument that as the nature of enemies and the technology they use have changed, so must the standards applied to methods of defence. In September 2002 the President published *The National Security Strategy of the United States of America*. It referred to the need to defend the US, 'the American people, and our interests at home and abroad by identifying and destroying the threat before it reaches our borders'. While attempting to operate in conjunction with the international community, 'we will not hesitate to act alone, if necessary, to exercise our right of self-defense by acting pre-emptively against . . . terrorists'. It was necessary to 'adapt the concept of imminent threat to the capabilities and objectives of today's adversaries'. The reason was that 'Rogue states and terrorists do not seek to attack us using conventional means . . . Instead, they rely on acts of terror and, potentially, the use of weapons of mass destruction – weapons that can be easily concealed, delivered covertly, and used without warning.' Therefore, the 'option of pre-emptive actions to counter a sufficient threat to our national security' applied, 'even if uncertainty remains as to the time and place of the enemy's attack'.

Another possible supporting argument for a conflict is that it is being carried out for humanitarian ends. A doctrine for such action presently exists only in embryonic form. Bill Rammell, the Parliamentary Under-Secretary of State for Foreign and Commonwealth Affairs, told the Commons in March 2004 that

> *Over recent years, the UN has been developing its thinking, based on individual cases, on where military intervention is justified for humanitarian purposes. The Security Council can authorise the use of force in response to threats to international peace and security, breaches of the peace or acts of aggression. It has explicitly determined that widespread violations of human rights and international humanitarian law have contributed to situations threatening the peace, and mandated enforcement action in former Yugoslavia, Rwanda and East Timor. I think that most people regard that as*

*essentially just and correct. The Security Council also supported
enforcement action to return to power an elected Government that
had been overthrown, such as in Sierra Leone and in Haiti. Again, I
think that most people would accept those actions and propositions.*[29]

Allied actions in northern and southern Iraq in 1991 suggested a
belief in a limited ability to violate state sovereignty on humanitarian
grounds. Operation 'Provide Comfort' in northern Iraq claimed as
its basis UNSC Resolution 688 which insisted that 'Iraq allow
immediate access by international humanitarian organisations to all
those in need of assistance in all parts of Iraq' and appealed 'to all
Member States . . . to contribute to these humanitarian relief efforts'.
But the resolution did not justify or argue for using force, or refer to
Chapter VII of the UN Charter.

On the UNSC, Russia and China have been very reluctant to
endorse humanitarian intervention, opposing the NATO action in
Kosovo in 1999, intended to prevent atrocities against ethnic
Albanians. A resolution clearly providing for the operation was not
obtained. The best that could be arrived at was Resolution 1199,
which stated the Council's intention, 'should the concrete measures
demanded in this resolution . . . not be taken, to consider further
action and additional measures to maintain or restore peace and
stability in the region'. Operation 'Allied Force' was therefore carried
out by NATO, with a claimed humanitarian basis (although there
was also a suggestion that the stability of the region was under
threat.)

In the words of Rammell,

*in the case of Kosovo, we had to ask ourselves how to respond when a
Security Council decision could not be reached in the face of an
imminent humanitarian crisis in the form of appalling ethnic*

cleansing the like of which we had not seen on our continent since the second world war. At that time, we made clear our view that states do have a right, in exceptional circumstances, to take military action when it is the only way to avert an overwhelming humanitarian catastrophe, and that that is the case even in the absence of explicit authorisation from the Security Council.[30]

It is possible to legitimise and even facilitate a wide range of actions using one or more of the justifications suggested above. It is extremely likely that democratic leaders, given the principles associated with that form of government, such as the rule of law, will wish to present themselves as acting in accordance with international regulations. Sometimes such claims will be extremely controversial. The case presented by the British government for the invasion of Iraq in 2003 was strongly disputed. It is outlined below (as expressed in a Written Answer to a Parliamentary Question by the Attorney General):

Authority to use force was derived from the combined effect of three UNSC resolutions. The first two dated from the time of the Kuwait conflict in the early 1990s, the third from 2002 and the run-up to the Iraq War. Resolution 678 provided for military action against Iraq to eject it from Kuwait and make the area stable again. Following that, Resolution 687 set out the ceasefire conditions and imposed obligations upon Iraq to eliminate its weapons of mass destruction. It suspended the use of force permitted under Resolution 678, but did not terminate it. A material breach of the later Resolution revived the earlier one. Resolution 1441 stated that Iraq was in violation of Resolution 687, because it was not fulfilling disarmament obligations. In Resolution 1441, Iraq was given 'a final opportunity to comply', or 'serious consequences' would follow. It was determined that failure to cooperate fully with Resolution 1441 would constitute a further material breach of Resolution 687. Iraq failed to conform, it was argued, and the provision for force under Resolution 678 was, therefore, revived. Resolution 1441 did not specifically refer to the need for a further decision by the Security Council. In that case, all that was required prior to action was a report and discussion, but not an express decision. George W. Bush, when reporting to Congress, noted that Resolution 678 was used for military action in 1993, 1996 and 1998, as well as to enforce no-fly zones. (Bush added that, given the type of threat posed by Iraq, there was an additional right for the US to proceed under Article 51 of the UN Charter, which refers to the right of self-defence. The British government did not use such an argument in the way its US ally did.)

There were countervailing arguments. A group of international lawyers wrote an open letter to Blair on 6 March 2003, arguing that

> *On the basis of the information publicly available, there is no justification under international law for the use of military force against Iraq ... There are currently no grounds for a claim to use such force in self-defence ... Neither security council resolution 1441 nor any prior resolution authorises the proposed use of force in the present circumstances.*

The letter went on, 'Before military action can lawfully be undertaken against Iraq, the security council must have indicated its clearly expressed consent. It has not yet done so.' Finally, a warning was issued. 'A decision to undertake military action in Iraq without proper security council authorisation will seriously undermine the international rule of law.'[31]

4   War, the State and Society

- War may necessitate increased state intervention in society, of a sort that can conflict with democratic principles
- The approach can be justified as necessary for the broader preservation of liberty
- Executive activity of an arbitrary nature may prove counterproductive
- Societies engaged in longer-term conflicts, such as the War on Terror, may be forced to curtail certain freedoms on a semi-permanent or permanent basis
- Imprisonment without trial – often on a large scale – has been conducted by many democratic war governments. As a policy, it is frequently of dubious value
- Contingency powers are needed by government to respond to emergencies. They can be used for political purposes, too. But they may be turned against the same politicians who first introduced them
- Terrorism has prompted frequent repressive responses from the state. Special legislation can be resorted to, though it may be introduced in haste and contain flaws
- The new demands placed upon the state by war may necessitate changes to bureaucratic structures and personnel

- Coordination of the different specialist components of the intelligence machinery is vital. There are dangers associated with agencies being deployed to service predetermined policy objectives, and not being held publicly accountable
- A modern day British government will utilise at the senior level a mixture of permanent staff and temporary, political appointments. Both have particular useful qualities which must be balanced with one-another

Intervention

War leaders have frequently enhanced the power of the state for purposes such as a galvanised national effort and internal security. Such intervention can take various forms, including economic *dirigisme*, or encroachment upon individual liberties. As Hennessy notes of the Second World War,

> *Never before and never since has a British Government taken so great and so intrusive a range of powers over the lives of its citizens – where they worked, what they did in uniform or in 'civvies', what they ate, what they wore, what they could read in their newspapers, what they could hear on their wireless sets.*

The programme was enacted through the Emergency Powers (Defence) Act of 1939, which 'gave the Government power to make regulations and to issue orders'.[1] It represented an extension of tendencies which developed in the First World War.

A similar pattern developed in the US. In the early 1860s, among other measures Abraham Lincoln's administration closed post offices to 'treasonable correspondence', applied new passport regulations, suspended habeas corpus, pursued a policy of detaining individuals

believed to be disloyal and implemented a militia draft. During the
First World War, under President Wilson, conscription was used (as
it was again in the Second). Alongside that, the executive acquired
extensive controls over production, trade, utilities and transport.
Threatened or actual economic sanctions were used against participating workers to end strikes. The activities of aliens were
regulated, and censorship and restrictions on freedom of speech
applied. The measures in question were implemented in large part
through regulations, drawing on primary legislation for their
authority. There was much bureaucratic reorganisation and creation
of agencies to carry out the new functions. As one comprehensive
study of the subject puts it,

> *in the war crucible the more general principles of constitutional law
> and theory, those that ordinarily govern the delegation of legislative
> power, the scope of national power over the ordinary life of the citizen
> . . . become highly malleable, and . . . even the more specific
> provisions of the Bill of Rights take on unaccustomed flexibility.*[2]

But measures resorted to in the two previous serious conflicts proved
only a prelude to those of the Second World War, even before the US
began its official participation in hostilities. With his first inaugural
address in March 1933, President Franklin D. Roosevelt indicated
that he was disposed towards powerful action, if necessary extending
beyond conventional constitutional practice, to counteract dire
circumstances. At the time, that meant the prevailing economic
depression. He described himself as assuming 'unhesitatingly the
leadership of this great army of our people dedicated to a disciplined
attack upon our common problems'. Roosevelt proposed that 'an
unprecedented demand and need for undelayed action may call for
temporary departure from [the] normal balance of public procedure'.

If Congress proved unable to take the necessary measures, 'I shall not evade the clear course of duty that will then confront me. I shall ask the Congress for the one remaining instrument to meet the crisis – broad Executive power to wage a war against the emergency, as great as the power that would be given to me if we were in fact invaded by a foreign foe.'

During the Second World War, central direction of industry, for the defence purposes of the US and its allies, was practised, exercised in large part through the War Production Board. In order to ensure essential production, on occasion whole plants were requisitioned. One individual who acquired great power in the unusual circumstances of war administration was Paul McNutt, Chairman of the War Manpower Commission. In late 1942, control of the entire workforce not enrolled in the armed forces was vested in him (with each executive department and agency obliged to cooperate with the decisions he took). The following February, to remedy labour shortages in certain areas, he issued his 'work or fight' order. It obliged all whose activities were not deemed essential to accept transferral elsewhere, or be enlisted into the military. He enforced a 48-hour week. In order to achieve compliance with the decree that all male staff were to be recruited through the United States Employment Service (which was under the direction of the Commission) a variety of pressures were applied to firms. Failure to cooperate could lead to measures as extreme as their power, lighting and heat being cut off.[3]

Often, extreme interventionism practised by war leaders can be to some extent relaxed, as a military emergency recedes. Such was true for Britain and the US following the wars referred to above. However, if the conflict is long-term, the measures may have to be, too. This has been the case for the state of Israel, with many enemies in its close proximity. In her 1993 book, *Living Without a*

Constitution, Daphna Sharfman, the Chair of the Civil Rights Committee of the Israel Labor Party, referred to 'Defense Regulations of 1945 . . . enacted by the British mandatory government to aid it in its fight against the rebellious Jewish community in Palestine'. Included amongst them were 'limitations on immigration, freedom of the press, freedom of speech, freedom of movement, and the freedom to demonstrate.' While the 'prestate Jewish community strongly protested these arbitrary regulations, viewing them as an instrument of suppression', nevertheless 'once the state was established . . . it soon became clear that the government had no intention of abolishing them'. Following the War of Independence, in 1948, a military government was established, using the emergency regulations. Arab areas were divided into districts, between which movement was restricted and where curfews were enforced (though Arabs were given full Israeli citizenship). There was public debate in Israel as to whether such measures were a propaganda gift to enemies and if they were genuinely needed to guard against a 'fifth column' – that is enemies within. The military government was not completely abolished until 1966.

Another aspect of the Emergency Defense Regulations was restriction of the media. The administration was granted the ability to censor and prevent the publication of information. Inherited from the period of British Mandate – and retained – was a system of permits for, and state controls over, newspapers (the 'Press Ordinance', introduced in 1933 because the prior Turkish legislation was seen as inadequate). Various other laws facilitated tight limitations on the release of official information and promulgation of views. There have also been non-statutory agreements between editors and the government. It might be argued that the restrictions proved detrimental to public safety in the early 1970s. The Yom Kippur War caught the population by surprise. Press allusions to preparations for attack were prevented since the military did not generally believe it would happen. Journalists may have had information regarding the intentions of the Arab states, which they were not permitted to disseminate. A suspicion that censorship was being used for narrow political purposes, rather than for the national interest, has arisen at times.[4]

The War on Terror, too, is an open-ended engagement, encouraging leaders, as those in Israel have done, to adopt emergency devices on a more enduring basis. On 20 September 2001 President George W. Bush told a joint session of Congress that 'Americans should not expect one battle, but a lengthy campaign unlike any other we have ever seen.' In 2004 the British government argued that security measures introduced immediately after 11 September 2001 (discussed below) were still necessary. Osama bin Laden's recorded message, issued on 12 February 2003, was cited as evidence for their view. In it, he stated, 'We stress the importance of the martyrdom operations against the enemy – operations that inflicted harm on the United States and Israel.' Referring to 'whoever supported the United States . . . to kill Muslims in Iraq' – which presumably included Britain – he iterated, 'It is permissible to spill their blood and take their property.' Therefore, the official view was that 'the main threat to the UK and its interests overseas is international, likely to be of long duration, involving groups of people engaged in long-term planning, using sophisticated technology, science and communications available to them, skilled in practising deception and evading surveillance, and using multiple stolen or fraudulent identities.'[5]

How should war leaders approach and present their responses to emergency circumstances? While increased intervention may be regarded by some as an affront to liberal principles, it is possible to argue that adherence to democratic values requires it. As one official committee in Britain, charged with reviewing the Anti-terrorism, Crime and Security Act 2001 (ATCSA) put it recently, 'The state has a duty to protect the public from harm, even at the expense of some individual rights. After all, terrorists curtail the rights of those affected by their activities. Aspects of this obligation are codified in international law. For example, Articles 1 and 2 of the European Convention on Human Rights, in combination, require the state to ensure that "Everyone's right to life shall be protected by law".'[6]

During the American Civil War, on not entirely dissimilar lines, in his 4 July 1861 message to Congress, Lincoln justified his suspension of habeas corpus, noting that 'the legality and propriety of what has been done under it are questioned, and the attention of the country has been called to the proposition that one who is sworn to "take care that the laws be faithfully executed" [the President] should not himself violate them'. Yet, he went on, because of the Southern secession,

> The whole of the laws which were required to be faithfully executed were being resisted and failing of execution in nearly one-third of the States. Must they be allowed to finally fail of execution, even had it been perfectly clear that by the use of the means necessary to their execution some single law, made in such extreme tenderness of the citizen's liberty that practically it relieves more of the guilty than of the innocent, should to a very limited extent be violated? To state the question more directly, Are all the laws but one to go unexecuted, and the Government itself to go to pieces lest that one be violated?

The recurring theme, that leaders engaged in war of various forms may feel compelled to engage in activities which curtail some civil liberties, continues to the present. In February 2004 the British government issued a discussion paper that dealt with the dilemma of ensuring security against terrorism in a democratic society.[7] In his foreword, the then Home Secretary, David Blunkett, noted that

> *Democratic governments have always had to strike a balance between the powers of the state and the rights of individuals. In more extreme times, the American Civil War of the mid 19th century saw Abraham Lincoln suspending the right of habeas corpus . . . while in World War II UK citizens were interned on British soil.*

He went on, 'The challenge today is of course different,' since 'the threat to our freedoms does not come in the main from conventional warfare from enemy states. The September 11 hijackers . . . had not issued a set of demands or previously publicly associated themselves with their cause . . . their murderous allegiances were secretive, allowing them to strike with maximum effect.' As Home Secretary, his 'first responsibility' was 'to do everything I can to ensure our common security'. 'But,' he asked, 'is this security worth having if the price is a series of unacceptable restrictions on our hard-won freedoms?' In the main text of the paper it was argued that 'sophisticated terrorist action . . . threatens the very democracy which protects our liberty. But that liberty may be exploited by those supporting, aiding, or engaging in terrorism.'

Though they may be able to justify intervention on such grounds, war leaders should be aware of the dangers of its excessive, unchecked, deployment. In the words of the ATCSA review:

> *The authorities are not infallible so their powers must include limitations and safeguards to reduce the danger that they could be misapplied. Misuse of such powers:*

results (by definition) in individual cases of injustice or harm;
leads to a false sense of security (because the actual terrorists are still
going about their business);
brings the use of those powers into disrepute (undermining the case for
their use where they are genuinely needed to protect the public).

The report cited a recent example of such flawed activity. Police used Section 44 of the Terrorism Act 2000 (TA) to search protesters outside the Arms Fair in Docklands, London, in October 2003. Events of that sort are undesirable for war leaders since they can damage the credibility of policies. They can in turn cause further embarrassment, bringing inconvenient information into the open. In a High Court case related to the Docklands incident, it emerged publicly for the first time that the powers afforded by Section 44 had been renewed in London every 28 days since the TA had come into force. The use, it seems, was far more extensive than some in Parliament had envisaged when agreeing to pass the law.[8]

Another outcome that is more likely if the executive is acting without restraint is the commission of errors possibly undermining its own objectives. Following the invasion of Kuwait in 1990, senior policy makers in Britain, in the words of Major, 'dared not rule out the [Iraqi] use – even prior to the conflict – of chemical weapons as an instrument of terror in population centres in the UK'. Presumably partly as a consequence, 'Undesirable Iraqis were expelled, although we soon realised that some mistakes in identifying them were made, through either haste or excessive caution.'[9] A decade later one individual, believed to be a risk to national security, could have been detained under part of the ATCSA which came into force in November 2001. But because a file had been lost, it was decided that it was inappropriate to proceed against him and he was not confined until April 2002.

As the ATCSA review stated, 'Neither do more extensive powers always lead to greater public safety. The East German Government may have had files on a quarter of their population, but it failed to predict or prevent its own demise. If there is too much information, it can be difficult to analyse effectively and so can generate more leads than can be followed up or trigger too many false alarms.' Additionally, 'Sophisticated terrorists change their profile and methods to avoid presenting a static target. For example, al Qaeda is reported to place particular value on recruiting Muslim converts because they judge them to be less likely to be scrutinised by the authorities.'[10] More of the different types of security measures a war leader may take – while being advised to consider the drawbacks associated with them – are considered here.

Internment

Detention without trial has been employed in various democratic societies at times of conflict. It is most advisable to do so on the basis that the individuals subject to it pose an immediate security risk. That will certainly be one possible motive for doing so. Such a policy may be a means of allaying public fears regarding 'fifth columns' of potential traitors, or attacking particular political or social groups. It is very likely to lead to harmless persons being detained in unpleasant circumstances. Genuinely dangerous ones may remain at liberty. There is a possibility that the leader who ordered the confinements may be criticised and feel remorse for doing so.

British governments have long carried out executive detention. It was frequently employed in Ireland, until the 1860s through 'Habeus Corpus Suspension Acts' or the introduction of martial law. The so-called 'Westmeath Act' of 1871 allowed the governors of Ireland to detain people temporarily in or around that county who were believed to be members of the Ribbon Society. In 1881 'An Act for the Better Protection of Person and Property in Ireland' enabled the incarceration of individuals in specific areas suspected of treason or disrupting law and order. It was targeted in particular at the Land League. There were nearly a thousand internees, including five MPs, before the Kilmainham Treaty of 1882. Then the Special Commission Court was introduced, consisting of three judges with no jury, an approach taken a century later with the 'Diplock' courts.

World war, too, spurred a similar approach. In 1914, the 'Defence of the Realm Act' (DORA) was passed, under which Regulation 14B was issued the following year. Initially the intention was to direct DORA at Germans, or those of German descent or connection. Using 14B, around 160 persons on mainland Britain were detained, many of whom were held in St. Mary's Institute, a poorhouse in Islington, with their names not made publicly available. Ireland then came back into the picture with the rebellion of 1916 and 14B was turned to a different purpose. Around eighteen or nineteen hundred individuals were held on suspicion of their associations. The authorities claimed, in May 1918, to have uncovered a German plot involving Sinn Fein. Around a hundred leaders of the party, including Eamon de Valera and seven MPs, were imprisoned. For official purposes, the war was prolonged until 1921. The Restoration of Order in Ireland Act of 1920 was passed in the light of worsening difficulties there. By the following year, about three thousand were interned (and the Irish Free State continued that policy). In 1922, the Civil Authorities (Special Powers) Act was first introduced, supplanted in 1973 by the Northern Ireland (Emergency Provisions) Act. It permitted exclusion, residence and internment orders.

During the Second World War 'enemy aliens', that is citizens of countries with which Britain was at war, were interned in large numbers. By October 1940 there were 28,000 in custody, around three times the regular prison population. Furthermore, under regulation 18B (1A) of the Defence (General) Regulations, the British government imprisoned – indefinitely, without charge or trial – nearly two thousand individuals believed by the Home Secretary to threaten national security. Arrests began in May 1940. Predominantly, the incarcerated comprised members of fascist groups, most famously Sir Oswald Mosley, the aristocratic former Labour minister and leader of the British Union of Fascists and National Socialists. Captain Maule Ramsay, a Conservative MP and founder of the Right Club (a group set up in opposition to Jewry, Freemasonry and Bolshevism) was also confined.

The internment policy of World War Two remains controversial. In his study of the subject, A. W. Brian Simpson refers to 'as gross an invasion of British civil liberty as could be conceived, only justifiable, if at all, by the grim necessity of the time.'[11] As Simpson suggests, in May 1940 the position was dire. Britain was soon to be isolated in Europe. But the course pursued seems as much as anything else to be motivated by the desire of the incoming Prime Minister, Churchill, to show he meant business. Mosley's wife, Diana (one of two of Churchill's own cousins to be locked up), wrote that the policy could be explained thus: 'Summer 1940 was a time of panic; German armies swept west, the Low Countries and France fell. Stories of fifth columns in defeated countries were believed, though subsequently found to be fantasies.'[12] David Cannadine's views of the programme are mixed. 'Detention,' he writes,

> was a bitter part of valour. Many of those who were incarcerated had never done anything wrong, and were never likely to. The conditions in which they were held were often appallingly squalid. They were not told the grounds on which they were locked up, and were given

114

no indication as to when they might be set free. They were denied adequate legal representation, let alone an impartial hearing. When they were released, they were given no apology, and no compensation. There were some who never got over it. In the words of one contemporary, this was a 'bespattered page in our history'.

But, Cannadine argues, 'a nation fighting for liberty can only do so by limiting those very freedoms it stands pledged to defend, by itself becoming, to some degree, a totalitarian state.' The policy was unfair in another respect:

most of those detained . . . were of relatively humble social origin. Yet there were many in the higher echelons of society whose loyalty was at least as suspect, especially among the aristocracy where dim, arrogant, rabidly anti-Semitic admirers of Hitler were often to be found. But thanks to their friends in high places, most of these fellow travellers of the far Right somehow avoided detention. Of all the injustices . . . that may well have been the greatest.[13]

When, in the wake of 11 September 2001, the Home Secretary, David Blunkett, sought to detain foreign terrorist suspects who could not be deported, critics drew comparisons with practices during the Second World War. In a talk at Gresham College, David Pannick QC noted that

In November 1943 . . . Winston Churchill . . . observed that 'the power of the Executive to cast a man into prison without formulating any charge known to the law, and particularly to deny him the judgment of his peers, is in the highest degree odious and is the foundation of all totalitarian government whether Nazi or Communist.'

Pannick went on, 'Parliament should have given the same response to the proposals by the Home Secretary, David Blunkett, for detention without trial of terrorist suspects.'[14]

Democratic leaders in many other countries have pursued policies of executive confinement in circumstances of conflict. The expansion of state powers under Abraham Lincoln was described above. In his message to Congress of 4 July 1861, he referred to the decision 'to authorize the Commanding General in proper cases, according to his discretion, to suspend the privilege of the writ of habeas corpus, or, in other words, to arrest and detain without resort to the ordinary processes and forms of law such individuals as he might deem dangerous to the public safety'. Under Lincoln, 'According to the best recent estimate, at least thirteen thousand civilians were held under military arrest.' But, while 'Many of these arrests were justifiable . . . glaring instances of abuse are not hard to find'. One individual was detained for stating that he 'wouldn't wipe [his] ass with the stars and stripes'. Another, while drunk, had made a disloyal remark about the President. It transpired that he was the writer of a well-known patriotic song. Military tribunals were used, not only in Southern or contested border territory, but the North. They extended to 'all Rebels and Insurgents, their aiders and abettors within the United States, and all persons discouraging volunteer enlistments, resisting militia drafts, or guilty of any disloyal practice, affording aid and comfort to Rebels against the authority of the United States'. Those tried and sentenced to death by military tribunal included members of a secret society called the 'Order of American Knights' (later the 'Sons of Liberty'), formed by Peace Democrats, a group that did not believe in fighting to preserve the Union. Some of them had planned insurrectionary action, but it is not clear that all who were prosecuted did.[15]

The Japanese attacked the US naval base at Pearl Harbor, Hawaii, on 7 December 1941, killing around 2,300 Americans, prompting

US entry into the Second World War. On 19 February 1942 Franklin D. Roosevelt signed Executive Order 9066, allowing the designation of military zones 'from which any or all persons may be excluded'. That March, the 'forced removal of over 110,000 persons of Japanese descent from the West Coast states and part of Arizona' began. They were kept in 'assembly centers' and 'holding pens' until the 'relocation centers' were prepared. The latter have been described as

> *ten concentration camps scattered throughout the western and southern states from California to Arkansas. Accommodations in the camps [were] a grade above the malodorous horse stalls of the assembly centres: barracks, one family to a twenty-by-twenty-five-foot room, without private plumbing facilities and with little protection against the extreme rigors of climate in the remote regions where the camps have been built. The camps [were] ringed by barbed wire; searchlights [swung] from the watchtowers manned by armed military guards.*[16]

Emergency Powers

A war leader must ensure that there is sufficient power held in reserve by the state for particularly grave circumstances, along with plans for its deployment. Since potential threats change, approaches to them must be kept up to date. A government may choose to be vague about what is meant by an emergency, defining it widely, in order to cover all eventualities. Pressures will be exerted by various institutions and groups, calling for limitations on powers on grounds such as civil liberties. Nevertheless, measures must be designed in such as way as to be effective and possible to implement without obstruction.

There is potential for exploiting emergency legislation for political purposes. Following a failed putsch attempt by generals in Algeria in

1961, Charles de Gaulle utilised extensive powers he had granted himself for such a contingency in the Constitution of the Fifth Republic. He maintained a 'state of emergency' from April to September, despite the fact that the mutiny only lasted for ten days. De Gaulle was able to govern without reference to the legislature and stated in April that the National Assembly could not discuss circumstances in Algeria. Then, in August, that was the only subject it was allowed to debate, seemingly in order to keep them away from the topic of a farming crisis that had occurred.

More recently, in September 2004, following the Beslan school siege in which terrorists caused more than three hundred deaths, President Vladimir Putin announced his intention to end regional elections, replacing the leaders with central government nominees, and change the electoral system for the Duma. Justified in the name of security, the measures were judged likely to have the effect of concentrating considerable power in his hands.

The suspicion of abuse of emergency measures may meet with political protest or judicial obstacles. Identity cards were compulsory in Britain from 1939 to 1952 (the present government intends to reintroduce them). In 1951, though the High Court upheld the conviction of an individual for refusing to produce his credentials, the acting Lord Chief Justice stated that 'to use Acts of Parliament, passed for particular purposes during war, in times when the war is past . . . tends to turn law-abiding subjects into lawbreakers, which is a most undesirable state of affairs.'[17] In 1969 the European Commission on Human Rights ruled that the government established by the Greek colonels who had staged a coup two years previously was not correct in its derogation from the ECHR in order to take measures it deemed necessary for the preservation of order.

A politician determined only to utilise contingencies power for the purpose for which it is officially intended should bear in mind that future administrations to which it is bequeathed may not be of the same mind. All leaders, whatever their attitude to the appropriate use of emergency authority, are well advised to consider that, at some point in the future, when they no longer hold office, it may be directed against them. The Weimar Constitution drawn up in Germany in 1919 was largely the work of 'Left-liberal lawyers'. Article 48 granted the President the power to issue emergency legislation and use the armed forces to restore order. In the words of Michael Burleigh, 'This last stipulation was ominously vague . . . At the time few thought of the potential misuse of this . . . power.' It was deployed to protect democracy, for instance in 1923, the year when Adolf Hitler first attempted to seize power. In 1933 the Nazis, now in government, interpreted a terrorist act to serve their own purposes. Following the Reichstag Fire, the Decree of the President for the Protection of People and State was issued on 28 February. It 'abolished rights guaranteed by the Weimar constitution . . . suspended freedom of assembly and expression, authorised wiretaps and opening of mail, and sanctioned search and indefinite detention without warrants. This formed the basis of police power, until the police became so powerful that they eventually required no written authorisation at all.' Those on the receiving end of the deployment of arbitrary executive authority included the same groups who had created the Weimar constitution.[18]

During Blair's second term there was a major overhaul of emergency policy. It was needed. A press article from late 2002, stating that 'Britain is massively unprepared for a catastrophic terrorist attack', suggested that much work was to be done. It claimed that a series of (leaked) reports produced by the Civil Contingencies Secretariat described 'how after the end of the Cold War "most civil defence infrastructure and initiatives were scrapped or suspended", and [concluded]: "Civil defence effectively no longer exists in the UK as a stand-alone practical activity."' In the story's account, the documents referred to the fact that 'Britain's emergency legislation is "out of date". They say that "though useful and common internationally", the "ability to declare a state of emergency effectively does not exist in the UK" because the 80-year-old law under which it would be done is "anachronistic".' The Secretariat had supposedly urged the introduction of new legislation to rectify the shortcomings.[19]

Accordingly, the government produced the Civil Contingencies Act 2004. It replaced two existing pieces of legislation which were designed for the requirements of earlier eras. The Emergency Powers Act 1920, providing for central government action, was drawn up at a time of international revolutionary socialism and widespread trades union militancy. Local preparation was covered by the Civil Defence Act 1948, which, in the words of Douglas Alexander, Minister for the Cabinet Office, was 'perhaps the final vestige of cold war civil defence architecture'.[20]

The process leading to the Civil Contingencies legislation had begun before 11 September 2001. The Act was not, therefore, purely a response to terrorism. Rather, it formed part of a government strategy for eventualities including large accidents, extreme weather conditions, electronic viruses, fuel protests, and human and animal epidemics. In accordance with such an approach, it provided a broad definition of an emergency, describing it as 'an event or situation which threatens serious damage to . . . human welfare . . . the environment [or] security'. The classification put forward initially was wider still, taking in incidents endangering 'political, administrative or economic stability'. Amongst the critics of that proposal, the human rights pressure group, Liberty, commented, 'Although unlikely in this country, it is chilling that the Government could, in principle, declare a state of emergency . . . if faced with potential political instability.' There was a reasonable fear that a future administration could exploit the law, using it against the general population, to preserve its own existence. The government took the point and removed that section of the text.

Part Two of the Civil Contingencies Act updated provision for central government to make immediate legislation in relation to a particularly grave event. No longer preceded by the official declaration of a state of emergency, regulations are to be formally introduced by the monarch or – if that is difficult – a senior minister. They will be able to modify or overrule existing law. Initially, as a means of avoiding judicial obstacles, it was contemplated that, for the purposes of the Human Rights Act 1998, the measures would be treated as if they were primary legislation, so that they could not be struck down by a court on human rights grounds. But the idea that judges might allow themselves to become accomplices in the hampering of genuine efforts to mitigate the effects of an emergency is not borne out by past experience. The government, seemingly persuaded of the fact, dropped the plan. Nevertheless, the Civil Contingencies Act does not specify that regulations should be compatible with the ECHR. The official explanation was: 'Making express provision in this case might cast doubt on the application of the Human Rights Act [which provides for the ECHR in UK law] to other legislation where no express provision was made.' A war leader attempting to utilise the act for purposes other than those for which it is officially intended may meet with judicial obstacles.

Regulations under the Civil Contingencies Act must be laid before Parliament as soon as possible and approved within seven days, or else they lapse. They may be amended by resolutions of both Houses. Yet, given the absence of a genuine separation of powers as between the executive and legislature in Britain, the latter may not prove to be a problematic restraint on the use of the law. In the wake of a serious incident, perhaps even an attack on the House, with MPs dead or detained, a war leader need not fear that Parliament would acquire the capacity for independent action it lacks in more regular circumstances.

It is possible and perhaps wise to retain a high degree of official reticence regarding the range of potential applications of emergency legislation. A reluctance to place examples of plans in the public domain exists in Britain, on the grounds that 'access to draft emergency regulations could highlight [to terrorists, protesters etc.] both potential weaknesses and targets or likely counter-measures.' Possible actions under the Civil Contingencies Act seem to include the confiscation or destruction of property (perhaps without compensation), forced evacuation and the cordoning off of areas, the prohibition of assembly and travel, the creation of offences relating to the obstruction of emergency powers, the conferring of jurisdiction upon a court or tribunal, and the deployment of the armed forces. There is, therefore, enormous scope for infringement upon democratic principles, which some war leaders will wish to avoid. Others might accept it as necessary, or indeed seek to bring it about.

A concern exists that, as the Joint Committee on the Draft Civil Contingencies Bill noted, 'In the wrong hands [the power to disapply or modify acts of Parliament] could be used to remove all past legislation which makes up the statutory patchwork of the British constitution.' In other words, a constitutional *coup d'état* might be executed, with a new, non-democratic regime utilising the Act to establish itself on a permanent footing. The committee argued that elements fundamental to the UK settlement possibly subject to alteration or annulment included:

- Magna Carta
- The Bill of Rights
- The Acts of Union
- The Parliament Acts
- The European Communities Act
- The Representation of the People Act
- Acts bringing about devolution
- The Civil Contingencies Act itself

In response, the government stated, 'Emergency powers should not be used to make major modifications to the constitutional fabric of the United Kingdom.' However, it went on, the necessary protection already existed, since

> *each proposed exercise of [the power to modify or disapply an enactment] must be assessed by reference to whether or not it is within the class of action that Parliament must have contemplated when conferring the power . . . in the unlikely event of needing to use this power, Parliament will not permit interference either with a general presumption [of common law] or with a 'constitutional' enactment.*

The possibility of altering 'such a statute if the interference is trivial' was left open. While 'the Civil Contingencies Bill is unlikely to be treated as a "constitutional enactment"', it was not 'appropriate for emergency regulations to modify . . . the Bill itself'.

Is there an overall set of principles limiting official reactions to incidents, and if so, where can it be found? The government holds that its so-called 'Triple Lock' will prevent abuses, through laying down three conditions which must be met:

- A serious threat of damage to human welfare, the environment or security must have occurred, be occurring or be about to occur.
- It must be necessary to make special provision for the purpose of preventing, controlling or mitigating the emergency as existing legislation is ineffective or risks serious delay and the need for effective provision is urgent.
- The effect of the provision must be in due proportion to that aspect or effect of the emergency it is aimed at.

Discretion remains for a war leader not wishing to breach the requirements. The tests must contain an element of subjectivity. Provision for the 'Triple Lock' is not grouped together in a single part of the Bill, on the grounds that this would 'distort the drafting'.

With some of the issues raised above in mind, Lord Lucas, speaking in Parliament in July 2004, asked, 'Are we opening up our system to the equivalent of what happened in Germany in 1933, where it became possible for an extreme party legitimately to hijack a democracy and turn it into something totalitarian?' In his view, it was possible that, at some point in the future, following a severe terrorist attack killing most senior government ministers, a demagogic politician could exploit the powers contained in the Act. Lucas continued,

> We can run on from there and ask at what point we recover our democracy. We have created a Bill under which the first thing you do is, by order, amend the Bill, removing the safeguards in it using the powers in the Bill. You censor the press and suspend the courts. Faced with that sort of behaviour, what are the only real powers that remain in the land to do? What will the police and the Army do? Will they be able to read from the Bill the subtleties of constitutional interpretation in which the Government indulge . . . Is it really right

to expect a general to understand how the whole thing works, or do
we need to write our protections for the preservation of our democracy
much more clearly, in plain English, in the Bill, so that it is quite
clear to everyone when lines have been overstepped?

He concluded, 'we are signing our death warrant as a democracy.'

Combating Terror

Internal security may have to be directed against terrorism, something of which Britain has long experience. The early twenty-first-century fear of a religiously motivated attempt to destroy the Houses of Parliament was not novel; the Gunpowder Plot of 1605 has an important place in our culture. Following the uncovering of the supposed 'Papist' attempt on the Palace of Westminster, repressive measures were introduced against Roman Catholics in England. That terrorism should be associated with severe responses from government – in Britain and elsewhere – is, therefore, within a long-established pattern. From 1986 the Irish Republican Army (IRA) began obtaining Semtex – a light but powerful explosive material – and was engaged in increased violence. Thatcher records a meeting of ministers and officials being held on the subject on 6 September 1987. Possibilities considered included

the proscription of Sinn Fein [the political wing of the IRA] . . . the
removal of British citizenship from undesirables with British/Irish
dual citizenship . . . the introduction of minimum sentences for
terrorist offences . . . cutting back on the 50 per cent remission for all
prisoners in Northern Ireland, ensuring that those convicted of
certain terrorist offences would serve consecutively with a new
sentence the unexpired portion of an earlier remitted sentence,

measures to deal with terrorist finance, improvement of intelligence coordination.

In October, the government announced its controversial 'prohibition of broadcast statements by Sinn Fein and other Northern Irish supporters of terrorism.' While it 'immediately provoked cries of censorship', Thatcher had 'no doubt that not only was it justified but that it has worked, and there is some reason to believe that the terrorists think so, too'. Measures 'to change the "right to silence" in Northern Irish courts were also introduced'.[21]

There may be public pressure upon a political leader to act in such a way. But where to direct this activity is not always clear, partly because of limited intelligence. Particular groups within society might be singled out – on a basis of characteristics including their religious or political beliefs, or foreign national associations – as special threats. Reacting to an attack, a government might choose rapidly to introduce specific legislation and attempt international coordination. Aspects of its policies may be controversial, unnecessary, ineffectual, or counterproductive.

Around the latter two decades of the nineteenth century there was an international wave of anarchist attacks. Though not a successful precursor to the destruction of capitalism and the state – the outcome intended by the perpetrators – the worldwide impact of the various assaults on individuals and public targets was considerable, perhaps even of a comparable degree and manner to that of Al-Qaeda presently. A doctrine of 'propaganda of the deed', of which terrorism was an extreme manifestation, was developed. In 1881 a conference of leading revolutionaries met in London. They advocated illegal methods and discussed studying bomb making. As James Joll notes, 'It is from anarchist actions over the next twenty years that the traditional picture of the anarchist is derived – a slinking figure with his hat pulled over his eyes and a smoking bomb in his pocket.' In that period there was divergence between the activities of intellectuals within the movement and the small groups that were set up in Europe and America. Though they were sometimes held responsible for them, the former knew little of the latter. Police use of *agents provocateurs* was common, forming groups to trap people or even (in France) setting up a revolutionary newspaper. For that reason, in the words of Joll, 'It is often impossible to tell whether some anarchist groups . . . ever existed at all outside the imagination of the police.'[22] Nevertheless, the list of senior assassination victims included the French President, Marie François Sadi Carnot (1894) and the US President, William McKinley (1901).

After the murder of Carnot, the French police took stern action against suspected anarchists, searching houses and banning publications. There was an attempt to accuse a number of intellectual theorists of carrying out common crimes, which proved unsuccessful. McKinley, who was shot on 6 September 1901, was succeeded by his Vice-President, Theodore Roosevelt, who delivered his first State of the Union Message on 3 December 1901. In it, he called upon

the Congress that in the exercise of its wise discretion it should take into consideration the coming to this country of anarchists or persons professing principles hostile to all government and justifying the murder of those placed in authority. Such individuals . . . perpetrate a crime, and the law should ensure their rigorous punishment. They and those like them should be kept out of this country; and if found here they should be promptly deported to the country whence they came; and far-reaching provisions should be made for the punishment of those who stay. [Anarchist] crime should be made an offense against the law of nations, like piracy and that form of man-stealing known as the slave trade; for it is of far blacker infamy than either. It should be so declared by treaties among all civilized powers.

Congress subsequently passed a law excluding any individual from the US 'who disbelieves in or is opposed to all organized governments'.

A scent of nineteenth-century anarchist terror prompted the consideration of an authoritarian response in Britain, too. There were eleven major explosions in France between 1892–4, including the bombing of the Chamber of Deputies (1893) and the Café Terminus, near the Gare Saint-Lazare in Paris, injuring nineteen and killing one, on 12 February 1894. Then, in Britain, previously spared such incidents, three days later there was an explosion in Greenwich Park. In what may have been a botched attempt on the famous Observatory, Martial Bourdin, a 26-year-old Frenchman, managed only to blow himself up, but succeeded in making news headlines both here and abroad.

With its tradition of political tolerance, Britain was a haven for dissidents, who congregated on London from around the world, with the area around Tottenham Court Road a centre for anarchists. This liberal approach was unpopular in countries where attacks occurred, but a theory seemed to exist that extremists would not jeopardise the hospitality from which they were benefiting by perpetrating outrages in their host nation. Greenwich threw such a view into doubt and heightened public concern was aroused.

There were lurid descriptions in the press of the 'Autonomie Club' ('as pretty a collection of scoundrels as are to be found on the face of the earth'), a society based in Windmill Street, off Tottenham Court Road, supposedly a nerve centre for international terrorism, of which Bourdin reportedly had been a member. A *Times* editorial referred to 'the abuse of the right of asylum in this country by foreign Anarchist conspirators'. It demanded harsher measures, stating that 'we doubt if there would be any serious resistance to the passing of a law making the offence of throwing explosives among a crowd . . . punishable with death'. The newspaper lamented 'the laxity of the police in dealing with some notorious nests of anarchists'. Asquith, then the Home Secretary – vulnerable to criticism because of what had just happened – promised, among other things, that the government was 'ready and anxious to cooperate with other countries in any practical measures that can be devised for dealing more effectively with Anarchists'. He called for 'a more constant and concerted inter-change of information and combined action . . . between the Governments and the police authorities of the different Nations of the world'.[23] International coordination for such a purpose has frequently been sought, but not always with satisfactory outcomes for war leaders. Thatcher notes that, in combating Irish Republican terrorism during the later 1980s, 'It slowly became clear that . . . greater support by the . . . Irish Government and people for the fight against terrorism [was] not going to be forthcoming . . . in fighting terror we would have to stand almost alone.'[24]

The manner in which media and government responded to Greenwich in 1894 was mirrored in Britain a century later, when fear of global terrorism was high once again. As with the anarchists of the Autonomie Club, there was a press fascination with Islamic radicals, notably Abu Hamza, 'the self-proclaimed Imam, or Holy Man . . . who is at the centre of an international Fundamentalist movement determined to destroy the decadence of the West'. Based at a mosque in Finsbury Park, north London, the Egyptian-born Hamza was famed for 'his iron-hook hands [sic] and single scarred eye'.[25] In addition to the likes of Hamza, as in the nineteenth century, aliens in general were singled out as likely culprits. Two days before 11 September 2001 the *Sunday Express* ran a story claiming that British intelligence agencies 'fear Iraqi spies posing as asylum seekers are entering Britain carrying deadly chemical weapons'.[26] Such fears were heightened by the Al-Qaeda attacks in the US and subsequent strikes. In November 2003 the *Sunday Times* reported, 'Security services are hunting two cells of Al-Qaeda terrorists whom they believe are preparing to carry out "spectacular" terrorist attacks in Britain.' There were up to ten suspect individuals, from north Africa and Saudi Arabia, believed to be based in the Midlands and north of England. It referred to Al-Qaeda 'sleepers' implanted 'so deeply into the Muslim community that they are proving almost impossible to detect. Some are believed to be British citizens.' Terrorist surveillance of possible targets – including large banks and shopping centres, synagogues and Jewish schools and community centres – was supposedly being carried out. The Security Service had 'so far failed to penetrate the units'.[27]

David Blunkett, Blair's Home Secretary on 11 September 2001, encountered circumstances, then, which would in some respects have been familiar to his predecessor, Asquith. Like him, Blunkett promised more coordinated international action 'on arrest, on joint investigation, on shared information', as he put it to the Labour Party Conference on 3 October 2001. He appeared less squeamish than Asquith had done where supposed threats to individual liberty were concerned, saying on the same occasion, 'What a farcical situation we face when it can take five, seven, ten years to extradite someone who is known to have been engaged in, or perpetrating, terrorism.' He described the need to prevent suspect individuals arrested at airports from 'using the asylum laws to be able to claim sanctuary' and criticised the 'constant use of judicial review, which has frankly become a lawyer's charter'.

Repressive policies in response to terrorism and those who implement them may be the subject of criticism. Joseph Conrad used the incident in Greenwich in February 1894 as source material for his 1907 novel, *The Secret Agent.* The character of the minister responsible for security, Sir Ethelred, was inspired – in part, at least – by Sir William Harcourt rather than Asquith. (Conrad set the novel in 1886, not 1894, though Harcourt was only Home Secretary until 1885, first appointed by Gladstone in 1880). Though not a negligible figure, Harcourt was popularly regarded as possessing comic qualities (which Conrad invested in Sir Ethelred) and his judgement over terrorism has been questioned. Anarchists were not the major concern for Harcourt during his term as Home Secretary, but he did face the Feinians. (Historically, Irish-related incidents have been by far the most significant problem of their sort for British ministers.) Harcourt has been described by Roy Jenkins as 'On criminal justice matters . . . on the whole liberal'. Yet he was, Jenkins argues, guilty of

> *an overreaction to Feinian terrorist threats . . . and . . . an immature enthusiasm for turning himself into a police generalissimo. His instinctive dislike of the Irish and his unrestrained boisterousness came together in an immoderate combination . . . he was susceptible to the idea of prancing police chiefs in the heart of the metropolis. He even instructed the Commissioner of Police to ride alongside the Queen's carriage whenever she was in London, a form of protection more ostentatious than efficient.*

Harcourt's administrative response to terrorism was to form the Special Branch of the Metropolitan Police for surveillance purposes. A legal measure he introduced was the Explosives Bill of 1883, which passed through Parliament in a single day on 9 April. It followed what was described in the press as 'The almost simultaneous discoveries made in Cork, Liverpool, Birmingham and London of explosives, leaving little doubt of the existence of a widely ramified conspiracy to intimidate the British Government and people by the destruction of public buildings'.[28] There was a view that organisation and funding for the so-called 'dynamite party' was being provided from individuals located in the US. *The Times* praised Harcourt's parliamentary exertions, stating on 10 April, 'The House of Commons gave proof yesterday that, when it so pleases, it is able to get through its work with an energy and a promptitude that could scarcely be matched in any other legislative assembly.'[29] Jenkins notes, 'I cannot . . . cite the Explosives Bill as an example of Harcourt's over-excited approach to police powers and Irish threats without remembering that, ninety-one years later, another Home Secretary introduced at short notice a Prevention of Terrorism (Temporary Provisions) Bill and carried it through all its parliamentary stages by breakfast time the next morning.'[30] And as Jenkins's comment – with which he was referring to activity during his own tenure at the Home Office – shows, Harcourt's decision to produce new statute was taken by others who followed him.

Many terrorist acts are proscribed by regular law (killing, for example, can be prosecuted as murder). However, they are arguably qualitatively different from other sorts of crime, partly because they are directed at the political system itself. The nature of the groups involved – perhaps based abroad, often well organised and funded – makes their detection particularly difficult. The crafting of specific legislation, therefore, may be deemed necessary. Since it is drawn up in particular circumstances, as they change, it can date. Moreover, perhaps because such security laws are often produced rapidly, in response to attacks and campaigns, they can contain flaws which require subsequent correction.

Three decades ago the Northern Ireland Troubles were the main concern of policy makers. In 1973 and 1974 respectively, the

Emergency Powers (EPA) and Prevention of Terrorism (PTA) Acts were introduced. Prompted by the rise of the IRA and attacks including the Birmingham pub bombings, they extended the powers of the police and armed forces. Jenkins, then Home Secretary, describes how he was in a Westminster restaurant when the news of the attack in the West Midlands, leading to 200 injuries and 24 deaths – 'a different order of casualties from anything we had previously known' – reached him. He and a Home Office minister, Lord Harris, 'spontaneously and jointly agreed that an emergency bill would now be both necessary and acceptable'. Jenkins was determined that the IRA should be made a banned organisation. He sought to allow police to detain terrorist suspects for longer without formulating charges; and to tighten up border controls. Jenkins wanted to enable 'the Home Secretary to exclude from Great Britain citizens of the Republic of Ireland or those originating in Northern Ireland where it appeared to him . . . that they were involved or likely to be involved in acts of terrorism'. The PTA became law, with certain modifications, 180 hours later. Though intended to be temporary, Jenkins notes, 'circumstances . . . regrettably made it necessary to keep on the statute book'.[31]

By the late 1990s the focus of anti-terrorist statute had to be widened. While the possibility of Loyalist or Republican acts had not vanished altogether, other concerns had increased in relative prominence. There was a perceived threat from international and domestic non-Irish groups (including Welsh and Scottish nationalists, and animal rights activists) and a possibility that more deadly weapons, leading to greater casualties, could be used (in the mid 1990s the Aum Shinrikyo religious cult carried out poison gas attacks in Japan). As Butler noted, in June 1995, the Joint Intelligence Committee (described below) reported, 'Selective interpretation of the Muslim faith enables [Islamist extremist] groups to justify terrorist violence and to recruit "martyrs" for suicide attacks.'

A view had emerged that the definition of terrorism in existing statute was inadequate. The PTA defined it as 'the use of violence for political ends, and . . . for the purpose of putting the public or any section of the public in fear'. The description of motive ('political') was too narrow, while the act ('any use of violence') was too wide. The Terrorism Act 2000 (TA) took into account changing concerns and the need for a more sophisticated definition. It referred to 'the use of threat or action . . . designed to influence the government or to intimidate the public or a section of the public . . . made for the purpose of advancing a political, religious or ideological cause'. The reference to 'religious' and 'ideological' objectives – in addition to 'political' ones – firmly extended the scope of the law beyond Irish terrorism.

Developments in the perceived nature of the peril were reflected in a number of additions to the list of organisations to which it was illegal to belong or support under the TA, made in March 2001. A number of Loyalist and Republican outfits were already outlawed. The Home Secretary added, by Order, various Islamic, Sikh, Tamil, Basque and Kurdish organisations. Further bans were made in November 2002. The approach of exhaustive proscription has pitfalls: there is a risk of leaving an organisation off the list. In May 2004, members of the 'Real IRA' were acquitted on the grounds that it was not specifically banned. The ruling was overturned, but the four men in question remained free.

Perceptions of and responses to the security threat were already changing by the early twenty-first century. Then, 11 September 2001 saw, in the words of one official document, the appearance of 'a new dimension to the terrorist threat, the infliction of mass casualties by horrific means, by suicide terrorists who struck without warning, without any claim or pretence to be advancing a negotiable cause'.[32] In the new climate, extensive use was made of the existing law. As a whole, between 11 September 2001 and the end of January 2004, 544 individuals were arrested under the TA, of whom 98 were charged for a total of 155 offences.

But the government believed fresh legislation was needed, too. In November 2001 the Anti-Terrorism, Crime and Security Bill, which marked a significant extension of the British state's reach into civil society, was published. Like some of its predecessors, it was moved rapidly through Parliament. Included in its provisions were:

- Official powers to seize the funds and freeze the assets of suspect individuals, organisations or even foreign governments.
- Greater availability of confidential information, held by public bodies and financial institutions, to police and intelligence agencies; and an extension of the period for which communications service providers could retain traffic data such as itemised telephone bills and records of emails.
- Indefinite detention, without charge or trial, for foreign nationals whom the Home Secretary deemed threats to national security and whose deportation was not possible. (Meaning a derogation from the ECHR was necessary, only a year after the Human Rights Act 1998, which incorporated it into British law, came into force.)
- The widening of racially-related crimes such as assault and the incitement of hatred to take account of incidents which were religiously motivated (ultimately scaled down just to certain attacks and public order offences).
- A requirement for laboratories and other premises to provide notification of their holdings of certain disease-causing organisms and toxins, and who had access to them.
- Enhanced authority for police and customs officers in carrying out such acts as expelling persons from airports or aircraft, or forcing

the removal of objects believed to be worn for the purpose of disguising identity.

- A tightening up of the law on the bribery of foreign public officials.

Part 4 of the Anti-Terrorism, Crime and Security Act 2001 (ATCSA) – which enabled the detention, without trial or charge, of foreign nationals, certified by the Home Secretary as 'suspected international terrorists' – proved particularly controversial. Aimed at 'people in the UK whose presence is not conducive to the public good' (as the government's Explanatory Notes to ATCSA put it) it necessitated, as noted, derogation from Article 5 of the ECHR. Such an opt-out was allowed for in Article 15 of the same convention, in circumstances of 'war or other public emergency threatening the life of the nation'. The government argued that a sufficiently precarious 'public emergency' existed. Its view was upheld by the Special Immigration Appeals Commission (SIAC) in the first appeals against confinement that were brought. The numbers involved, by comparison with earlier internment programmes, were small. Seventeen individuals had been certified under Part 4 of the Act by autumn 2003. As at mid-2004, the total actually in custody was twelve. Normally, the reason detainees could not be forcibly returned to their place of origin was the fear that they might undergo torture or inhumane treatment, forbidden by Article 3 of the ECHR, to which, unlike Article 5, there could be no exceptions. Individuals detained were free to leave the country at any time (although, by late 2003, only two had chosen to do so, for France and Morocco).

Such a practice inevitably caused unease, even among those who felt it was a necessity. It contradicted basic judicial principles and could have a harmful impact upon the mental health of the suspects concerned. One was transferred to Broadmoor, the high-security psychiatric hospital; another granted bail and subject to effective house arrest. Given that foreign nationals were involved, there was a sense of discrimination, not eased by evidence that the TA was being directed disproportionately against the Islamic community. During 2001–2, according to Metropolitan Police Service figures, the number of Asians subject to stop-and-search in London increased by 41 per cent, while for whites the total rose by only 8 per cent. Some within the law enforcement community were of the view that, owing to the nature of the threat, the trend was to be expected. As is discussed in the next chapter, racial tension in Britain had reached a high level, which was associated in part with the War on Terror.

In theory, new protection was introduced by the religiously aggravated offence element in ATCSA, but it was a curious law in which to include such a provision. It was not spectacularly effective, with only 24 successful convictions by the end of 2003. An unforeseen aggravating domestic aspect of the War on Terror was the seizure of suspected terrorist assets. In order to facilitate the compensation of individuals who were deemed not to have such links, the money was placed in bank accounts that contravened Islamic rules on the accrual of interest. Further legislative measures which were aimed at aliens of terrorist association included the Extradition Act 2003, to enable suspects to face trial abroad; and Section 4 of the Nationality, Immigration and Asylum Act 2002, introducing a power to strip dual-nationals who originated from another country of their British citizenship.

Targeting particular groups in the interests of security may prove self-defeating, even to the detriment of the personal safety of the leader. In 2004 Amnesty International USA produced a report criticising the use of 'Racial Profiling' by law enforcement agencies in the US, which it found had expanded since 11 September 2001. It noted, 'When law enforcement officials focus on what people look like, what religion they follow, or what they wear, it puts us all at risk.' Historical examples supported the view. Notably, in 1901, the assassin of President McKinley, 'a white man born in Michigan, was able to conceal the murder weapon in a bandage wrapped around his arm, pass through security, and go undetected until he shot the president because secret service agents had decided to focus their attention on a "dark complexioned man with a moustache".'[33]

What were the limitations to the power bestowed upon the Home Secretary by Part 4 of ATCSA and what rights did detainees have? First, it followed from the ECHR derogation that it was available only for use against threats of the type which appeared on 11 September 2001, that is against those suspected of links to bin Laden and Al-Qaeda. It was subject to annual review by Parliament: given the government's majority in the Commons, not a great hurdle to overcome. Internees had the right to appeal to the SIAC. In such cases, sensitive intelligence material could be presented in closed sessions, though the presumption was for open hearings. When classified information of that sort was examined, the internees were represented not by the Counsel of their choice (as was the case in open session) but by a Special Advocate appointed on their behalf. In theory, evidence obtained through torture was admissible, since the proceedings were not criminal. Rulings by the SIAC could be challenged through the Court of Appeal, House of Lords and then the European Court of Human Rights, where appropriate. Reviews took place, first after six months, then at three-monthly intervals. Bail could be sought.

It might be asked, why were powers of detention only applied to aliens? Was there not a threat from British subjects? The government's response was that 'the threat came predominantly but not exclusively from foreign nationals.'[34] Another problem was that only individuals believed to be associated with Al-Qaeda could be detained. Other groups were not covered. It could be argued that in allowing, indeed encouraging, supposed terrorists to leave the country, a danger was being irresponsibly exported. (The assassination of President Carnot of France in 1894 was carried out by Santo Jeronimo Caserio, who had been expelled from Italy for his anarchist ideas.) But that was because the powers being used related to immigration. The only other possible detention was for the purpose of police enquiries and was limited to fourteen days. Ideally, it could be argued, individuals would be prosecuted for crimes, rather than interned indefinitely. There were a number of obstacles to doing so in the cases under examination. Presently, intercepted communications cannot be used as evidence in British courts. Revealing intelligence in such proceedings, it is believed, might endanger national security, compromise sources and impose extra burdens upon the agencies responsible for its collection.

The policy of detention was deemed illegal by the highest court in the country. On 16 December 2004 the Law Lords held, by an eight-to-one majority, that the opt-out from the ECHR was unjustified since it represented a disproportionate response to the threat, and that detention of immigrants was incompatible with the Convention, on grounds of discrimination. But they could not actually strike down the legislation.

What were the motives for the decision? One of the Law Lords, Lord Hoffmann, noted, 'There have been times of great national emergency in which habeas corpus has been suspended and powers to detain on suspicion conferred on the Government. It happened during the Napoleonic wars and during both world wars.' But, he went on,

There had to be a war or public emergency threatening the life of the nation . . . I do not underestimate the ability of fanatical groups of

> terrorists to kill and destroy, but they do not threaten the life of the
> nation. Whether we would survive Hitler hung in the balance, but
> there is no doubt that we shall survive al-Qaeda.

Lord Walker, the one dissenter, conceded, 'Whether or not patriotism is the last refuge of the scoundrel, national security can be the last refuge of the tyrant.' But he noted, 'in a period of nearly three years no more than 17 individuals have been certified . . . Of course every single detention is a matter of concern, but in the context of national security the number of persons actually detained is relevant to the issue of proportionality.'[35]

How did the British legal response to 11 September 2001 compare with other countries'? First, it was notable that no other signatory to the ECHR, though many had taken security measures, felt it necessary to derogate from Article 5. That may be evidence of overreaction on the part of Britain. On the other hand, Britain was perhaps more of a centre for terrorist operations than other Council of Europe members. It may have been an extremely likely target for an attack. In the wake of a major Al-Qaeda strike, carried out by foreign nationals when intelligence existed suggesting they posed a threat, few would have paused to congratulate the Home Secretary for not exercising the right to opt out of part of the ECHR. While Britain's response may have been unusually strong, a number of countries including Canada, the US, France and Germany all introduced special legislation in autumn 2001. Some nations, such as Australia, Belgium, Canada, Denmark, Finland and Sweden, resorted to specific anti-terrorist law where none existed previously.

A democratic society in which very stringent measures were taken was the US, unsurprisingly since that was where the 11 September attacks occurred. Individuals, believed to number around six-hundred, captured largely during the invasion of Afghanistan in the autumn of 2001, were held in 'Camp Delta', at the navy base in Guantanamo Bay, Cuba. Initially, Bush held that the Geneva Convention applied to Taliban, but not Al-Qaeda suspects; subsequently the US has argued that neither are subject to it. Consequently, more extensive interrogation methods than would otherwise be permitted were used on them. Bush authorised military tribunals to try some of the captives. Such measures, while falling outside the immediate scope of the present work, nevertheless reveal a severity of approach that has developed.

'Fifth column' fears manifested themselves in the US after September 2001. The 9/11 Commission, reporting in July 2004, referred to two participants in the plane attacks who were previously tracked by US intelligence. It noted, 'Because these two Al-Qaeda operatives had spent little time in the West and spoke little, if any English, it is plausible that they or KSM [Khalid Sheikh Mohammed, an Al-Qaeda field commander who first proposed the 'planes operation' to bin Laden] would have tried to identify, in advance, a friendly contact in the United States. We explored suspicions about whether these two operatives had a support network of accomplices in the United States. The evidence is thin – simply not there for some cases, more worrisome in others.'[36]

In October 2001 the USA Patriot Act (or to give it its curiously convoluted full title, the Uniting and Strengthening America by Providing Appropriate Tools Required to Intercept and Obstruct Terrorism Act) was introduced. Among its many provisions were the creation of offences of harbouring, concealing or supporting terrorists. New grounds for refusing entry to the US were established. The law extended the definition of 'terrorist organisation' to take in a group of as little as two people, organised or not; and enhanced investigative powers. Similarly to Britain, the Attorney General was granted the authority to detain aliens on national security grounds. The use of 'material witness' status enabled the indefinite confinement of possibly over a thousand individuals, as observers of offences. Much opposition to the Patriot Act was voiced by civil liberties groups.

War and administrative revolution

Just as it demands extraordinary action by the state, war may expose weaknesses in the machinery of government, which must be rectified. Poor official coordination can be disastrous, as the report of the US 9/11 Commission indicated. It catalogued a variety of shortcomings, stating, 'The 9/11 attacks were a shock, but they should not have come as a surprise. Islamist extremists had given plenty of warning that they meant to kill Americans indiscriminately and in large numbers.' It drew attention to various incidents, starting with the 1993 attack on the World Trade Center, as signals of intent, as well as Osama bin Laden's issuance of a 'self-styled fatwa' against Americans, of February 1998. The Commission noted that 'During the spring and summer of 2001, US intelligence agencies received a stream of warnings that Al-Qaeda planned, as one report put it, "something very, very, very big." Director of Central Intelligence George Tenet told us, "The system was blinking red."' But it was believed that the threat was to US interests abroad, not domestically.

Opportunities to stop the attacks were missed. In August 2001, an individual who had sought instruction on flying jet planes was arrested for immigration violations. The authorities became aware that two terrorists who had been sighted and then lost by US intelligence in Southeast Asia in January 2000 were now in the US. In fact, they had arrived in Los Angeles on 15 January and lived openly in San Diego under their own names. However, 'These cases did not prompt urgent action.'

On 11 September itself the nineteen perpetrators all successfully passed through security checks. The crews and cockpits of the planes they boarded were not ready for the possibility of suicide hijacks. Neither were the plans of the Federal Aviation Administration and North American Aerospace Defense Command prepared for such a contingency. Authorisation to shoot down aircraft came too late and was not communicated to pilots. Planes that were scrambled did not know where to go or the targets to intercept. The emergency response, despite the heroic efforts of individuals, was hampered by 'weaknesses in preparations for disaster, failure to achieve unified incident command, and inadequate communications among responding agencies'. At the Pentagon, too, 'problems of command and control' could be detected. The Commission argued that, in advance of 11 September 2001, 'Across the government, there were failures of imagination, policy, capabilities, and management.'

One US response to 11 September 2001 was the establishment of a new government department, discussed below. Similarly, on a number of occasions in its history, British engagement in armed combat has led to considerable upheaval in the Civil Service, often with significant long-term implications for that institution's development. Arguably, the origins of a body of permanent Whitehall staff lie in the reaction to perceived administrative shortcomings during the Crimean War. Faced with a popular movement demanding change, in 1855 the government of the day, through Order in Council, established the Civil Service Commission, a panel of three which certified senior appointments and was answerable to the Crown, not the Prime Minister. A significant early step had been taken towards a politically impartial career Civil Service. In time, the Commission would wrest from ministers influence over recruitment, thereby eliminating patronage and jobbery from the process.

Yet – though an early impetus in its long emergence was difficulty with one military engagement – shortcomings on the part of the permanent Whitehall staff were twice exposed by the exigencies of total war. Consequently, both the 1914–18 and 1939–45 conflicts saw considerable structural changes to the Civil Service, along with the large-scale introduction of temporary personnel, some of whom attained great personal prominence. In the First World War the Ministry of Munitions was established under Lloyd George in 1915, who made a habit of recruiting outsiders to official posts. One admirer of Lloyd George has noted that he used 'men of great ability and expertise advising him directly – a method . . . of bypassing bureaucratic obstacles in the way of winning the war'.[37] Lloyd George's formation of a War Cabinet, subsequently leading to the appearance of the Cabinet Office, and his personal team, the 'Garden Suburb' have been discussed (as has Churchill's Prime Minister's Statistical Section, set up in 1940). In the Second World War there was greater upheaval still in Whitehall. One significant development which followed Churchill's assumption of the premiership was a reduction in the importance of the Treasury, which had become dominant within the Civil Service. As the office of government responsible for control of spending, it traditionally emphasised thrift, whereas total war demanded primary attention to the most effective allocation of resources. The Lord President of the Council was made responsible for economic coordination, with a committee served by a team of economists, the Economic Section of the War Cabinet, including in its staff economists and statisticians drawn from academia. Across the Civil Service as a whole, hundreds of thousands of 'irregulars' were recruited, serving both in older departments and wartime ministries such as Information, Food and Economic Warfare. Two intellectuals who – having re-entered Whitehall after long periods on the outside – were able to achieve enormous impact on the course of economic and social policy were William Beveridge and John Maynard Keynes.

The expansion of the role of the state in the US during the Second World War has been discussed. To bring it about, numerous bodies were set up, within which prominent staff members were drawn from outside the existing official machine. They included the Office of Price Administration, Office for Emergency Management, Board of Economic Warfare, National Housing Agency, National War Labor Board, the Office of Censorship, Office of Civilian Defense, Office of Defense Transportation, Office of Facts and Figures, Office of War Information, War Manpower Commission, Office of Economic Stabilisation, and Office of War Mobilization and Reconversion. The proliferation of agencies was constitutionally difficult, with their exact status unclear. There was a tendency for them to wield, behind a supposed but fictitious purely advisory role, genuine authority. For example, the War Labour Board acted as a tribunal in labour disputes, arbitrating between the public interest, management and workforce. To perform that role effectively, the counsel it supplied had to be accepted without revision.[38]

The tendency for war to lead to the establishment of new bureaucratic entities has continued to the present. After 11 September 2001, the US was forced to reassess its approach to possible attack, a fact reflected in machinery of government changes. In March 2003 the Department of Homeland Security (DHS), the fifteenth department of the federal government, was formed, taking on the bulk of 180,000 employees from 22 agencies. The purpose of the DHS was to 'lead the unified national effort to secure America' against terrorism.

In Britain, though much thought has been given to prevention of and readiness for disaster, there was no equivalent to the DHS set up. The Home Secretary has primary responsibility for safety and security, with particular departments taking the lead according to the nature of the problem. He chairs the Ministerial Committee on Civil Contingencies (CCC), attended by various departments and agencies, including the devolved administrations, depending upon the subject under discussion. The CCC is serviced by the Civil Contingencies Secretariat, which coordinates work across government from the Cabinet Office, reporting to the Prime Minister through the Security and Intelligence Coordinator, Sir David Omand (a post created after 11 September 2001). There are seventeen cross-departmental capabilities, including food and fuel supply, and mass-evacuation measures. The Conservative Party have argued that there should be a British version of the DHS, that only a single ministry can provide the focus which is required. On the other hand, it could be that the British model, whereby the Home Office has overall responsibility for safety and security, with different departments taking the lead according to the nature of the problem, provides more flexibility. After all, no purpose-created body, even on the scale of the DHS, can take in every potential type of future emergency in its functions.

Another function important to war, performed by one part of the machinery of government, is the acquisition and processing of information not publicly available, that is, intelligence. Different types of agency perform varying tasks, such as internal and external ones, and communications interception. Such specialisation is necessary, but there is a need for coordination between them in order to provide a war leader with the most complete picture possible.

A lack of coordination in the intelligence machinery can be fatal. Douglas Porch notes that, in the Second World War, French intelligence did not accurately predict the time and place of the German attack of 1940. He argues that this 'must count, along with the absence of guidance on the Schlieffen Plan of 1914, as one of its historic failures'. Problems may have been caused by the fact that 'The central command of the French armies . . . was . . . splintered into four different geographical locations, five if one included the War Ministry on the Left Bank in central Paris. Communications between the various command posts were primitive, and assured in the main by goggled motorcycle dispatch riders who crisscrossed the French countryside with orders, reports, papers, and documents to be signed in their satchels.' The intelligence services themselves had 'two separate headquarters' with 'a third section . . . dispatched to North Africa'. It seems that 'fragmentation of the intelligence services' was, in the view of 'French intelligence veterans . . . fairly critical' to 'France's ultimate failure to stop Hitler in 1940'.[39]

The US President, Harry Truman, set up the Central Intelligence Agency (CIA) in 1947. His motive, he told a journalist while in retirement, was that

> *I needed . . . at that time a central organization that would bring all the various intelligence reports we were getting in those days, and there must have been a dozen of them, maybe more, bring them all into one organization so that the President would get one report on what was going on in various parts of the world . . . that's why I went ahead and set up what they called the Central Intelligence Agency.*[40]

But it would seem that the more effective coordination Truman sought did not exist on 11 September 2001. Consequently, the 9/11 Commission recommended a 'National Counterterrorism Center' for 'unifying strategic intelligence . . . across the foreign-domestic divide'. It advocated 'unifying the intelligence community with a new National Intelligence Director.' The move was needed, it was argued, because 'the intelligence community is not organised well for joint intelligence work' failing to use 'common standards and

practices'. Another proposal was for the creation of a cross-departmental information-sharing network, for all engaged in the effort
against terrorism. As the Commission put it, 'The system of "need to
know" should be replaced by a system of "need to share."'

British agencies are traditionally more effectively coordinated than
their US counterparts, thanks to the Joint Intelligence Committee
(JIC), which processes the various contributions and produces single
assessments for ministers. But the Butler Review identified some
weaknesses. It noted that the resources available to the JIC
Assessments Staff were 'very slight in relation to those of the
collecting agencies. Moreover, for the most part the Assessments
Staff is made up of officials from departments on short-term
secondments.' The report therefore advocated a review of 'the size of
the Assessments Staff, and in particular . . . whether they have
available the volume and range of resources to ask the questions
which need to be asked in fully assessing intelligence reports and in
thinking radically . . . whether there should be a specialism of analysis
with a career structure and room for advancement'. Butler drew
attention to the fact that the Defence Intelligence Staff (DIS), a part
of the Ministry of Defence, 'has in the past perhaps been seen as
rather separate from the rest of the intelligence community'. The
Review recommended 'further steps . . . to integrate . . . the DIS
more closely with the rest of the intelligence community'.

A war leader may be faced with public demands to bring
intelligence material into the open. The parliamentary Joint
Committee on Human Rights, in a discussion of the derogation
from the ECHR, noted in 2004 that 'we have never been presented
with the evidence which would enable us to be satisfied of the
existence of a public emergency threatening the life of the nation, but
have proceeded on the basis that there might be such evidence.' It
went on, 'If . . . the threat is likely to remain indefinitely, then we

consider that democratic legitimacy demands some independent confirmation that the emergency remains at the level which justified unusual measures.' The committee requested that ways be found in which Parliament and public could be provided with 'the gist of the intelligence . . . without prejudicing legitimate security interests'. Further, it wondered, could 'the Government . . . give careful consideration to whether there is a role for the Intelligence and Security Committee to scrutinise the material on which the Government's assertions about the level of the threat are based'.[41]

Potentially, war leaders, appearing to respond to such pressure, can do so in a manner which leads to the deployment of intelligence in support of predetermined policy objectives, which were not in fact based on such information. Some observers have argued that the tendency has developed recently both in Britain and the US. The approach, if publicly suspected, is likely to prompt controversy. It is also dangerous, since it might lead to the neglect of other functions, such as the detection of threats.[42] The Butler Review provided evidence that in 2002–3, the intelligence agencies in Britain were servicing political requirements in a manner detrimental to the objectivity of their contribution. As Hennessy puts it, 'the road to Baghdad was *not* paved with the intelligence product.'[43] It could be argued that the impartiality of the JIC was compromised. Butler found fault with the arrangement whereby 'the Chairman of the JIC should be outranked not only by the heads of the agencies but also by two other heavyweight Permanent Secretaries on his Committee.' As noted in Chapter 2, it was concluded that the post ought to be 'held by someone with experience of dealing with Ministers in a very senior role, and who is demonstrably beyond influence, and thus probably in his last post'.

In advance of the Iraq War, intelligence was used to publicly validate a particular approach. The method was also intended, in the words of Straw, 'to meet the [public] demand for intelligence-based information about Iraq'. In the process the government associated itself with claims which turned out to be inaccurate. On 24 September 2002 it published a dossier drawing on the authority of the intelligence agencies, *Iraq's Weapons of Mass Destruction*. This was the first – and possibly last – ever publicly produced JIC document. The Butler Review found that it was not 'explicitly intended to make a case for war', but that the dossier was 'a broadly-based document which could support a range of policy options'. However, it did note that Geoff Hoon, the Secretary of State for Defence, told them that 'if we were going to be able to make out a case for war against Iraq, we were going to have to publish the material.'

The document was not a great success as a propaganda tool. At the time of its publication, it did not significantly shift the balance of debate. After the war, some of its claims, relating to Iraq's capabilities and procurement activities, became the subject of intense dispute. Its production caused internal problems, too. Butler concluded, 'The Government wanted an unclassified document on which it could draw in its *advocacy* of its policy. The JIC sought to offer a dispassionate *assessment* [italics in original].' The tension between the two objectives placed a 'strain' upon the JIC. In translating its assessments into the dossier, 'warnings were lost about the limited intelligence base on which some aspects of these assessments were being made . . . the language in the dossier may have left with readers the impression that there was fuller and firmer intelligence behind the judgements than was the case'. Had appropriate caveats been included, Butler subsequently told the *Spectator*, the dossier would have been 'weakened'. He believed,

> *What the government was saying is, we really think this guy [Saddam Hussein] is a threat, because he's got this terrible stuff, he's a very bad*

man, nobody's got any idea what he may do with it, and then if you say that we're only drawing this conclusion on the evidence we've got, and the direct evidence we've got is thin because Iraq is a very difficult country to penetrate that would have weakened it.[44]

There was further evidence of intelligence providing the means for achieving, rather than the basis for formulating, policy objectives. The Butler report noted that, on 18 December 2002, the JIC produced an 'Initial Assessment' of Iraq's statement on the status of its weapons of mass destruction programme. But, 'despite its importance to the determination of whether Iraq was in further material breach of its disarmament obligations' under UNSC Resolution 1441, 'the JIC made no further assessment'. This was something the Butler Review found 'odd'. Perhaps because the political leadership was intent upon war, further investigation of the Iraqi declaration was less of a priority. When Iraq was taken, no weapons of mass destruction were to be found there.

In Chapter 3, there was discussion of how the Intelligence Services Act 1994 established the Intelligence and Security Committee (ISC), responsible for examining expenditure, administration and policy. War leaders may be uncomfortable with such scrutiny and can obstruct it or minimise its impact in the ways outlined in the previous chapter. They may wish to grant their intelligence services the maximum discretion in such matters as determining individuals to be interned without trial. But it is wise to ensure some degree of accountability, whether through a body such as the ISC, a parliamentary select committee or other means. Agencies with an abundance of autonomy are likely to become a problem, even causing political destabilisation, or turning on war leaders themselves.

The unrestrained pursuit of a political agenda by an intelligence agency had an unsettling effect on the French Third Republic. In

1894, Alfred Dreyfus, a Jewish captain in the French army, was charged with spying for the Germans, at the behest of the so-called 'Statistical Section' of the French general staff. Porch argues, 'While some of the officers of the Statistical Section were certainly anti-Semitic, the origins of the Dreyfus affair can be found rather in a weakness common to counterintelligence officers. Those whose job it is to search for spies begin to see them everywhere. Paranoia becomes an occupational hazard.' He goes on, 'The consequences for France of Dreyfus' twelve-year calvary of court-martial, incarceration on Devil's Island, retrial, presidential pardon and eventual rehabilitation were profound. The anti-Semitic passions it aroused, the attacks on the honour of the army, precipitated a political realignment which shaped French politics for much of the twentieth century.' Porch states,

> the question raised by the Dreyfus Affair from a secret service perspective was 'Who guards the guards?' This was to pose the great dilemma for France in the twentieth century . . . the Dreyfus Affair, which envenomed French politics at the turn of the century, was a clear indication to France that she could never be certain of the loyalties of her secret services, convinced of their objectivity, persuaded that their competence and integrity were absolute.[45]

In Britain in the 1960s and 1970s, certain operatives developed a view that the Labour Prime Minister, Harold Wilson, had been recruited by the KGB (the Soviet Committee for State Security). A small number seem to have carried out covert operations against him. President Truman, who formed the CIA, later privately expressed the view that the decision to do so

> was a mistake. And if I'd known what was going to happen, I never would have done it . . . it got out of hand. [President Dwight

Eisenhower] never paid any attention to it, and it got out of hand . . . those fellows in the CIA don't just report on wars and the like, they go out and make their own, and there's nobody to keep track on what they're up to. They spend billions of dollars on stirring up trouble so they'll have something to report on . . . it's become a government all of its own and all secret. They don't have to account to anybody . . . That's a very dangerous thing in a democratic society, and it's got to be put a stop to. The people have got a right to know what those birds are up to. And if I was back in the White House, people would know. You see, the way a free government works, there's got to be a housecleaning every now and again, and I don't care what branch of the government is involved. Somebody has to keep an eye on things.[46]

A lack of accountability can lead to public questioning of the intelligence agencies. Events in the US in the 1970s might suggest that Truman had a point. Revelations emerged in 1974 regarding CIA participation in a coup in Chile in 1973 and illegal domestic operations against political activists. In 1975 President Gerald Ford himself admitted that assassinations had been organised by the CIA over a number of years, in a comment to senior *New York Times* figures which he hoped to keep off the record. Later in the same year CIA intervention to prevent Angola falling into Communist hands was exposed. Embarrassing, high-profile public inquiries were prompted.[47] If such circumstances transpire, the agencies may be subjected to the bulk of the criticism for what has taken place, rather than a war leader who was perhaps complicit in them – the better outcome from the latter's perspective.

Official personnel

War leaders should give consideration to the type of staff employed inside the bureaucracy. While in the US, at senior level they are largely political appointments, in present-day Britain there will be both career civil servants and those employed on a temporary basis. The advantages permanent officials bring include their knowledge of functions and procedures. Their attention to correct practice can help facilitate a smoothly running administration. They are bound to give impartial advice, which may enable a thorough examination of policy options. On the other hand, permanent civil servants are not supposed to be committed to the party of government or individual ministers in such a way that they could not serve their successors. In theory, it could mean that British war leaders find civil servants reluctant to oblige them at all times. The *Civil Service Code* refers to a range of binding considerations, including 'the duty to comply with the law, including international law and treaty obligations'.

If concerned about ministerial instructions, ultimately, it seems that officials will often be required to go along with them, or resign and remain silent. When they believe that they are being asked to carry out actions which are 'illegal, improper, or unethical . . . in breach of constitutional convention or a professional code . . . may involve possible maladministration; or . . . [are] otherwise inconsistent with this Code', they 'should report the matter in accordance with procedures laid down in the appropriate guidance or rules of conduct for their department or Administration'. Once the departmental route has been exhausted, a final appeal can be made to the Civil Service Commissioners. At that point, 'Where a matter cannot be resolved by the procedures set out . . . on a basis which the civil servant concerned is able to accept, he or she should either carry out his or her instructions, or resign from the Civil Service.' They are told not to air their concerns in public (there is a threat of prosecution under the Official Secrets Act if they do so). The fundamental tenet is, 'Civil servants should not seek to frustrate the policies, decisions or actions of the Administrations by declining to take, or abstaining from, action which flows from decisions by Ministers.'

Particularly contentious military campaigns may provoke some protest within Whitehall. In an era before the promulgation of the *Civil Service Code*, but when the values it described existed, there were two resignations from the Foreign Office over the Suez action of 1956 and the surreptitious manner in which it was planned. Inside the Treasury William Armstrong, subsequently Head of the Home Civil Service, wore a black tie in protest for the duration of the operation, but stayed on.

Elizabeth Wilmshurst, a deputy legal adviser in the Foreign and Commonwealth Office, resigned over the invasion of Iraq. She has declined to be interviewed on the subject, issuing the following statement:

> *I left my job . . . because I did not agree that the use of force against Iraq was lawful, and in all the circumstances I did not want to continue as a legal adviser.*[48]

A number of others within the Civil Service shared her concerns.

The Intelligence and Security Committee (ISC) stated in its 2004 annual report, 'A total of three members of staff at GCHQ and the SIS, who objected to working on the Iraq conflict, were moved to other work either at their own request or as the result of a management decision.' Shortly before the invasion Katharine Gun, a translator at GCHQ, disclosed that the American National Security Agency had asked the British government to help in the surveillance of six delegations to the UN Security Council. She was charged under the Official Secrets Act but the case was dropped in February 2004. The ISC remarked,

> *The arrest and charging of Ms Katharine Gun, who worked at GCHQ, attracted considerable publicity as a prosecution was first mounted and then discontinued. We have discussed this case with the Foreign Secretary, the Attorney General and the Director of Public Prosecutions. We also saw a note from counsel concerning his advice. We agree that the case had to be discontinued for evidential reasons not in any way related to the Attorney General's advice on the lawfulness of invading Iraq.*

Supposedly, there was a misunderstanding 'in the initial stages of the investigation . . . between GCHQ and prosecuting counsel about' a matter the details of which could not be publicly revealed.[49]

Successful prosecutions under the Official Secrets Act have always been difficult. Embarking on one at all may cause more embarrassment to a war leader than it is worth. In July 1984 Clive Ponting, a Ministry of Defence official, sent documents to Tam Dalyell MP relating to the sinking of the Argentinian warship, the *General Belgrano*, during the Falklands conflict. Ponting's motive was disapproval of the ministerial misleading of Parliament, which he believed was taking place. He was charged and brought to trial. Though the judge directed the jury that Ponting's duty was to carry out the policy of the government of the day, not to any broader conception of public interest, they reached a unanimous verdict of not guilty in February 1985.

Special advisers, unlike their career Civil Service counterparts, are usually overt in their partisanship. They are recruited by particular politicians, on temporary contracts. The personal connection between aide and political head of department, then, is clear. It is in the interest of the special adviser that the administration is politically successful and that the minister prospers personally. There may be a tension between the two tendencies. A government can be undermined by aides participating in and even aggravating conflicts between their respective Cabinet bosses. Special advisers are officially recruited for the purpose of providing 'only . . . advice'. That would seem to restrict their being deployed in formal positions of power over career staff, thereby limiting the uses to which they can be put. But if such aides are given clear backing from ministers and are able to speak on their behalf, they can exert *de facto* authority in their dealings with permanent civil servants. They may be used as channels for the communication of instructions; perhaps an effective means of ensuring that the policies of the war leadership are implemented. However, if ministers become isolated from the bulk of their departmental staff, they may be deprived of valuable impartial advice.

Across Whitehall as a whole, special advisers are greatly outnumbered by permanent staff. Expanding the former group is likely to encourage charges that the Civil Service is being 'politicised'. It may lead to an increased number of counterproductive power struggles between temporaries and established elements. As discussed in Chapter 2, the Prime Minister can appoint more special advisers than other Cabinet members, with Blair served by as many as twenty-six. The total complement at No. 10 and its annexe, including menial and clerical workers, is less than two hundred. A Prime Minister, therefore, can determine the composition of his staff to a considerable extent. Since senior career officials at Downing Street are seconded from elsewhere, premiers can create teams which are their own. Blair's extensive use of his close group of aides has been discussed. On coming to power in 1997, he exempted up to three special advisers in the Prime Minister's Office from the 'only . . . advice' stipulation, taken up by Alastair Campbell and Jonathan Powell. The purpose was formally to confer authority upon them, making it explicit that they could perform tasks such as communicating decisions, and carry out a coordinating role, both within No. 10 and across Whitehall. As the Iraq crisis developed, Campbell chaired the Iraq Communications Group, composed of senior officials from a number of departments, with responsibility for presentation strategy.[50] Much controversy surrounded allegations regarding his role in the production of the *Iraq's Weapons of Mass Destruction* dossier of September 2002. The Hutton Inquiry found that, though they did not determine the process in an inappropriate way, presentational requirements may have subconsciously influenced the Chairman of the JIC, John Scarlett, who was formally responsible for the document.

Despite the undoubted value of special advisers to a war leader, it is advisable to ensure that they are not used to the extent that career officials – and the qualities they bring, particularly the duty to provide impartial advice – are eclipsed. In the words of Butler in a press interview in December 2004,

> *Good government in my view means bringing to bear all the knowledge and all the arguments you can from inside and outside, debating and arguing them as frankly as you can, and to try to reach a conclusion . . . it's clear that politically appointed people carry great weight in the government, and there is nothing necessarily wrong with that, but if it's done to the exclusion of advice from civil servants, you tend to get into error, you make mistakes.[51]*

5 Justification and Dissent

- War leaders can justify their campaigns as conducted in pursuit of the cause of democracy
- They should present their cases in a proactive manner – and seek generally supportive media coverage for their administrations
- Presentation may be regarded as of more value than veracity – but if such an approach undermines government credibility, it is self-negating
- News management techniques available to a present-day democratic war government are limited as compared with earlier periods, but methods do exist
- Greater freedom of information may prove to be an effective means of communication with the public, bypassing media outlets
- War leaders can face dissent within their own party. Labour has split on many occasions over the issue of armed conflict – but it benefited politically from both world wars
- There is a possibility for cross-party consensus, as between Labour and the Conservatives over the invasion of Iraq. At the same time, a growth in support for smaller parties can occur, filling the void left by such agreement
- Fundamental shifts in the political landscape are possible, with ideas changing, and parties rising and being eclipsed

- War can destroy the careers of political leaders and military defeat can result in the supplanting of the democratic system itself

The Case for War

In presenting their war policy, leaders can portray it as conducted for the sake of democracy. They should emphasise that universal issues are at stake and exhort other countries who share their values to support them. On 11 September 2001 Blair stated that

> mass terrorism is the new evil in our world. The people who perpetrate it have no regard whatever for the sanctity or value of human life and we, the democracies of the world, must come together to defeat it and eradicate it . . . This is not a battle between the United States of America and terrorism but between the free and democratic world and terrorism . . . We therefore, here in Britain, stand shoulder to shoulder with our American friends in this hour of tragedy and we like them will not rest until this evil is driven from our world.[1]

On 18 March 2003, explaining his support for the invasion of Iraq and portraying it as closely linked to the War on Terror, Blair said in the Commons that

> there are two begetters of chaos: tyrannical regimes with weapons of mass destruction and extreme terrorist groups who profess a perverted and false view of Islam . . . there are several countries – mostly dictatorships with highly repressive regimes – that are desperately trying to acquire chemical weapons, biological weapons or, in particular, nuclear weapons capability . . . We all know that there are terrorist groups now operating in most major countries . . . Those

two threats have, of course, different motives and different origins, but they share one basic common view: they detest the freedom, democracy and tolerance that are the hallmarks of our way of life . . . The possibility of the two coming together – of terrorist groups in possession of weapons of mass destruction or even of a so-called dirty radiological bomb – is now, in my judgment, a real and present danger to Britain and its national security.[2]

Lincoln, in his message to Congress of 4 July 1861, argued that the Southern challenge to the Union

embraces more than the fate of these United States. It presents to the whole family of man the question whether a constitutional republic, or democracy – a government of the people by the same people – can or can not maintain its territorial integrity against its own domestic foes. It presents the question whether discontented individuals, too few in numbers to control administration according to organic law in any case, can always, upon the pretenses made in this case, or on any other pretenses, or arbitrarily without any pretense, break up their government, and thus practically put an end to free government upon the earth.

In his first State of the Union Address, made on 3 December 1901, the US President Theodore Roosevelt, referring to the assassination of his predecessor, William McKinley, by an anarchist, declared his own war on terror, stating that

President McKinley was killed by an utterly depraved criminal belonging to that body of criminals who object to all governments, good and bad alike, who are against any form of popular liberty if it is guaranteed by even the most just and liberal laws, and who are as

hostile to the upright exponent of a free people's sober will as to the tyrannical and irresponsible despot . . . Anarchy is a crime against the whole human race; and all mankind should band against the anarchist.

Almost exactly a century later, on 20 September 2001, George W. Bush addressed Congress, saying that

Our war on terror begins with al-Qaeda, but it does not end there. It will not end until every terrorist group of global reach has been found, stopped and defeated. Americans are asking 'Why do they hate us?' They hate what they see right here in this chamber: a democratically elected government. Their leaders are self-appointed. They hate our freedoms: our freedom of religion, our freedom of speech, our freedom to vote and assemble and disagree with each other . . . We have seen their kind before. They're the heirs of all the murderous ideologies of the 20th century . . . they follow in the path of Fascism, Nazism and totalitarianism. And they will follow that path all the way to where it ends in history's unmarked grave of discarded lies . . . Every nation in every region now has a decision to make: either you are with us or you are with the terrorists . . . This is not . . . just America's fight. And what is at stake is not just America's freedom. This is the world's fight. This is civilisation's fight. This is the fight of all who believe in progress and pluralism, tolerance and freedom. We ask every nation to join us . . . Freedom and fear are at war. The advance of human freedom, the great achievement of our time and the great hope of every time, now depends on us.

An important moment in the emergence of the Cold War was Truman's address to a joint session of Congress on 12 March 1947. It described the US decision to provide aid to Greece. The British could no longer meet their commitment to do so and there was a fear that the country might be subject to a Soviet-inspired Communist takeover. In his memoir, Truman notes, 'This declaration of policy soon began to be referred to as the "Truman Doctrine". This was, I believe, the turning point in America's foreign policy which now declared that wherever aggression, direct or indirect, threatened the peace, the security of the United States was involved.' Truman stated in his address that

> *it must be the policy of the United States to support free peoples who are resisting attempted subjugation by armed minorities or by outside pressures . . . we must assist free peoples to work out their own destinies in their own way . . . Our way of life is based upon the will of the majority, and is distinguished by free institutions, representative government, free elections, guarantees of individual liberty, freedom of speech and religion and freedom from political oppression . . . The second way of life is based upon the will of a minority forcibly imposed upon the majority. It relies upon terror and oppression, a controlled press and radio, fixed elections, and the suppression of personal freedoms . . . The free peoples of the world look to us in maintaining their freedoms . . . If we falter in our leadership, we may endanger the peace of the world — and we shall surely endanger the welfare of our own nation.*[3]

In the words of Graubard, Woodrow Wilson, with his refusal to recognise the dictatorial Mexican regime of General Victoriano Huerto, 'in effect, initiated the human rights policy that later presidents would also invoke to justify their military intervention against dictators'.[4] Continuing in a similar vein, in January 1918 Wilson declared to Congress that the US had entered the First World War

because violations of right had occurred which touched us to the quick
. . . What we demand in this war . . . is nothing peculiar to ourselves.
It is that the world be made fit and safe to live in; and particularly
that it be made safe for every peace-loving nation which, like our
own, wishes to live its own life, determine its own institutions, be
assured of justice and fair dealing by the other peoples of the world as
against force and selfish aggression. All the peoples of the world are in
effect partners in this interest, and for our own part we see very clearly
that unless justice be done to others it will not be done to us.

He issued his 'Fourteen Points', intended to form a basis for the
peace. Stipulations included 'Open covenants of peace, openly
arrived at'; free trade; 'A free, open-minded, and absolutely impartial
adjustment of all colonial claims'; and 'A general association of
nations . . . formed under specific covenants for the purpose of
affording mutual guarantees of political independence and territorial
integrity to great and small states alike'. In holding such objectives,
Wilson saw the US as 'intimate partners of all the governments and
peoples associated together against the Imperialists'.

A war leader who believes in such a programme, as Wilson
appeared to, may find difficulties in enlisting others, domestically
and abroad, in its pursuance. It may also be difficult to bring about,
appear hyperbolical, or lack credibility. The European associate
powers of the US – who themselves possessed colonial empires –
were not enthusiastic about the 'Fourteen Points' and the Treaty of
Versailles was rejected by the Senate.

Franklin D. Roosevelt may have found his British allies similarly
reluctant fully to embrace post-colonial values. On 14 August 1941
he and Churchill jointly issued the 'Atlantic Charter', condemning
territorial aggrandisement, and advocating the 'freely expressed wishes
of the people concerned' in the settlement of borders and determining

forms of government. It called for international collaboration to bring about social and economic rights, universal access to resources and trade, freedom of navigation on the high seas and the banishing of the use of force by nations. A 'permanent system of general security' was to be established. Yet Churchill clearly felt – and publicly indicated – that the Atlantic Charter's references to principles of self-determination ought not to apply to the British Empire, of which he was a devout supporter. In more recent times many have noted a contradiction between the rhetoric deployed in support of the War on Terror and the willingness to collaborate with allies which made habitual use of torture, even utilising information extracted in the process. The policy of collusion with Russian security agencies in the period of anarchist attacks of the late nineteenth and early twentieth centuries was unpopular with sections of the French public, who disliked what they saw as Czarist oppression.

If faced with sustained criticism of a military action, even after its completion, a war leader may choose to argue that, whatever objections there might be, an unpleasant enemy was defeated and a desirable outcome secured. When the Butler Review team reported in July 2004, the Prime Minister told Parliament that 'as the months have passed, it has seemed increasingly clear that, at the time of invasion, Saddam did not have stockpiles of chemical or biological weapons ready to deploy'. That led to the question whether, 'even if we acted in perfectly good faith, is it now the case . . . the war was unjustified?'. Blair had

> *searched my conscience . . . in the light of what we now know . . . My answer would be this: the evidence of Saddam's weapons of mass destruction was indeed less certain and less well founded than was stated at the time. However, I cannot go from there to the opposite extreme. On any basis, he retained complete strategic intent on*

WMD and significant capability . . . I say further that if we had backed down in respect of Saddam, we would never have taken the stand that we needed to take on weapons of mass destruction, we would never have got the progress on Libya, for example, that we achieved, and we would have left Saddam in charge of Iraq, with every malign intent and capability still in place, and with every dictator with the same intent everywhere immeasurably emboldened . . . for any mistakes made, as the report finds, in good faith, I of course take responsibility, but I cannot honestly say that I believe that getting rid of Saddam was a mistake at all. Iraq, the region and the wider world are better and safer places without him.[5]

Theodore Roosevelt took a comparable approach. In 1903 he dispatched navy vessels to ensure the success of a revolution leading to the separation from Colombia of Panama, the intended site of a transcontinental canal. A small number of troops were landed. Roosevelt later argued that the action, regarded as illegal by some, was justified on a number of grounds. Columbia was a dictatorship which was unable to maintain the peace, and had breached treaty obligations with and forsaken the trust of the US. In his words, 'Colombia was solely responsible for her own humiliation; and she had not then, and has not now, one shadow of claim upon us, moral or legal; all the wrong that was done was done by her.' The end result, namely the construction of the waterway, was a desirable one. As Roosevelt put it, 'the canal would not have been built at all save for the action I took. If men chose to say that it would have been better not to build it, than to build it as the result of such action, their position, although foolish, is compatible with belief in their wrongheaded sincerity. But it is hypocrisy, alike odious and contemptible, for any man to say both that we ought to have built the canal and that we ought not to have acted in the way we did act.'[6]

Presenting the Case

Whatever particular justifications they have developed for their actions, war leaders ought to give considerable attention to presenting them, and communications designed to achieve the more general maintenance of public support. In the words of Cassar, to Asquith

> *the thought of courting the press was something that never entered his mind. He never drew attention to his own achievements and, in fact, had an aversion to any form of self-advertisment . . . He intensely disliked interviews and rarely agreed to sit through one. He made no effort to answer his press critics, let alone to try to influence them in his favour . . . Asquith's neglect of the press made him particularly vulnerable to criticism when the tide of war took an unfavourable turn.*[7]

Other war leaders have taken different approaches to Asquith's. Woodrow Wilson established a Committee on Public Information in 1917. Its staff, which grew to number hundreds, was engaged in propaganda and censorship. In Britain during the Second World War, the specifically created Ministry of Information (MoI) was used for similar purposes. The diaries of Harold Nicolson, a Parliamentary Secretary at the MoI, serve to illustrate some of the techniques and difficulties associated with concerted propaganda campaigns.

It may be deemed necessary to communicate particular messages, regardless of their veracity. Nicolson considered it possible that

> *if our propaganda is to be as effective as that of the enemy, we must have at the top people who will not only command the assent of the Press, but who will be caddish and ignorant enough to tell dynamic*

lies. At present the Ministry is too decent, educated and intellectual to imitate [Joseph] Goebbels [Hitler's propaganda minister]. It cannot live by intelligence alone. We need crooks.[8]

Such methods can be hazardous. On 11 March 2004, around two hundred were killed and more than a thousand injured in a terrorist attack on Atocha railway station in Madrid, days before a general election. The conservative government, led by José Maria Aznar, which had participated in the Iraq War, instantly blamed Basque separatists,

and continued to do so even as evidence mounted that it was more likely to be the work of al-Qaeda. Aznar did not want voters to link his support for Bush and Blair in Iraq with insecurity on the streets. Three days later [Aznar's party] were dramatically defeated by the socialists, who had pledged to withdraw Spanish troops from Iraq.

John Kampfner refers to the view held by 'Many in Spain' that 'The outgoing administration had been punished at the ballot for lying, and for seeking to exploit a tragedy for political ends.'[9]

Nicolson's account shows how the requirements both of presentation and the individuals charged with carrying it out may conflict with the approach and values of other government staff. In June 1941 the MoI complained to the Admiralty 'that there are no photographs of the sinking of [the German battleship] the *Bismarck*', which had taken place the previous month. The response was

that the official photographer was in the Suffolk and that the Suffolk was too far away. We say, 'But why didn't one of our reconnaissance machines fly over the ship and take photographs?' [The Admiralty representative] replies 'Well you see, you must see, well upon my word, well after all, an Englishman would not like to take snapshots of a fine vessel sinking.'

Government propaganda and the machinery for its implementation may themselves become the subject of negative publicity. On 3 August 1940 Nicolson referred to politically motivated attacks in the press on the MoI. He complained that its 'value to our war-effort will be diminished by this constant sniping from the rear . . . A Ministry of this character cannot really be conducted efficiently if the majority of the Press are out to sabotage it.'[10]

It is unlikely that the level of control over public communications during both world wars, in Britain and elsewhere – which included both statutory and informal censorship – could be applied in a modern-day democracy. Nor do newspapers in particular display the same degree of deference towards politicians that they have at points in the past. What propaganda techniques are presently at the disposal of a war government? Among the media there is a high premium placed on exclusivity derived from privileged contact with informed sources. In Britain the tendency is probably enhanced, where political coverage is concerned, by a strong tradition of official secrecy. The selective granting of access can be used to exploit this, in attempts to secure desired coverage. It may be targeted at journalists and outlets considered sympathetic, or used as a type of favour, in order to secure goodwill. Information can be provided in a form which encourages a particular interpretation. An example of strong support for Blair over Iraq was provided by the *Sun*. (As it was by another Rupert Murdoch-owned title, *The Times*.) On 18 March 2003 the *Sun* pronounced that Bush and Blair 'are united in their resolve to make the world a safer place. The world should rejoice that it is in such capable hands.'[11]

However, success is not guaranteed. Such methods may not work, even leading to confused or critical coverage. Sometimes, suppliers of informal briefings will be officials or ministers acting without the approval of the war leader and pursuing their own agendas. The material might be presented in a way that was not intended by the provider. In such a culture, some journalists may imply or claim on behalf of their stories a stronger basis in genuine inside knowledge than they actually possess. Those who feel they are being neglected while others receive privileged access may consequently become more hostile. In Britain there is a convention that, while Parliament is sitting, the government is supposed to make policy announcements there. Perceived neglect of the rule may lead to criticism.

To what extent was the technique used under Blair? When asked by PASC about his supposedly 'feeding stories selectively to newspapers in order to get the kind of coverage that you wanted to see', Alastair Campbell stated that there were 'some journalists that you can have a sensible, adult, mature conversation with. They might think they are getting a more informed briefing from you, but it is just a misrepresentation to say that the whole time there was this systematic briefing to selected journalists who were being favoured.' He conceded that 'If I am sitting down, on a one to one basis, with one journalist, and I am talking to them, they could argue and you could argue they are going to be better informed as a result of that. It might inform what they write.' But, 'This idea that big decisions are coming up, big speeches are being made and we are sitting there thinking, "We will give this bit to this paper and this bit to that paper and cut across Parliament" – It just was not like that.'[12]

Aside from selecting particular outlets for stories, war governments might wish to time releases of information according to the amount of attention it wants them to receive. Under Blair, the Strategic

Communications Unit was set up at No. 10, maintaining a computerised grid of coordinated cross-departmental announcements. Again, the approach can create problems. One departmental special adviser saw the 11 September 2001 attacks as an opportunity for the release of unpalatable news. Unfortunately, she wrote an email to that effect which was leaked to the press, seemingly by one or more of her enemies within the department. The incident became a major media event in its own right – certainly not a successful piece of presentation. (Part of the problem was the tension that can develop between those engaged in presentation who are committed to the government of the day and those who aspire more to the role of dispassionate information-givers.)

A war leader and his staff are likely to feel that they are receiving unfair treatment from the media, even that sections of it are deliberately campaigning against them. Lyndon Johnson, the US President during part of the Vietnam War, wrote of coverage of the 'Tet' offensive by the North Vietnamese and Viet Cong in early 1968 that

> *There was a great deal of emotional and exaggerated reporting . . .
> in our press and on television. The media seemed to be in
> competition as to who could provide the most lurid and depressing
> accounts. Columnists unsympathetic to American involvement in
> Southeast Asia jumped on the bandwagon. Some senatorial critics
> and numerous opponents of America's war effort added their voices
> to the chorus of defeatism. The American people and even a number
> of officials in government, subjected to this daily barrage of bleakness
> and near panic, began to think that we must have suffered a
> defeat.*[13]

Johnson himself regarded Tet as 'a military debacle for the North Vietnamese and the Viet Cong.'[14]

Particular tensions may develop between the government and individual outlets. Campbell's loathing of the *Daily Mail* was vehement. He told PASC, 'You still hear journalists who ought to know better saying, "Say what you like. It is a very professional product." It is not; it is vile. It is the worst of British values posing as the best. It has a backward looking view of the world that I think anybody with progressive values should not respect. It systematically undermines and runs down the country and anybody in public life. I am going to carry on saying that because it is what I believe.' The dislike was returned. When it was suggested to Paul Dacre, editor of the *Daily Mail*, by a member of PASC that there was a 'striking similarity between yourself and your great opponent Alastair Campbell', Dacre responded, 'I do hope not! That is a gross slander.' Asked, 'You have got this thing about Alastair Campbell?', Dacre said, 'No, he has got a thing about the *Daily Mail*.'[15]

Not only the press but broadcasters may cause war leaders and their aides displeasure. Bernard Ingham, Thatcher's Press Secretary, writes that the BBC was 'the most awkward organisation I was ever likely to deal with'. In his view, because it was publicly funded, the BBC was 'determined to demonstrate [its] independence of government'. During the Falklands War he found it 'rather trying when . . . the BBC gave an impression of neutrality as between Britain and the Argentine . . . and the Prime Minister herself was not best pleased'. He 'feared that every suggestion by the likes of me to the BBC would be a criticism or interference, every criticism a provocation and every complaint an incident'.[16]

Blair, too, experienced difficulties with the BBC, which developed into a considerable 'incident', to apply Ingham's term. Blair told Hutton of 'a feeling, but I do not doubt we are not the first Government to be in such a situation, that there were parts of the BBC that were not covering it [Iraq] in as objective a way as we thought.'[17] Writing in the *Guardian* on 18 March 2003, David Aaronovitch, who agreed with Blair's stance on Iraq, complained of media distortion. He wrote,

> *the impression has been given, on the BBC in particular, that public and expert opinion is strongly and almost exclusively opposed to military action. This expectation has entered the cultural stratum that the majority of broadcasters exist in, and so dominates that it has become that most dangerous of wisdoms – not so much orthodox, as axiomatic . . . Yet today's poll for the Guardian has the gap between pros and antis at just 6 per cent in favour of the latter.*[18]

The following day, Campbell wrote to Richard Sambrook, Director of News at the BBC, drawing attention to Aaronovitch's column (Campbell sent a number of similar letters to the BBC at other times). Campbell argued, 'The point [Aaronovitch] was making was underlined several times on this morning's [BBC Radio 4] *Today* programme.' He asked Sambrook to justify 'five incidents', including a statement by the journalist Andrew Gilligan that 'innocent people' would die in Iraq 'in the next few hours'. After making a more detailed point regarding coverage of the legality of the war by the Corporation, 'to illustrate the selection towards anti-war, anti-government stories', Campbell stated that 'I know you will try to justify this. You always do. But it is wrong.' He signed off with a warning:

> *You may be interested to know that the Prime Minister has also expressed real concern about some of the reports he has seen and heard. I feel strongly that if the BBC reporting continues as it is, this will become a public controversy, which I am sure neither of us particularly want.*[19]

Campbell's prediction was fulfilled to a greater extent than he could have imagined. In the summer of 2003 he engaged in a public dispute with the BBC over a story it had run, reporting allegations from a supposedly well-placed source that Downing Street had interfered in the production of the *Iraq's Weapons of Mass Destruction* dossier of September 2003 against the better judgement of intelligence staff, and suggesting that it contained information the government might have known was wrong. The Ministry of Defence scientist, David Kelly, came forward as having spoken to Gilligan. After his appearance before the FAC, Kelly committed suicide. Faced with a political crisis, the government chose to establish the Hutton Inquiry, which found very much in the Blair administration's favour, condemning the BBC. But the turn of events was politically damaging to the government.

As Nicolson's diary shows, a war leader's efforts to secure helpful media coverage can themselves become the subject of criticism. Such was the case for Blair. He did not establish a formal department such as the MoI. Around half the expanded number of special advisers he took on from 1997 – approximately forty, of a total which eventually exceeded eighty – were deployed to some extent on presentational duties, with a quarter of them engaged exclusively in such tasks. As discussed in the previous chapter, compared with career officials, they were more directly committed to the government of the day and their ministers, therefore possessing a clearer interest in the active promotion of policy. In addition, after Blair came to power a number of new departmental heads of information were appointed. Some took these developments, along with other factors such as the powerful position of Campbell, as evidence that Blair was excessively concerned with presentation and neglecting constitutional propriety, to self-defeating and damaging effect. Dacre complained to PASC of how, in his view,

Labour flag waving journalists from the Mirror were put in charge of ministry press machines. You should not be doing that. You should be going back to the day where you had civil servant press officers observing Civil Service objectivity; they would then be much more respected by the specialist journalist reporters who dealt with them.

Clare Short told the FAC that, under Blair, presentational concerns were afforded an inappropriate primary importance:

Alastair Campbell is responsible for the presentation of government policy, and that soon becomes propaganda and there is a place for that. Once proper decisions have been made, then the Government should put forward what it is trying to do as well as it can and communicate to the public, but the two often conflate and they were conflated [over Iraq].

Ingham was reported in the *Daily Telegraph* in March 2003 as saying, 'Of course we should be going to war. This country's gone mad when everyone from schoolchildren to old colonels seems to be backing Saddam.' He blamed the government's use of 'spin' for the problem it was experiencing in communicating its case. He went on, 'The spin has gone all wrong for the Prime Minister. He's the little boy who cried wolf once too often. The wages of spin is a serious loss of trust by the public.'[20]

As Ingham's comment suggested, by the time of the Iraq War, there was much anecdotal and opinion poll evidence to the effect that public credence with respect to government information was extremely low. A long-term trend, it could not be attributed solely to an over-use of news management methods by Blair. But the problem was not helped by the failure to discover weapons of mass destruction in Iraq and allegations that intelligence material was compromised by presentational requirements. *An Independent Review of Government Communications*, produced under the chairmanship of Bob Phillis of the Guardian Media Group, was presented to the government in January 2004. In the words of the report, it was commissioned in the atmosphere of a 'three-way breakdown in trust between government and politicians, the media and the general public'. It listed certain principles that ought to be adhered to in order to help rectify the difficulty. They included 'Openness, not secrecy . . . More direct, unmediated communications to the public . . . Positive presentation of government policies and achievements, not misleading spin . . . Reinforcement of the Civil Service's political neutrality, rather than a blurring of government and party communications'. Many of the methods Phillis opposed were those that war leaders have utilised. But if they are likely to prove self-defeating, damaging the perceived reliability of official communications, then different ones need to be used.

A future war leader might consider adopting a more liberal approach. One means of doing so would be through encouraging accedance to requests under the Freedom of Information Act, and forbearance with regard to the ministerial veto. Rather than waiting for applications, government could attempt to anticipate them. Through more proactive disclosure, with material placed directly in the public domain, for instance on websites, individual journalists and outlets could be bypassed and their importance as conduits for communications from the administration to the outside world reduced. Campbell, following his experiences, now advocates greater openness, telling PASC that

> *I was never a great devotee of freedom of information. I have had a bit of a change on this . . . I think maybe the Hutton Inquiry showed that if you veer towards openness and you find that the world does not*

come to an end, it may be no bad thing. I think maybe on freedom of information you have to hold your nose and take a huge leap and see what happens.

. . . Nobody can say the Government was not being open at the Hutton Inquiry. Every single piece of paper that anybody could find that related to any of those issues was put out there . . . If you went through everything that had been put in the public domain with a fair mind, the Government came out of it pretty well. Maybe the lesson from that is: do not worry so much about what the papers are going to say about what comes out in the public domain. Just be a bit more trusting of the public because I think they are canny enough to see where they are being spun a line, wherever it is coming from, whether it is a politician or a newspaper.

A culture of proactive official disclosure might mitigate a tendency commonly associated with war which can cause governments presentational difficulties, namely conspiracy theorising. In September 2003, the Labour MP Michael Meacher wrote an article for the *Guardian* arguing that the 'conventional explanation' for the invasion of Iraq did 'not fit all the facts. The truth may be a great deal murkier.' Meacher portrayed some of George W. Bush's closest allies as having a 'blueprint for the creation of a global Pax Americana' prior to his becoming President. It entailed taking 'control of the Gulf region whether or not Saddam Hussein was in power'. The intention was 'US world domination'. Meacher went on, 'it is clear the US authorities did little or nothing to pre-empt the events of 9/11.' He then posed the following questions: 'Was this inaction simply the result of key people disregarding, or being ignorant of, the evidence? Or could US air security operations have been deliberately stood down on September 11? If so, why, and on whose authority?' He added, 'No serious attempt has ever been made to catch Bin

Laden.' Meacher's view was that 'None of this assembled evidence
. . . is compatible with the idea of a real, determined war on
terrorism.' However, it did 'fall into place' if set against the view 'that
the so-called "war on terrorism" is being used largely as bogus cover
for achieving wider US strategic geopolitical objectives'.[21]

Ideas of the sort expressed by Meacher had been circulating widely
(especially on the internet) ever since 11 September 2001, but were
associated more with the fringe than the mainstream. That an MP
for the governing party in Britain – who had, moreover, served as
Environment Minister from 1997 to 2003 – should promote them
(and in a national daily broadsheet) was inevitably far more
controversial. He received widespread criticism. In the same paper
which had run the original piece, Aaronovitch wrote, 'this is all
rubbish.'[22] Mick Hume commented in *The Times*, 'Meacher's
"revelations" are a tired rehash of the sort of gossip and paranoid
fantasies that fill internet chatrooms.'[23] Meacher's response was, 'I
did not say at any point, and have never said, that the US
government connived at the 9/11 attacks or deliberately allowed
them to happen. It need hardly be said that I do not believe any
government would conspire to cause such an atrocity.'[24] Yet his
article had posed certain questions in such a way that many reading
it understandably thought that he felt the answer to them might be
'yes'.

Meacher's feature probably served to fuel ongoing conspiracy
theories, the like of which have long possessed a certain political sex
appeal. Their possible use to a war leader is that they may help
discredit by association more sensible criticism. Were a government,
as part of a general approach of greater openness, to reveal details of
the policy-formation process, it would serve to reveal the complex
considerations that make the fully coordinated pursuance of a single
overriding agenda, such as global domination, unlikely, even if

leaders wanted to do so. Few would find the bulk of internal Whitehall papers exciting enough to merit reading, but if they were available, claims of a cover-up might be harder to sustain.

Dissent

Blair's participation in the invasion of Iraq saw him experience arguably the most severe political difficulties of his premiership. On a basis of opinion poll evidence, there was less public support for the action than there had been for his earlier engagements. It was widely criticised, from a variety of sources. Some were those who tended to regard all actions by Western governments, particularly the US and its allies, with suspicion. Radical forms of resistance were advocated. John Pilger's *New Statesman* article from 17 March 2003 attacked 'an illegal and immoral war against a stricken nation with whom we have no quarrel and who offer us no threat: an act of aggression opposed by almost everybody and whose charade is transparent'. He argued that since '11 September 2001, the consciousness of the majority has soared. The word "imperialism" has been rescued from agitprop and returned to common usage. America's and Britain's planned theft of the Iraqi oilfields, following historical precedent, is well understood.' Bush, Pilger wrote, employed advisers, drawn from the American Enterprise Institute, who were 'crypto-fascists'. He described a future 'Pax Americana . . . policed with nuclear, biological and chemical weapons used "pre-emptively", even in conflicts that do not directly engage US interests'. Pilger went on, 'There is only one form of opposition now: it is civil disobedience leading to what the police call civil unrest.'[25] Certainly, there were very large public demonstrations (though not widespread 'civil unrest'). But, in themselves, such events need not prevent action by a war leader with a majority in the House.

Perhaps the most problems for Blair came from his own party, both within and beyond Parliament. War has disrupted and divided Labour at many points in its history. Ramsay MacDonald resigned as chairman over his opposition to British participation in the First World War. George Lansbury's disagreement with the use of force in defence of international order, at a time of rising fascism, led to his being forced out of the Labour leadership in 1935. Clement Attlee's administration participated in the Korean War, necessitating a reallocation of resources to defence, away from social services, in the 1951 budget. The move prompted three Cabinet resignations. In time, Korea helped prompt the emergence of the Bevanite group within Labour, which fought with the more right-wing Gaitskellites. Though Harold Wilson did not commit British troops to the Vietnam War, he was nevertheless criticised for not actively opposing it. Disagreement over policy on nuclear weapons divided Labour for many years. One motive for the formation in 1981 of the Labour breakaway group, the Social Democratic Party, was opposition to unilateral disarmament.

Conflict has divided parties of the Left in other countries, as the emergence of the Cold War did the Democrats in the US. Henry Wallace, who had served in Roosevelt and Truman cabinets, ran as a Progressive in the presidential election of 1948, against Truman. Wallace argued that the President's policy of opposing the Soviet Union through economic aid and the formation of military alliances would lead to war. When announcing his candidacy at the end of 1947, he stated that

> *a vote for a new party in 1948 will be the most valuable vote you have ever cast, or ever will cast. The bigger the peace vote in 1948, the more definitely the world will know that the United States is not behind the bipartisan reactionary war policy which is dividing the world into two armed camps and making inevitable the day when*

> *American soldiers will be lying in their arctic suits in the Russian snow.*
>
> *There is no real fight between a Truman and a Republican. Both stand for a policy which opens the door to war in our lifetime and makes war certain for our children.*
>
> *Stop saying 'I don't like it but I am going to vote for the lesser of two evils.'*

It was widely believed that Truman would lose the 1948 contest. Potentially, Wallace could split the left vote, letting in the Republican candidate, Thomas Dewey. After an initial promising start, the Progressive campaign lost momentum. Some Democratic supporters were probably reluctant to register a protest vote which might result in a Republican victory. Furthermore, Wallace was identified by the public with the Communist Party.[26]

It would be wrong to suppose that divisions over war within Labour have been along entirely clear left- and right-wing lines. Initially, some on the Labour left, who disliked the Communist regimes, including the future party leader Michael Foot, enthusiastically supported intervention in Korea. Though his success was limited, Blair attempted to appeal to those towards the left of the party who had campaigned against Saddam Hussein since the 1980s, offering them the final removal of his regime. He was able to win the support of Ann Clwyd MP on such terms. Equally, disagreement with the Iraq War spread across the party as a whole and was not confined to one wing of individuals who were opposed to Blair's leadership in general.

Dissent within Labour was provoked, in part, by the fact that the action was carried out in conjunction with a Republican US administration and opposed by many European allies, including socialist governments. There were additional doubts over the wisdom, necessity and legality of the action, and the implications for multilateral international co-operation. Some sensed a lack of even-handedness that was unfair and provocative in the respective treatments meted to Iraq and Israel.

In the issue of the Labour, left-leaning, *Tribune* dated 3 April 2003, its editor, Mark Seddon, wrote 'Tony Blair and his Cabinet have taken Britain into an unlawful war, making this country a rogue state.' He also viewed the action as 'unnecessary'. While many opponents of the war muted their criticism once the action had begun, on grounds of loyalty to the British troops who were engaged, Seddon insisted 'Those who demand the immediate return of British troops can claim the moral high ground . . . their desire is to save lives.' He argued 'Forces under the auspices of the UN should be sent in while weapon inspectors return to continue with their jobs.' While 'the world would be a better place without despots such as Saddam Hussein . . . they should be brought to justice before a war crimes tribunal in The Hague.'[27]

The *Mirror*, a Labour-aligned tabloid, opposed involvement in 'A war without international support, or the backing of the British public'. Though acknowledging that Saddam Hussein was a brutal dictator, the *Mirror* questioned the justifications that had been offered for the action against his regime, imploring the reader to

> *ask yourself whether anything we've heard from Bush and Blair in the last few months has persuaded you that this is justified. They told us Saddam has got weapons of mass destruction. We haven't seen any. They told us he was linked to Osama bin Laden and al-Qaeda. But have singularly failed to prove it. They told us it's not about oil. But Iraq's oil reserves are the second largest in the world and Bush is*

desperate to control them. They told us that they would get a second UN resolution and would not go to war without one. They didn't and they are. Tony Blair has even tried convincing us that Saddam poses a clear and present danger to Britain. He quite obviously doesn't. In short, just about everything they've told us to validate this conflict has turned out to be nonsense. Is it any wonder the world is in uproar at what is about to happen?

Blair, the *Mirror* argued, was committing a grave error in aligning himself with the current US leader, who was 'fraudulently' elected, 'likes blood' and could be characterised as 'a not very bright Texan oil man' at the head of a 'terrifyingly right-wing administration'. The newspaper warned 'It could be a lengthy, bloody, terrible battle.'[28]

The Labour MP, Peter Kilfoyle, spoke in the Commons on 18 March for the cross-party group who felt that 'the case for war against Iraq has not yet been established'. An early supporter of Blair for the Labour leadership in 1994, he was a minister from 1997, but resigned from the government in 2000, seemingly disillusioned with what he saw as its failure properly to assist the very poorest members of society. Kilfoyle noted that 'this is one of those issues that come along once in a generation. Indeed, it is an issue that transcends many normal ties of party, friendship and even family.' The policy pursued by the government was ill-conceived, Kilfoyle believed, referring to 'the idiocy of fighting the wrong war in the wrong place at the wrong time against the wrong enemy . . . We are having a 19th-century gunboat war in the Gulf when the real dangers of terrorism should be isolated and dealt with as the first priority.' Participants in the present US administration, he noted, had advocated an attack on Iraq before coming to power following the 2000 presidential election. That fact, Kilfoyle believed, would suggest that the atrocities of 11 September 2001 were more an excuse than a motive for the proposed invasion. Kilfoyle concluded that 'this act would be illegal, immoral and illogical.'

The opposition Blair met with from within his own Cabinet was discussed in Chapter 2. Only Robin Cook resigned in advance of the invasion. Though his career was in decline, Cook was a significant figure within Labour, regarded by some as a lost leader. In March he informed Blair that he would quit the Cabinet if a fresh UN mandate was not secured for the intended action. He duly did so on 17 March, when the US, Britain and Spain announced that they had abandoned the attempt to obtain a further resolution from the Security Council. He became one of the most eloquent exponents of opposition to the war of a Labour – and more generally progressive – political perspective.

Cook wrote to Blair referring to how

> *At Cabinet for some weeks I have been frank about my concern over embarking on military action in the absence of multilateral support . . . the evident importance that we attached to a second resolution makes it all the more difficult now to proceed without one, and without agreement in any other international forum. As I cannot give my support to military action in these circumstances, I write with regret to resign. You and I have both made the case over the years for an international order based on multilateral decisions through the UN and other forums. In principle, I believe it is wrong to embark on military action without broad international support. In practice I believe it is against Britain's interests to create a precedent for unilateral military action . . . I am dismayed that once again Britain is divided from our major European neighbours. As President of the Party of European Socialists, of which the Labour Party is a member, it troubles me that I know of no sister party within the European Union that shares our position.*

In response, Blair acknowledged the fact that 'You were good enough to tell me some days ago that you would resign in the event of our failure to secure a new UNSCR that authorised military action.' The Prime Minister insisted that

> *I have always tried to resolve this crisis through the UN . . . But I was always clear that the UN must be the way of dealing with the issue, not avoiding dealing with it. The Government is staying true to Resolution 1441. Others, in the face of continuing Iraqi non-compliance, are walking away from it. As I have said to you, the threatened French veto set back hugely the considerable progress we were making in building consensus among UNSC members. I passionately believe that if the international community had stayed rock solid in its determination and unity around Resolution 1441, Saddam could finally have been disarmed without a shot being fired. But, just as he has done for the past 12 years, he has divided the international community and used his dictatorship to exploit our democracies and weaken our will. My will is as strong as ever that he must be disarmed.[29]*

On the evening of 17 March Cook made his resignation statement to the House, explaining 'why I cannot support a war without international agreement or domestic support'. As well as iterating the concerns about the lack of international consensus on the action that he had expressed to Blair, Cook argued that

> *Iraq probably has no weapons of mass destruction in the commonly understood sense of the term – namely a credible device capable of being delivered against a strategic city target. It probably still has biological toxins and battlefield chemical munitions, but it has had them since the 1980s when US companies sold Saddam anthrax*

agents and the then British Government approved chemical and munitions factories. Why is it now so urgent that we should take military action to disarm a military capacity that has been there for 20 years, and which we helped to create?

Cook pointed out that 'it is more than 30 years since resolution 242 called on Israel to withdraw from the occupied territories' and argued that there was a 'strong sense of injustice throughout the Muslim world at what it sees as one rule for the allies of the US and another rule for the rest'. He went on, 'Nor is our credibility helped by the appearance that our partners in Washington are less interested in disarmament than they are in regime change in Iraq.' He was most troubled by the feeling that, were it not for Bush's controversially close election victory in 2000, 'we would not now be about to commit British troops'.[30]

The discontent within the Labour Party which Cook exemplified manifested itself in two historically huge backbench rebellions. Partly because many within Labour disagreed with the war, two votes on substantive motions were held in Parliament. Their outcome underlined the fact that considerable opposition existed among Conservatives, too. On 26 February 2003, MPs were asked to register that the Commons 'supports the Government's continuing efforts in the United Nations to disarm Iraq of its weapons of mass destruction; and calls upon Iraq to recognise this as its final opportunity to comply with its disarmament obligations'. Selected for consideration was an amendment, to the effect that the statement should read 'supports the Government's continuing efforts in the United Nations to disarm Iraq of its weapons of mass destruction; *but finds the case for military action against Iraq as yet unproven* [italics added].' It was tabled in the name of Chris Smith, a Labour MP and former Cabinet member (Secretary of State for Culture, Media and

Sport from 1997 to 2001). He was one of the figureheads of a group of Labour and Conservative rebels who defied their party whips to oppose the war. Other leaders were, on the Labour side, two former ministers, Graham Allen and Kilfoyle (who seemingly originated the wording of the February amendment) and Douglas Hogg, a Conservative. On 26 February, ultimately, 122 Labour and 14 Conservative MPs supported the 'as yet unproven' view (with, respectively, 256 and 129 against it). Had the Conservatives who voted against the amendment done the reverse, it would have been passed with a majority of 64. In its issue of the following day, *The Times* referred to 'the biggest revolt against any governing party in parliamentary history', which, it argued, 'left Tony Blair facing a perilous moment in his premiership' and 'served notice on the Prime Minister that he will have to win a second UN resolution to avoid his future being called into question.'[31]

The new record set in February did not last long. By tradition, after such an expression of discontent, the following occasion on which an issue is considered, the number defying the whip declines. The opposite happened on 18 March 2003. Having abandoned its attempt to secure further UN endorsement, the government produced a long motion including the statements that 'Iraq's weapons of mass destruction and long range missiles, and its continuing non-compliance with Security Council Resolutions, pose a threat to international peace and security . . . despite sustained diplomatic effort . . . it has not proved possible to secure a second Resolution in the UN because one Permanent Member of the Security Council [France] made plain in public its intention to use its veto whatever the circumstances.' It noted 'the opinion of the Attorney General that . . . the authority to use force [under an earlier UN resolution] has revived and so continues today'. Support was therefore requested for 'the decision of Her Majesty's Government that the United Kingdom should use all means necessary to ensure the disarmament of Iraq's weapons of mass destruction'. An amendment, again in Smith's name, asserted that 'the case for war against Iraq has not yet been established, especially given the absence of specific United Nations authorisation.' In order to avoid the charge of disloyalty to personnel about to be deployed in the battlefield, it pledged 'total support for the British forces engaged in the Middle East . . . and hopes that their tasks will be swiftly concluded with minimal casualties on all sides'.

The *Guardian* speculated on the coming revolt within the Parliamentary Labour Party. Up to a hundred 'would be a huge rebellion by previous standards, but far smaller than expected today'. A figure of 122 would equal 'The number of rebels last month. This would be seen as a boost for Tony Blair because this time there is no prospect of a fresh UN security council resolution.' If the total reached 132, 'the Prime Minister would have lost the confidence of half of his backbenchers – a serious, but not fatal, blow to his authority'. At 173, 'Mr Blair would need Tory support to win the Commons vote'. Finally, 206 would be 'A devastating result for Mr Blair. He would have lost confidence of half his parliamentary party and would depend heavily on Conservative support to win the vote.'[32]

In the event, the amendment was supported by 139 Labour MPs (34 per cent of the total) and 16 Conservatives (10 per cent). With the support of all 164 Conservatives, it would have been passed by 109 votes. *The Times* wrote, 'the Prime Minister suffered the biggest anti-government rebellion in parliamentary history.'[33]

At times of conflict, there may be a higher than normal degree of cross-party consensus, motivated in part by a feeling that the national interest is at stake. Dissent may be regarded by some as disloyalty. As one newspaper put it on the day of the second parliamentary vote on the invasion of Iraq:

the time has passed when war could be averted, so any vote against war cannot be effective or persuasive. Such a vote turns, then, from being an expression of principle to being an act of defeatism. We have 45,000 servicemen 'in theatre', many of whom will be in action within days, even hours. They need to know that the Parliament which represents their fellow countrymen at home supports them as steadfastly as they are about to fight abroad. At this late hour, the parading of consciences by those who will not have to fight starts to look like bad taste to those who will.[34]

Leaders should try to cultivate such a tendency. In the First and Second World Wars in Britain, coalition governments were formed and elections postponed. Even in less severe circumstances there are often attempts to ensure a degree of cooperation. John Major describes how, as the action to remove Iraq from Kuwait which took place in 1991 loomed, 'I wanted to obtain the widest possible public and parliamentary support for the hazardous undertaking that lay ahead.' To that end, 'I sought a cross-party consensus, and was determined to keep Neil Kinnock, as leader of the opposition, and Paddy Ashdown for the Liberal Democrats, fully briefed.' Both backed the policy. The Prime Minister took his drive for inclusiveness beyond party politics when he 'invited the Archbishop of Canterbury, Robert Runcie, and Cardinal Basil Hume to the Cabinet Room to secure their support for an action that was now only a few days away'. Major's move was successful. Though apprehensive, the religious leaders 'gave me their public and private support and, in so doing, their reassurance that this would be a just war'.[35]

Military conflict may have a beneficial effect on poll outcomes. Conservative victory in 1900 seems to have been associated with a public rally at the time of the Boer War. Lloyd George's performance in the 1918 General Election, though assisted by the deal between his followers and the Conservatives, was strong. In 1982 Thatcher's recovery from extremely low popularity ratings (followed by a massive poll success in 1983) coincided with the Falklands conflict – though whether the former was caused by the latter has been disputed. Attempts to benefit from patriotic unity may not be successful. Woodrow Wilson appealed to voters to provide backing for his war leadership in the congressional elections of 1918. But the Democrats lost their majorities in both House of Representatives and Senate. Despite military success, Churchill was defeated in the 1945 General Election.

Blair did not enjoy the same backing from senior churchmen as Major. But he was supported, sometimes grudgingly, by the official opposition. The Conservative Party, by 2003, had endured a decade of internal division and political failure. After two successive election disasters, it continued to seem unable to establish itself credibly as the alternative government. The invasion of Iraq, though less popular with the public than Blair's earlier military engagements, was not particularly promising material for a recovery strategy; the party was not noted for its pacifist tendencies and it had strong atlanticist urges. Bush was, after all, a Republican, for whom William Hague, the Conservative leader from 1997 to 2001 – in what was an unusual move – had indicated his support when the former received the presidential nomination in 2000.

The Conservative Party, then, officially supported the war. Its leader, Iain Duncan Smith, speaking in the Commons on 18 March 2003, acknowledged 'the heavy responsibility that the Prime Minister and the Government have to bear' and was keen to 'make it clear from the outset that the official Opposition will vote tonight in the same Lobby as the Government'. Nevertheless, he recognised that 'there are honestly felt and genuinely carried differences of view on both sides of the House about further military action in Iraq.' It was the case that

> the official Opposition could somehow have sought to manoeuvre themselves into the No Lobby tonight. After all, we have argued consistently that Ministers have failed to convince the public of their case, and we have sought to hold the Government to account in the House for their mistakes. In particular, we have also pointed out the failures with regard to the humanitarian consequences of war. However, I believe that when the Government do the right thing by the British people, they deserve the support of the House, and particularly of the main Opposition.

In an editorial of 18 March, the Conservative-supporting *Daily Telegraph* could not resist gloating at the Prime Minister's difficulties: 'There is a certain justice in the fact that Tony Blair, the Prime Minister who, more than any other in history, has ignored the House of Commons, is to be judged by it today.' Yet, it went on, 'everyone who cares about the future of this country as a brave and honourable influence in the world should hope that he prevails.' The publication argued that 'the agreement of the Security Council to a second resolution would have been nice, but was never necessary.' It went on, 'The fall of Saddam . . . will present a great opportunity . . . it will send out a message to Islamist and anti-Western despots that they are not safe.' The action was seen by the *Telegraph* as a means of achieving 'The planting of the rule of law, plural civil society, the beginnings of democracy' in the Middle East.[36]

Amongst Conservatives, some genuinely did not agree with the action and did not approve of Bush. There was a sense that a chance to inflict damage on a politically vulnerable Blair was being wasted, both before the action and afterwards, when the intelligence basis for it, and the way that had been presented, was under scrutiny. In a revealing article for the *Spectator* in February 2004, the Conservative MP, George Osborne, described how 'many Conservatives don't much like Bush'. That did not include Osborne himself, the Conservative leader Michael Howard, or his two predecessors in the post. The reasons for the tendency were complex. First there was the relationship which had developed between Bush and Blair. As Osborne put it, 'we're behaving like a child whose best friend has just gone off and become friends with the popular kid we hate.' The conflict in Iraq was an influence: 'Conservatives supported the war, but not with universal enthusiasm. I was a hawk, and remain one, but I remember a very lively debate in the 1922 Committee about whether we should back Tony Blair in the crucial vote. That debate reflected a broader Conservative ambivalence about foreign policy crusades and interfering in another country's affairs.' While 'the great majority of Tory MPs ended up casting their vote for war . . . they now want to get at the truth and (let's be honest) try to exploit the uncomfortable position Tony Blair and George Bush find themselves in'.[37]

As Osborne's article suggested, opposition parties which claim to be supportive of an action may at the same time criticise the war leader for the way it has been conducted. The approach is likely to be regarded as opportunistic and can be attacked as such. On 8 March 2004, commenting on the Conservative Spring Forum, *The Times* argued that

> *The attack by Michael Ancram, the Shadow Foreign Secretary, on the Prime Minister and his 'deception' was disappointing. It is absurd for the Tories to suggest that Mr Blair's actions in Iraq are right but that he lied about the reasons for them. This implies that there exists another set of arguments for war, true ones, which Mr*

Blair did not deploy but that the Tories find privately convincing. If these exist, perhaps Mr Ancram might care to share them with the rest of us.[38]

During the Commons debate on the Butler report in July 2004, Howard asked, if Blair sought to go to war in future, 'would the country trust him? The issue is the Prime Minister's credibility. The question that he must ask himself is: does he have any credibility left?' Blair responded 'The right hon. and learned Gentleman thinks even now that it was right to go to war, does he not? So . . . leave aside his usual opportunism and understand that we both agreed that Saddam was a threat, we both still think Saddam was a threat and we both think the war was justified. Let us therefore concentrate on making Iraq better, not on point-scoring that has nothing to do with the central issues.'[39]

There is a history of smaller parties making political progress in wartime, though not necessarily through opposing the conflict itself. Labour, first conceived of in a Trades Union Congress motion of 1899, emerged from the First World War as the main opposition. During the Second World War a new political party, Common Wealth, was launched, obtaining at its peak four MPs. There was a truce between the established parties, meaning that they did not contest by-elections. Common Wealth filled the vacuum. For some active members, in the words of Addison, 'it was no more than a staging-post along the highway of left-wing causes'. However, it contained many idealists – predominantly middle class – who sought 'a libertarian form of socialism in which all property beyond what was necessary for personal use would be taken into common ownership'.[40] The Communist Party achieved its best electoral performance – with two MPs returned – in the election held in the closing stages of the Second World War.

The Liberal Democrats – the third party in Britain, with only moderate representation in terms of parliamentary seats because of the electoral system – disagreed with the invasion of Iraq in 2003. On 18 March Charles Kennedy, its leader, argued in the House for pursuing 'the course of disarmament on the ground in the presence of weapons inspectors'. Referring to a 'huge public anxiety in Britain', he noted that all MPs 'know that the kind of people contacting us are very different from many of those with whom we deal regularly. They . . . say, "I have never contacted a Member of Parliament before" or "I've never been politically active before." They . . . have never gone on a march or attended a vigil before.' Kennedy concluded,

> *But much as they detest Saddam's brutality, they are not persuaded that the case for war has been adequately made at this point, they are worried about the new doctrine of regime change, they are wary of the Bush Administration's motives, and they do not like to see Britain separated from its natural international allies.*[41]

The Liberal Democrats seemed to benefit from the considerable public unease Kennedy referred to, but which neither Labour nor the official opposition voiced, performing well at by-elections after the invasion. The trend was broader still. At the 2004 European election there was a considerable growth in support for smaller and new parties, at the expense of established ones. A number of factors encouraged such an outcome, but both the invasion of Iraq and the War on Terror were certainly influences. There were a total of 33 parties or candidates, the most significant of which, either in electoral performance or their relationship to conflict, have been included in the table below. Some of the smaller groups are then described.

	% Vote	% Change on 1999	Total popular vote
Conservative	26.7	-9	4,397,090
Labour	22.6	-5.4	3,718,683
UK Independence Party	16.1	+9.2	2,650,768
Liberal Democrats	14.9	+2.3	2,452,327
Green	6.3	0	1, 028,283
British National Party	4.9	+3.9	808,200
Respect – The Unity Coalition	1.5	N/A	252,216
Peace Party	0.1	+0.1	12,572

A new group, Respect, grew out of the Stop the War Coalition, which organised mass protests over the invasion of Iraq. Its most public face was George Galloway, the MP who had been expelled from the Labour Party for the nature of his opposition to the policy in Iraq. Respect's 'Founding Declaration'[42] indicated that its objectives went beyond mere opposition to war. On the one hand, it stated that

Tony Blair's New Labour has taken us to war five times in the last six years, each time with calamitous consequences. The bloodshed, the waste of precious economic resources, the lying and hypocrisy that have accompanied the attack on Iraq have brought many to the conclusion that they must rethink their traditional political allegiance.

But, it went on,

the yearning for a political alternative is even wider than the anti-war movement. Pensioners, students, trade unionists, Muslims and other faith groups, socialists, ethnic minorities and many others have been deeply disappointed by the authoritarian social policies and profit-centred, neo-liberal economic strategy of the government.

Much of Respect's policy content (renationalisation of the railways and utilities, repeal of trades union legislation) would be familiar to the observer of hard-left politics. The reference to 'Muslims and other faith groups' was the more novel part of the statement, the significance of which is discussed below.

It has been argued that Respect was controlled by the Trotskyist Socialist Workers Party (SWP), as the Stop the War Coalition had been before it. In the words of the comedian and left-wing activist Mark Thomas, 'It was not surprising that the party dominated the Stop the War Coalition; its leaders are old hands at controlling "popular fronts". They have to be. Without fronts like Globalise Resistance . . . the SWP would have shrivelled into political oblivion long ago.' Thomas wrote, 'the SWP is totally incapable of co-operation. Coalition partners would be presented with decisions as faits accomplis: the SWP would call a demonstration, then inform everybody after the press release had gone out. Moreover, it actively undermined protests and demonstrations that it didn't control.'[43]

Critics of the SWP saw similar naked opportunism in its participation in Respect, further arguing that its supposed values were incompatible with those of some of its new-found allies. Writing in the *New Statesman* during Respect's embryonic phase, Nick Cohen drew attention to the Stop the War Coalition's supposed overtures to the Muslim Association of Britain, an offshoot of the fundamentalist Muslim Brotherhood.[44] Then, in June 2004, he wrote that 'for the first time since the Enlightenment, a section of the left is allied with religious fanaticism and, for the first time since the Hitler-Stalin pact, a section of the left has gone soft on fascism.' He went on, 'The price you pay when you ally yourself with religious fundamentalists is a downgrading of the aspirations of women and gays.' Cohen also criticised what he saw as Respect's failure to distance itself from the Saddam Hussein regime.[45] Unsurprisingly, Cohen's latter article prompted letters of response, one of which stated that 'The Muslim Association of Britain is not part of Respect and does not give it blanket support. It's not that stupid. It generally backs the Lib Dems in local elections, and backs Respect only in London . . . Yorkshire and Humberside . . . North-East . . . and West Midlands. But . . . the SWP and Galloway wanted these fundamentalist reactionaries in their "party" and were desperately disappointed when the MAB turned them down.'[46]

Despite the grandiose, epochal claims it made for itself, Respect would be best regarded as another instalment in the history of factional, opportunistic, revolutionary socialism in Britain. With an electoral performance that was generally unspectacular (though it did gain around 250,000 votes in the 2004 European elections), its significance was as a noteworthy but minor political realignment occurring in response to a military conflict, more than a hugely successful movement in its own right.

A more obscure group, the Peace Party, could claim the support of more than twelve thousand voters at the 2004 European election; not bad for a local organisation with a universalist programme appealing to no particular social group or faction. It started life in 1996 when a small group of activists in Guildford formed the Pacifist Campaign and ran a candidate, John Morris, in the forthcoming general election. In 2001 it became the Pacifist Party and, in 2003, changed its name to (in full) 'The Peace Party – Non-violence, Justice, Environment'. It described itself as advocating 'respect and love for all life . . . non-violence . . . willingness to contribute to a stable environment . . . the absolute acknowledgement of all human rights, as defined in the United Nations Charter . . . reduction of conflict with the environment through better ecological awareness'. It was 'a secular political group' which 'welcomes people of all faiths – and none'. A major objective was ending the production, trade and ownership of arms. Money that would thereby be saved could be used to 'abolish economic and social differences' worldwide. Like a number of idealists of the previous century, the Peace Party favoured supranational institutions, seeking the establishment of 'world government'. Its electoral performance in June 2004 was surely largely attributable to the invasion of Iraq and the War on Terror.

Though it did not use the term, the British National Party (BNP) was a neo-fascist organisation. The BNP supported 'an immediate halt to all further immigration' and a repatriation programme. It promised to 'clamp down on the flood of "asylum seekers", all of whom are either bogus or can find refuge nearer their home countries'. Another policy was withdrawal from the EU. Also on its agenda were corporal and capital punishment; import controls; repatriation of assets and capital; profit-share schemes; traditional educational values; autarky in agricultural produce; improvements to the National Health Service; phasing out development aid; and ending defence cuts. It distanced itself from the mainstream parties, which it labelled 'Liars, buggers and thieves'.

Never before had the BNP performed as well in a national election as it did in June 2004, though the media largely concentrated on the achievements of the United Kingdom Independence Party. The BNP had experienced a growth in support (including winning council seats in areas such as Blackburn) over recent years which must have been in part attributable to heightened racial tension following the terrorist attacks of 11 September 2001. In its propaganda, the party referred to supposed 'ethnic cleansing . . . thousands of brutal, unprovoked, racist attacks on innocent young whites – overwhelmingly by gangs of young Muslims'. Yet, while parties claiming to represent the interests of the Islamic community opposed the invasion of Iraq, the BNP, courting the anti-Muslim vote, did not, according to statements issued on its website, support the action.

Professing 'no love of Saddam', the BNP was nevertheless 'totally opposed to using British troops in any forthcoming war by the USA on Iraq. Not a single drop of British blood should be spilt in Bush's personal vendetta against Saddam Hussein as it is definitely not a war that will serve British interests.' Another description of the invasion offered by the BNP was 'the Bush/Blair Crusade to make the Middle East safe for US oil consumers and Israel'. Attacks on Jewry and capitalism were firmly within the ideological tradition represented by the BNP; so was dislike of any policy pursued by a Labour government. The BNP drew attention to the fact that 'Iraq does not have any military capability of striking targets in the British Isles.' Where it diverged most clearly from other anti-war parties was in its view of domestic circumstances. 'If Blair is concerned about the extremist threat to Britain he would be well advised to look not for bogeymen overseas but here in his own backyard'; that is, among Islamic fundamentalists. The BNP argued 'Employing only a fraction of the resources and cost of a major war with Iraq it would be easy for him to extradite those wanted for crimes abroad, easy to stop the flow of funds to terror groups based in this country . . . we cannot accept a 5th column of extremists in our very midst.' A slogan employed by the BNP was 'Keep Britain out of foreign wars, Keep foreign wars out of Britain'.

As well as prompting a growth in smaller groups, leaders should be aware that war has helped bring about fundamental structural and ideological shifts in British politics. Like the Iraq invasion, the Boer War prompted political controversy and a series of public inquiries. G. R. Searle writes that as a consequence of 'The reverses suffered by the British Army during the Second Boer War . . . [British] national complacency received a severe jolt from which it never fully recovered'.[47] This encouraged the appearance of the cross-party 'National Efficiency' movement, calling for the reordering of society in order to reverse imperial decline. Early demands for what became the welfare state were made, intended to appease a potentially revolutionary working class. Despite the hopes of some, the formation of a new party was never brought about. As has been noted, Labour became the main opposition after the First World War. The conflict itself contributed to the demise of the Liberals as a party of government. It necessitated activities such as state interference in society which were a source of ideological discomfort. Having been supplanted by him in the midst of the war, Asquith's differences with Lloyd George were difficult to reconcile. Therefore, though Lloyd George was successful in the 1918 election, he had no firm party base, and once he lost office in 1922, he never returned.

The impact of the Second World War upon prevailing political assumptions has been judged by some to be great. Paul Addison writes that, during 1940–5, 'popular opinion swung towards Labour and gave the party its "landslide" victory at the 1945 general election'. In the interwar period, 'politics were under the spell of the Conservatives and their ideas'. But 'World War II broke into the pattern'. The fact of 'popular mobilisation for total war . . . bred the demand for a better society when the fighting was done . . . swung opinion decisively from Conservative to Labour, dismissed Churchill from office and made Attlee Prime Minister'.[48] The Suez crisis arguably helped bring about a prolonged obsession in Britain with the idea of national decline. The Cold War encouraged division in the Labour Party. Internationally, groups on the left were arguably tainted by association with communism. In the 1990s, after the collapse of the Soviet Union, progressives on both sides of the Atlantic were more successful.

Some advocated that another twist of the political kaleidoscope should be affected in response to the invasion of Iraq and the War on Terror. In March 2003, writing in the *New Statesman*, Neil Clark, described as 'unashamedly old Labour', predicted 'The war against Iraq will not be the war to end all wars . . . The neo-cons and their liberal imperialist allies appear unstoppable. They have hijacked the major parties on both sides of the Atlantic and have an entourage of journalists eager to peddle their propaganda.' 'Yet', Clark went on

the overwhelming majority on both sides of the Atlantic oppose the policy of 'endless war'. The demonstrations against war in Iraq have been the biggest since Vietnam, attracting people from all walks of life – not just the usual peaceniks, trade unionists and women's groups, but soldiers, farmers and businessmen, too. After initial squeamishness, conservatives and socialists, right-wingers and Trotskyists have marched together.

He called for 'The anti-war alliance . . . to be put on a more permanent and formal footing'. To bring that about, 'the left [had] to take a bold and historic step . . . and start to embrace warmly those at whom we have been hurling insults for the past 40 years'. Clark was, in his words, 'a committed, and totally unreconstructed, old leftist. Yet if [the right-wing, anti-war, US politician] Pat Buchanan announced he was standing for US president again, I would be on the next plane out to join his campaign team . . . Until the left is ready in its hordes to link up electorally with the "old" anti-war right, the brutal truth is that we have no chance of defeating the Bush/Blair axis.'

However, 'To make the Peace Party work . . . the left needs to jettison some baggage.' That meant abandoning social liberalism, since there was no reason 'why a belief in the mixed economy . . . also entails assenting to same-sex marriages, an open-door immigration policy and free abortion on demand'. Equally, 'Social conservatism and socialism, far from being contradictory, complement each other. The most destructive, anti-conservative force in our societies is not old left socialism, but unbridled free-market capitalism, which destroys communities, the environment and traditional ways of living.' On such common ground, a 'Peace Party', opposed to the presently ascendant 'War Party' – itself a coalition of previously antagonistic groups – might be founded.[49] As Nick Cohen's comments on Respect indicate, not all on the left approved of ideological alchemy of the sort advocated by Clark.

Another tendency that can emerge is for anti-war movements to develop attachments to the military enemy even in total contradiction of their initial objectives. Mark Gilbert has written how the Peace Pledge Union, set up in Britain in 1936, developed 'strikingly equivocal . . . views of Hitlerite Germany.' Its journal, *Peace News*, 'regularly went to extraordinary lengths to present the German case before British public opinion, on ocassion going so far as to permit its contributors to peddle German propaganda as unvarnished fact.'[50]

Though he had undergone various political ordeals, Blair retained his premiership through 2003–4. Perhaps opposition to the action in Iraq was too diffuse in form, spread as it was over outlets including the Liberal Democrats, Trotskyist, fascist and pacifist groups; but not finding an official vehicle in the Conservatives. The experiences of Asquith and Chamberlain suggest that the most likely replacement – and threat – for a war leader is inside the Cabinet. But the Chancellor of the Exchequer and widely acknowledged Labour dauphin, Gordon Brown, made no move against the Prime Minister. Had the action turned out to be a military disaster he may have done so (if Blair did not resign first). But Brown probably stood to lose too much, in terms of damage to the party, by making such a bid, rather than waiting in the hope of a more orderly succession. With his policy in Iraq subject to extreme criticism from all sides and assorted calls being made for his resignation, Blair liked to argue that in the end it was up to voters to judge him. Though his personal ratings suffered, Labour's opinion poll standing remained historically strong. In October 2004 he announced that he intended to contest one more general election and, if returned, stand down when his term was complete.

Though Blair lasted to fight for a final period of governemnt, armed conflict, and the controversy and dissent it brings with it, can destroy the political careers of leaders. The fact that campaigns were going badly contributed to the downfall of both Asquith and Chamberlain. Other forms of combat have helped undermine administrations, such as Aznar's in Spain in 2004. Involvement in the

Vietnam War was a subject of immense controversy and mass protest in the US. It inflicted considerable damage upon and contributed to the ending of the Johnson administration. Johnson argues that

> *Every President in this century has had to assume that there would be opposition to any war in which we became involved. That was true not only during the Korean War but also, though to a lesser extent, during World Wars I and II. It is never easy to accept the idea that fighting, with all its horrors and pain and loss, is preferable to the alternatives. I sensed that another idea was now influencing many Americans, including men who had played a major part in our critical decisions since 1965. They seemed to feel that the bitter and noisy dissension at home about Vietnam were too high a price to pay for honoring our commitment in Southeast Asia.*

Though he won an enormous victory in the 1964 presidential election, Johnson chose not to seek another term. He records that his announcement to that effect was motivated partly by the desire to be clear that his policy of a cessation of bombing

> *had been made without political considerations. I wanted that decision to be understood by the enemy and by everyone everywhere as a serious and sincere effort to find a road to peace. The most persuasive way to get this across, I believed, would be to couple my announcement of a bombing halt with the statement that I would not be a candidate for reelection.*

He hoped that 'the combined announcement' would reduce 'divisions and hostilities among Americans' over the 'issue of Vietnam'. On the evening of 31 March 1968 he made a televised broadcast, saying that

I have ordered our aircraft and our naval vessels to make no attacks on North Vietnam, except in the area north of the demilitarized zone, where the continuing enemy build-up directly threatens allied forward positions and where the movement of their troops and supplies are clearly related to that threat . . . With America's sons in the fields far away, with America's future under challenge right here at home, with our hopes and the world's hopes for peace in the balance every day, I do not believe that I should devote an hour or a day of my time to any personal partisan causes or to any duties other than the irksome duties of this office – the Presidency of your country. Accordingly, I shall not seek, and I will not accept, the nomination of my party for another term as your President.[51]

Vietnam cannot be recorded as a military success for the US, but an even more disastrous outcome than that experienced by Johnson and others is possible. The fall of France in 1940 led not only to the removal of Reynaud as Prime Minister, but the supplanting of the democratic system itself. Formed in 1931, the Spanish Republic was destroyed by civil war. In circumstances of European political polarisation and domestic class war, the republican-left Popular Front won the election held in February 1936. The Socialists, however, would not participate in the Cabinet. Strong government was lacking at a time of breakdown in public order, with violent clashes between the Falange (fascists) and anarchists. Military risings took place on the 17 and 18 of July, but what was intended as a swift reactionary power seizure turned into a full, bloody civil war between Republican and Nationalist forces. By 1939, the latter group, representing the anti-democratic interests of social and religious conservatism, won. Spain became a dictatorship under General Fransisco Franco.

Conclusion

Certain considerations apply to all democratic leaders making war. They include the following:

- War can bring about a suspension of normal political understandings, in the behaviour of parties and what is expected of government
- A higher than normal level of discretion is required by governments at times of armed conflict
- For the senior politician in an executive, whether or not constrained by a formally defined constitution, many means exist of achieving room for manoeuvre
- Disregard for rules, conventions, understandings and dissenting views can be counterproductive, producing tension and rancour, and leading to bad policy

A final interest may be addressed. During 2003–4 there was much discussion as to what Blair's role in history might be. It was generally believed that his involvement in combat would be an important determining factor. Many prime ministers or presidents will be concerned about their future reputations. The manner in which they operate with respect to armed conflict is likely to have a considerable impact upon assessments of them. Observers have judged war leaders to have made immense, unique personal contributions. Referring to the events of 11 September 2001 in a work which appeared in 2003, one author, in a study of Lincoln, writes that

> *Midway through the writing of this book came a brutal and frightening reminder that peace and security can never be taken wholly for granted ... In any emergency, some people will see the need to take harsh actions. Others will fear that individual rights and needs will be crushed in the rush to save the nation. Lincoln was extraordinary because he could see both at once ... It was Lincoln's character – his ability, judgment, courage, and humanity – that brought the Union through the war with the Constitution intact. It was as much dumb luck as anything else that placed Lincoln in the White House in this critical time. To expect another Lincoln would be foolish.*[1]

When the importance of one individual within a government is heightened, decisions can be made through opaque processes, with personal eccentricities coming to the fore. John Colville, his private secretary during the early period of his war premiership (and when he returned to office in peacetime) has provided a vivid portrayal of Churchill's leadership style. He was, Colville writes, 'entirely unpredictable' in his judgement, owing to 'some strange intuitive power which he held and which might induce him to take a line contrary, as it appeared, to logic and contrary to the normal mental workings of everybody else'. Such a trait was 'a frequent source of irritation as well as of astonishment to his Cabinet colleagues and to the Chiefs of Staff'. Yet, 'There were indeed a number of occasions when he showed a quite inexplicable facility for reaching the right decision on faulty logic and against all the best advice.'[2]

For Lincoln and Churchill, dynamic personal leadership has been regarded as a strength, even when it was associated with such activities as mass internment of innocent individuals or disregard for constitutional understandings. Characteristics which were – superficially, at least – similar, displayed by the likes of Anthony Eden during the Suez crisis, have been a basis for condemnation. Others, such as David Lloyd George and Woodrow Wilson, have been subject to mixed portrayals, even though the methods they used in the First World War provided models for their respective and more esteemed successors in the Second, Churchill and Franklin D. Roosevelt. Those judged generously may have been the beneficiaries of good fortune. Churchill probably tipped the odds in his favour by producing his own voluminous accounts of his exploits, soon after the events concerned, in an easily readable form. A war leader, if interested in securing as favourable a place in history as possible, has further reason for studying the detail of the approaches taken by predecessors, both those who have been subject to more and less subsequent flattery.

In the spring of 2005, as a war leader, Blair faced a number of concerns. Their satisfactory resolution would enhance his long-term reputation. Failure to deal with them properly would compromise it. Major criticisms of him were that he engaged in over-centralised, informal decision making; continued to utilise archaic constitutional power in the form of the Royal Prerogative; had breached international law; misled Parliament and the public; undermined civil liberties in the name of security against international terrorism; and split his own party and the country over Iraq. Preceding chapters have described how the senior figure in a government can work the existing political system. Blair had done so effectively, but was faced with intense criticism of his methods and policies. In seeking to counter such denigration, an option available to him was to alter the framework within which war leadership operated, without ceding a significant quantity of prime ministerial and executive power.

Most importantly for his future, Blair had to win another general election. If he was defeated, many would speculate that his participation in the Iraq War was to blame. Another problem was the fact that, late in 2004, the Law Lords ruled executive detention of foreign terrorist suspects incompatible with the European Convention on Human Rights (ECHR). The Law Lords could not strike down the legislation facilitating the internments, but simply ignoring the judgement was politically difficult for Blair's government. After all, it was Labour that had incorporated the ECHR into domestic law in the form of the Human Rights Act. At the same time Blair and his ministers could not overlook the security threat they believed was real. They kept the individuals concerned in detention while a solution was devised.

On 26 January, in a statement to the Commons,[3] the Home Secretary, Charles Clarke, noted that the House of Lords Judicial Committee had found the practice of internment 'incompatible with articles 5, on the right to liberty, and 14, on freedom from discrimination' of the ECHR. The reasoning behind the judgement was that 'the . . . powers were discriminatory in that they only applied to foreign nationals, and secondly, because they were not proportionate as a response to the threat that we faced from terrorism'. But, Clarke insisted, 'the powers have played an essential part in addressing the current public emergency, because they have been successful in containing the threat posed by those certified and detained under them.' He added 'It is clear from the intelligence reports that I have seen that the existence and use of the powers have helped to make the UK a far more hostile environment for international terrorists to operate in.' While accepting the Law Lords' declaration of incompatibility with the ECHR, he said 'there remains a public emergency threatening the life of the nation.' Such an assertion had been the basis for the British government's derogation from the ECHR in 2001 over the confinement of foreign nationals.

The government, Clarke revealed, now intended to pursue a 'twin-track approach'. It entailed deporting suspects wherever possible, obtaining assurances from the country of destination that they would not be treated in a manner contravening Britain's human rights treaty obligations. Coupled with the policy of removal was 'a new system of control orders' intended to enable the authorities 'to impose conditions constraining the ability of those subject to the orders to engage in terrorist-related activities'. The restraints would 'be capable of general application to any suspected terrorist irrespective of nationality'. By such means, unfair discrimination could be avoided, since British nationals were covered, too. In order to respond to the Law Lords' ruling about proportionality, 'The controls imposed would be proportionate to the threat that each individual posed.' No opt-out from the ECHR, it was believed, would be necessary.

The process would work as follows:

- The Home Secretary would consider Security Service evidence and decide whether 'there are reasonable grounds for suspecting that an individual is, or has been, concerned with terrorism'.
- 'If the answer to that question is yes' and if such action was deemed necessary for public safety, the Home Secretary 'would impose controls on that individual'.
- Controls would range from limitations on movement, association or communication with certain individuals; to curfews or tagging; to restrictions on use of telecommunications and the internet. 'At the top end, control orders would include a requirement to remain at their premises' – in other words, house arrest, though not 'detention in prison'. In response to criticism of the plan, the government subsequently stated it would not use house arrest, but

provided for it in the Prevention of Terrorism Bill it brought forward, in case such a practice became necessary. To introduce it would require derogation from Article 5 of the ECHR on the deprivation of liberty. If this decision was made, parliamentary approval would be required within 40 days.

- Limits on the power of the government included independent judicial scrutiny, with the hearing of evidence, in open and closed sessions, against the use of the order. A mechanism 'for reviewing and modifying conditions as circumstances warrant' was to be used. The Secretary of State would report regularly to Parliament on the orders made. Annually, the powers themselves would be subject to a report and renewal.

The government should ensure that its new approach rectifies certain problems. Wherever possible, individuals should be prosecuted for criminal offences. Such an approach is desirable from the perspective of democratic values and for political reasons. One route to doing so was through the intended treatment of breaches of control orders as criminal offences. It is possible that the government will set out to bring about the imprisonment of suspects through imposing restrictions in the hope that they will be broken.

Various means have been proposed for making more use of the judicial system against terrorist suspects. They include security-cleared investigative judges, extending custody times, video evidence from abroad, plea bargaining, and immunity for accomplices. The introduction of new offences, such as acts preparatory to terrorism, or an equivalent to the French crime of association with a wrongdoer has been suggested, too.

An obstacle to prosecuting the present detainees and individuals believed to be dangerous in the future is the fact that the intelligence information on which suspicion is founded cannot be heard in open court. Under the Regulation of Investigatory Powers Act 2000, domestic intercepted communications may not be used in such proceedings. At the time of writing, the government has refused to yield to widespread pressure to relax the ban, even though the idea of doing so seems to have support from the Security Service and the police. Clarke told the Commons in January of a 'misconception that if we could only adduce intercept as evidence, we would be able to prosecute those detained. However, the review of intercept as evidence found no evidence to support this'.

The position was difficult to sustain. It could be construed that the government was not confident of the very information upon which it had based its decisions to make internments – not a desirable perception for a war leader. Furthermore, it is curious that, as the Joint Committee on Human Rights (JCHR) noted in 2004, 'The UK is the only country in the world, apart from Ireland, to have an absolute ban on the use of such material.' Lord Carlile, who was responsible for reporting on the use of the detention powers, told the JCHR that the prohibition was 'a nonsense'. He said that, though many within the security community supported a change, it was believed that internal opposition came from Government Communications Headquarters (GCHQ), the agency responsible for collecting such data.

Carlile's view was echoed by Lord Newton, the chairman of the committee of Privy Counsellors which reviewed the Anti-Terrorism, Crime and Security Act, under which internment was carried out. In 2003, his report identified more puzzling inconsistencies in the rules on evidence.

The Regulation of Investigatory Powers Act 2000 forbids the use of domestic intercepts in UK court proceedings. There is, however, no such bar on the use of foreign intercepts obtained in accordance with foreign laws. Nor is there a bar on the admission of bugged (as opposed to intercepted) communications or the products of surveillance or eavesdropping, even if they were not authorised and were an interference with privacy. There is no bar on foreign courts using British intercept evidence if the intelligence and security services are prepared to provide it.[4]

As Newton put it to the JCHR, 'Clearly the principle worry [over the use of intercepted evidence] was compromising methods and sources and, I suppose at the extreme in rather more James Bond terms, revealing the identity of an agent and the possible effects for them.' But, he said, 'what puzzles me in respect of this issue is that nobody is suggesting that you should have to use intercept evidence in court if you form the judgment that you do not wish to do so and that there are dangers which prevent you from doing so.' Even if lifting the ban produces no extra prosecutions, criticism of the government for refusing to allow the use of this form of evidence would be neutralised.

An anomaly in the detention system was suggested when Carlile spoke to the JCHR in June 2004. He said a suspect (known as 'M') was released on appeal because, though 'a person who posed a terrorist threat, he was a member of a Libyan terrorist organisation. The Libyan terrorist organisation in question is not part of Al-Qaeda . . . and, as a result, it is outwith the derogation [from the ECHR] because the derogation has been carefully circumscribed to refer only to Al-Qaeda connections'. The JCHR interpreted the case differently, arguing that it turned on there being an inadequate intelligence basis for the detention. Nevertheless, Carlile's claim needs to be addressed, since terrorists are dangerous, whether or not they belong to one particular organisation.

Control orders were not a politically easy option. In the sense that they would be applicable to British subjects as well as foreign nationals, they represented an extension of the reach of government into society as compared with that provided by existing legislation, even though the practice of imprisonment would be ended. Clarke said he was was 'well aware that the proposals I am making today represent a very substantial increase in the executive powers of the state in relation to British citizens who we fear are preparing terrorist activities and against whom we cannot proceed in open court'. Labour MPs and others were uneasy about the proposal. One criticism was the fact that the Home Secretary, not a judge, initiated the procedure, something the government consequently amended. In fact, such an approach was in keeping with that taken under both Liberal and Conservative war leaders in the past.

The government justified its plans by arguing that it had access to confidential information demonstrating a continuing 'public emergency threatening the life of the nation'. Yet there is evidence that, following many decades of declining social deference, the public is less disposed towards taking ministers at their word. The media are certainly more prone to scepticism, as are MPs, including backbenchers of the ruling party. Morale in the War on Terror is threatened by such incredulousness. In order to counteract this tendency, there is a strong case for finding a way of fulfilling two JCHR suggestions. The first is that Parliament and public be provided with 'the gist of the intelligence . . . without prejudicing legitimate security interests'. Second, it was suggested that there be an investigation of 'whether there is a role for the Intelligence and Security Committee [ISC] to scrutinise the material on which the Government's assertions about the level of the threat are based'.[5] Clarke saw the latter proposal at least as worthwhile, saying 'I am considering separately what role the Intelligence and Security Committee of this House might play in' reviewing government powers.

It is significant that Clarke should refer to the 'Intelligence and Security Committee of this House'. In fact, the ISC is not – at present – a parliamentary body. But if it is to play a publicly convincing role as independent assessor of the intelligence basis for measures taken in the War on Terror, it should be reconvened as such. Concerns within Whitehall that the ISC would be less trustworthy if attached formally to the legislature could be allayed through security clearance and privy counsellorships for its members, if absolutely necessary.

Providing for greater parliamentary involvment in the War on Terror could reduce the likelihood of Commons revolts of the sort experienced in 2003 over Iraq. At the same time it would not necessarily alter the substance of the policy a war leader sought to pursue, especially if the intelligence basis for official concerns is as strong as is claimed by ministers.

Another possible means of establishing partnership and reducing tension between government and Parliament over armed conflict would be to establish more formal arrangements for consultating the legislature over the deployment of troops in potential or actual combat circumstances. Over recent years a number of MPs, including Graham Allen and Neil Gerrard, and the Public Administration Select Committee (PASC) have advocated their own variants on a British equivalent to the US 1973 War Powers Resolution (or War Powers Act, as it is commonly known). Blair told the Commons Liaison Committee on 8 February 2005 'I am slightly reluctant to go and bind whatever future governments may do . . . I think you have got always to have the ability, as a government, to take immediate action if that is necessary, which is why I do not actually myself favour changing the constitutional prerogative.'[6] But the history of the US since the War Powers Resolution was passed over Richard Nixon's veto demonstrates that such a measure need not prevent a leader from making premeditated war, let alone responding to an emergency. And, since their parties normally enjoy Commons majorities and they benefit from a lack of separation of powers, British prime ministers are more able to dominate their legislatures than US presidents. A premier would therefore have little to fear from a more entrenched parliamentary role in conflict, and there are a number of potential benefits. If the executive appeared to be consulting fully with the legislature, relations between the government and its backbenchers would improve, meaning a reduced likelihood of major rebellions. With some MPs taking part in the drafting of a war resolution from the early stages, they and their colleagues would be less likely to reject it when it was put to the House. There would be a presentational gain, with the impression created of an open, collegiate administration. A war leader obliged to engage more thoroughly and specifically with Parliament may find this process an effective means of testing policy, perhaps modifying it if flaws are exposed. The political implications of a decision could be assessed on the basis of its reception amongst MPs. Certain MPs and peers in possession of military, foreign affairs and other expertise could helpfully apply it when scrutinising the government's plans. Prime ministers could use the new position of the legislature to strengthen their hands in negotiations with international military allies, arguing that certain requirements are necessary in order to secure the support of Parliament for an action.

Another important occurrence for British governments and war was the implementation of parts of the Freedom of Information Act on 1 January 2005. Soon more than forty requests were made for the release of the full text of the Attorney General's advice on the legality of the invasion of Iraq. They were rejected. Given that a version of the counsel had already been presented to Parliament and presuming that this did not misrepresent or make significant ommission from the original, the decision to withold was a mistake. It could only serve to exacerbate doubts about the veracity of official assertions and communications in this particular case and generally, and undermine ministers' claims that they were committed to greater openess. Just as, to sustain morale in the War on Terror, it is advisable to diclose as much intelligence as prudently possible on the Al-Qaeda threat, for the same reason, the actual legal advice provided on the Iraq War – and future conflicts – should be published. Similarly, a cooperative attitude ought to be taken with select committees seeking access to witnesses and papers. The experience of the Hutton Inquiry shows that armed conflict and open government can mix.

(However, there was possibly good reason for the government's decision. In February 2005, one author claimed 'The attorney general's . . . statement was not a summary of [his] written advice . . . Rather, it [was] a recasting of a plausible argument into [a] succinct and decisive opinion of law.'[7])

A British Prime Minister wishing to go to war in future – especially one who leads a progressive party, be it Blair or a successor – ought to find a justification more effective than a complex construction based on UN Security Council resolutions, or intelligence material which is by its nature uncertain, or a right of pre-emptive self-defence as advocated by the US. Blair has partially developed a theory of humanitarian justification for conflict, as well as calling for adjustments to UN arrangements for collective security, taking into account the threat of international terrorism. The intention was to enable his activist foreign policy to be more readily reconciled with principles of international legality and cooperation. Giving a speech in his Sedgefield constituency in March 2004, he described how in Chicago in 1999 'following the Kosovo war . . . I called for a doctrine of international community, where in certain clear circumstances, we do intervene, even though we are not directly threatened'. He went on

> So . . . before September 11th, I was already reaching for a different
> philosophy in international relations from a traditional one that has
> held sway since the treaty of Westphalia in 1648; namely that a
> country's internal affairs are for it and you don't interfere unless it
> threatens you, or breaches a treaty, or triggers an obligation of
> alliance.

Blair argued 'It may well be that under international law as presently
constituted, a regime can systematically brutalise and oppress its
people and there is nothing anyone can do . . . This may be the law,
but should it be?' He called for better international organisation,
remarking 'The UN Universal Delaration on Human Rights is a fine
document. But it is strange the United Nations is so reluctant to
enforce them.' Blair also believed the UN should become more active
against terrorists, 'those who would exploit racial and religious
division to bring catastrophe to the world'.

The ideas expressed by Blair gained increased currency with the
report produced by the UN Secretary-General's High-level Panel on
Threats, Challenges and Change. It appeared in late 2004 and
endorsed 'the emerging norm of a responsibility to protect civilians
from large-scale violence . . . When a state fails to protect its
civilians, the international community then has a further
responbility to act . . . with force if necessary'. The Panel noted that
the UN Security Council 'has the authority to act preventively
[against threats such as terrorism], but has rarely done so. The
Security Council may well need to be prepared to be more proactive
in the future, taking decisive action earlier'.

If more international progress is made with the concepts put
forward by the High-level Panel, a British leader could incorporate
the values into domestic legislation, setting out the conditions under
which war can be waged. The law could be drawn in such a way as to

preserve flexibility for the executive, but include general principles, such as the duty to safeguard human rights and the custom of self-defence, to which it would be hard for many to object. Such an act would be a good place to include reference to parliamentary consultation over armed conflict and the circumstances under which the Law Officers' advice should be disclosed. It might refer to a need to engage the Cabinet collectively in decisions on combat.

The attractiveness to a war leader, especially one on the political left, of being able to present military action as in keeping with humanitarian values and international cooperation is great. Doing so convincingly will depend upon portraying a future foe as a threat to stability and security, or internally brutal. When an enemy genuinely fits into one of these categories, such a public relations task becomes easier. It was greatly beneficial to the Thatcher administration that General Galtieri's regime which invaded the Falkland Islands in 1982 was as dictatorial as it was.

If a British government appears inconsistent in the pursuance of its espoused democratic values, its credibility will be eroded. Controversy has arisen over allowing the export of arms where their possible end use is repressive. As a signal of intent it would be useful to acede to the request of one Commons committee and introduce 'a system of prior parliamentary scrutiny of export licence applications'.[8]

Taken together, the combination of domestic and international adjustments outlined above would comprise a substantial reform package for Blair, a war leader who has been criticised both for the substance of his policies and his style in implementing them. It could improve historical assessments of him, without inhibiting his ability to act. Indeed, the latter consideration may not arise, since by the time the changes were fully implemented, he might have chosen to stand down or have been forced out of office, leaving such alterations as a legacy to future war leaders, whether they liked them or not. If not taken on by him, then a successor, either of the same or a different party, could bring forward a similar programme, as a means of establishing a distinct identity at the outset of a premiership. On the surface it appears to be composed of fetters upon a Prime Minister. But central features of the task of leading an armed conflict in a democracy have remained constant, across different time periods and countries. They would continue to do so, even after the introduction of constitutional formalisation. It would not alter the substance of how to go to war.

Epilogue

The following is a brief for a British Prime Minister and Cabinet engaging in military conflict, to be read in conjunction with the preceding discussion of how to go to war. It draws partly on Peter Hennessy's six 'performance indicators for premiers as limited war leaders.'[1]

Brief for a future War Leader and Cabinet

The problems
1. The recent controversy around anti-terrorist security measures has illustrated the difficulty in reconciling war leadership with democracy. Premiers from Herbert Asquith, to Winston Churchill, to Tony Blair, and leaders abroad, have faced this problem.
2. The need for rapid, purposeful decision-making and secrecy suggests that the smallest number of ministers should be inside the loop of information and deliberation. But the convention of collective Cabinet responsibility says otherwise.
3. A war government in Britain does not require the formal approval of Parliament for actions it carries out under the royal prerogative. But, a discontent legislature can help destroy an administration, as it did that of Neville Chamberlain 1940. Blair, too, suffered the two largest Commons rebellions of the modern era over Iraq.

4. Investigation of the activities of government by parliamentary and other bodies has come to be expected in Britain and elsewhere. Such scrutiny can be unwelcome and disconcerting for a war leader, who may seek to keep official information secret.

5. Democratic states will wish to portray themselves as acting within the bounds of international legality – but may find organisations such as the United Nations (UN) unsuitable vehicles for achieving their military objectives.

6. Social intervention by the state can fashion a country into a more efficient, secure war machine, but compromise liberal values in the process. A bureaucracy accustomed to serving the peacetime requirements of the electorate may be unsuited to bringing about such organisation.

7. War leaders are likely to portray their actions as furthering the cause of democracy. But sustaining such an argument is difficult if it is deemed necessary to co-operate with repressive regimes.

8. Presentation is vital to sustaining public confidence, but the existence of a press free to criticise the government makes public relations tasks especially difficult. Media and public scepticism towards politicians is greater than it once was. Overselling a campaign, or disseminating misleading information which becomes exposed as such, is counterproductive. The requirements of advocacy can dangerously compromise the value of bodies including the intelligence agencies, and lead to the war leader being associated with inaccurate claims.

9. Armed conflict will benefit from some degree of national political consensus around its conduct. A multi-party system can make such agreement less likely. War may cause unrest which spreads across the regular partisan divisions.

Some approaches

1. Anthony Eden responded to the dilemma described above by resorting to methods which might be regarded as counter to democratic principles, including the deception of Parliament and public, minimising the importance of Cabinet, and acting without a secure basis in international law.

2. Asquith could be seen as Eden's polar opposite. He worked through full Cabinet, submitted himself to an inquiry while the First World War was taking place, and was not disposed towards media manipulation.

3. The administrations of both Asquith and Eden were destroyed by a military conflict. To avoid repetition of their experiences, rather than approaching the relationship between war leadership and democracy as a dichotomy, it should be treated as a symbiosis. The major armed struggles of the twentieth century, both world wars and the Cold War, saw defeat for the dictatorships (or, in the First World War, the conservative monarchies). These outcomes show that liberal societies, which sometimes have to wage war in order to survive, can do so effectively. Indeed, democracy can be an effective weapon in itself. Abraham Lincoln's Emancipation Proclamation, Franklin D. Roosevelt's and Churchill's Atlantic Charter, and the 'Truman Doctrine' were simultaneous statements of democratic principle and devices for fighting wars.

4. To utilise democracy as a weapon, war leaders must be willing to test their policies through honest discussion. If they feel their intentions, when fully revealed, would not withstand scrutiny, they should consider whether they are wise. 'Tunnel vision' and 'groupthink' are to be avoided.

5. The neglect of established procedure can be a tempting shortcut, but can weaken policy development and implementation.

6. The inner decision-making group must keep Cabinet, Parliament and public regularly and honestly informed as to developments. War cabinets work better if formed out of existing committee machinery, with a small (no more than six), fixed membership, and minuted meetings. They should convene regularly, and act decisively, with access to the relevant staff support, information, and papers.

7. If they are not receiving satisfactory briefings, preferably in written form, or are unhappy about developments, it falls to Cabinet members to force the issue with the Prime Minister.

8. Parliament must be consulted by the executive as fully as possible, and co-operated with when it seeks information. With the affirmative support of elected representatives, policy can become only more powerful. Rebellions are less likely with MPs involved in decision-making at the earliest possible stage. Parliament can act as a valuable double-check on government proposals, and should be given the opportunity to hold such bodies as the intelligence agencies to account.

9. There may be times when international organisations such as the UN are an obstacle to achieving military objectives. But to abandon them, rather than attempt to reform them, is to ignore the fact that they have, on occasions, helped facilitate the conduct of war. International law has a similar value which may be negated by the manipulation of concepts such as the right of self-defence.

10. Where it is necessary to abrogate certain democratic principles in the interests of security, adherence to the rules described here, such as the need to pursue maximum official openness, is yet more important. There is a particular need for clarity around emergency powers, to prevent their abuse.

11. Impartial advice, offered without fear or favour, of the sort permanent civil servants and the intelligence agencies are bound to provide, is useful.

12. Assessing intelligence information properly is as important as gathering it.

13. It is far easier to present policy as furthering the cause of democracy if the government's approach is genuinely and consistently directed towards that end.

14. Officially disclosing as much information as it is safe to do could undermine the opinion-forming power of often unhelpful media outlets, and reduce prevailing high levels of incredulity towards government, improving public morale.

15. None of the above rules apply absolutely. But war leaders and their ministers must pick their moments and reasons for breaking them carefully. Eden infringed upon too many principles for a purpose that many have considered objectionable. Lincoln, on the other hand, stretched constitutional understandings, but in order to preserve and fulfil that same constitution. The return to normality should be affected as soon as possible – prime ministers and their cabinets should be particular wary of emergency measures becoming permanent.

Notes

Foreword

1   Private information.

2   *Review of Intelligence on Weapons of Mass Destruction: Report of a Committee of Privy Counsellors*, HC898, Stationery Office, 14 July 2004.

3. Peter Hennessy, 'Informality and Circumscription: The Blair Style of Government in War and Peace', *The Political Quarterly*, Vol 76, No 1, January–March 2005, pp. 3–11.

Prologue

1   Peter Hennessy, *The Prime Minister: The Office and its Holders since 1945* (Allen Lane, London, 2000), p. 237. See pp. 207–47.

2   Tony Shaw, *Eden, Suez and the Mass Media: Propaganda and persuasion during the Suez crisis* (I.B. Tauris, London and New York, 1996), pp. 94, 150.

3   Nick Cohen, 'Without prejudice', *Observer*, 18 November 2001; Duncan Campbell, 'Anti-Saddam Arabs amongst detainees', *Guardian*, 23 January 1991.

4   Peter Hennessy, 'Shaken – and stirred', *Tablet*, 15 January 2005.

1 Introduction

1   John Kampfner, *Blair's Wars* (Free Press, London, 2004), pp. ix-x.

2   Peter Hennessy, 'The Lightning Flash on the Road to Baghdad: Issues of Evidence', in W. G. Runciman (ed.), *Hutton and Butler: Lifting the Lid on the Workings of Power* (The British Academy/Oxford University Press, Oxford, 2004), p. 63.

2 War, leaders, Ministers and Courtiers

1 Winston S. Churchill, *The Second World War:* Vol. II, *Their Finest Hour* (Folio Society, London, 2000), pp. 14, 15.

2 David Lloyd George, *War Memoirs*, Vol. III (Ivor Nicholson and Watson, London, 1934), p. 1060.

3 John Major, *The Autobiography* (HarperCollins, London, 2000), p. 233.

4 John Grigg, *Lloyd George: War Leader, 1916–1918* (Penguin, London, 2003), p. 11.

5 George H. Cassar, *Asquith as War Leader* (Hambledon, London and Rio Grande, 1994), p.32.

6 Edward S. Corwin, *The President: Office and Powers, 1787–1984* (New York University Press, New York and London, 1984), p. 268.

7 G. W. Jones, 'Introduction' to Herbert van Thal, *The Prime Ministers*, Vol. I, *From Sir Robert Walpole to Sir Robert Peel* (George Allen and Unwin, London, 1974), p. 14.

8 Corwin, *The President: Office and Powers*, p. 23.

9 David Lloyd George, *Memoirs of the Peace Conference* (Yale University Press, New Haven, 1939), pp. 146–7.

10 Harry S. Truman, *Year of Decisions: 1945* (Hodder and Stoughton, London, 1955), p. 253.

11 Peter Hennessy, *The Prime Minister.*

12 Philip Thody, *The Fifth French Republic* (Routledge, London and New York, 1998), pp. 17–9.

13 Corwin, *The President: Office and Powers*, p. 70.

14 Daniel Farber, *Lincoln's Constitution* (University of Chicago Press, Chicago and London, 2003), p. 115.

15 Stephen Graubard, *The Presidents: the transformation of the American Presidency, from Theodore Roosevelt to George W. Bush* (Allen lane, London, 2005), p. 7.

16 C. R. Attlee, *As it happened* (Odhams Press, London, 1956), p. 232.

17 *Ministerial Code* (Cabinet Office, 2001).

18 Uncorrected transcript, House of Commons (HC) Public Administration Select Committee (PASC), Oral Evidence, 21 October 2004.

19 Clare Short, *An Honourable Deception?: New Labour, Iraq, and the Misuse of Power* (Free Press, London, 2004), p. 71.

20 Truman, *Year of Decisions*, p. 253.

21 Burton J. Hendrick, *Lincoln's War Cabinet* (Little, Brown and Company,

Boston, 1946), pp. 79–81, 175–6.

22 Truman, *Year of Decisions*, p. 56.

23 Frances Perkins, *The Roosevelt I Knew* (Viking, New York, 1946), pp. 377, 380.

24 David Lloyd George, *War Memoirs*, Vol. III, pp. 1039, 1046, 1067.

25 Margaret Thatcher, *The Downing Street Years* (HarperCollins, London, 1993), pp. 185–6, 187.

26 John Colville, *The Fringes of Power: Downing Street Diaries,* Vol. One: *1939–October 1941* (Sceptre, London, 1986), p. 148.

27 Churchill, *Their Finest Hour*, p. 16.

28 Hendrick, *Lincoln's War Cabinet*, pp. 4, 6.

29 Ruth Gledhill, 'Archbishop rounds on Government over Iraq war', *The Times*, 20 April 2004.

30 *Review of Intelligence on Weapons of Mass Destruction.*

31 Lloyd George, *War Memoirs*, Vol. III, pp. 1060, 1080.

32 Margaret Thatcher, *The Downing Street Years*, p. 188.

33 Merle Miller, *Plain Speaking: An Oral Biography of Harry S. Truman* (Victor Gollancz, London, 1974), p. 303.

34 Colin Seymour-Ure, 'British "War Cabinets" in limited Wars: Korea, Suez and the Falklands', *Public Administration*, Vol. 62, Summer 1984, pp. 181, 199.

35 John Turner, *Lloyd George's Secretariat* (Cambridge University Press, Cambridge, 1980), p. 191.

36 G. D. A. MacDougall, 'The Prime Minister's Statistical Section' in D. N. Chester (ed.), *Lessons of the British War Economy* (Cambridge University Press, Cambridge, 1951), pp. 59, 68. See also: Thomas Wilson, *Churchill and the Prof* (Cassel, London, 1995).

37 Alfred Dick Sander, *A Staff for the President: The Executive Office, 1921–1952* (Greenwood Press, New York, 1989), pp. 24–5.

38 See table in Harold C. Relyea (ed.), *The Executive Office of the President: A Historical, Biographical, and Bibliographical Guide* (Greenwood Press, Westport, 1997), pp. 27–8.

39 Colville, *The Fringes of Power*, p. 145.

40 George Sylvester Viereck, *The Strangest Friendship in History: Woodrow Wilson and Colonel House* (Duckworth, London, 1933), pp. 4–5.

41 Philip Bobbitt, *The Shield of Achilles: War, Peace and the Course of History* (Allen Lane, London, 2002), pp. 367–8.

42 Lloyd George, *Memoirs of the Peace Conference*, p. 156.

43 Alexander L. George and Juliette L. George, *Woodrow Wilson and Colonel House: A Personality Study* (Dover Publications, New York, 1964), p. 112.

44 John Milton Cooper, *Breaking the Heart of the World: Woodrow Wilson and the Fight for the League of Nations* (Cambridge University Press, Cambridge, 2001), pp. 34–5.

45 Bobbitt, *The Shield of Achilles*, p. 410.

46 Robert E. Sherwood, *Roosevelt and Hopkins: An Intimate History* (Harper & Brothers, New York, 1948), pp. 202, 1, 4.

47 HC Liaison Committee, Oral Evidence, 16 July 2002.

48 Robin Cook, *The Point of Departure* (Simon and Schuster, London, 2003), diary entry for 7 March 2002, pp. 115–6.

49 HC Foreign Affairs Committee (FAC), Oral Evidence, 17 June 2003.

50 Short, *An Honourable Deception?*, pp. 149, 142.

51 FAC, Oral Evidence, 17 June 2003.

52 Short, *An Honourable Deception?*, pp. 146–7.

53 HC Written Answers, 16 July 2003, col. 32.

54 Peter Hennessy, 'The Lightning Flash on the Road to Baghdad', p. 74.

55 FAC, Oral Evidence, 25 June 2003.

56 Hutton Inquiry, Hearing Transcripts, 18 August 2003, morning.

57 HC Written Answers, 16 July 2003, col. 32.

58 Short, *An Honourable Deception*, pp. 151, p. 150.

59 Runciman (ed.), *Hutton and Butler*, p. 85. Jones's full statement was 'A Prime Minister who can carry his colleagues with him can be in a very powerful position, but he is only as strong as they let him be.' See: G. W. Jones, 'The Prime Minister's Power', in Anthony King (ed.) *The British Prime Minister* (Macmillan, London, 1985), p. 216.

60 Boris Johnson, 'How not to run a country', *Spectator*, 11 December 2004.

61 Runciman (ed.), *Hutton and Butler*, p. 85.

62 Hennessy, 'The Lightning Flash on the Road to Baghdad', p. 73.

3 Restraint and Scrutiny

1 'The Royal Prerogative' Memorandum from the Treasury Solicitor's Department to PASC, MPP09(a), in *Taming the Prerogative: Strengthening Ministerial Accountability to Parliament*, HC Public Administration Select Committee (PASC), HC 422 (Stationery Office, London, 2004).

2 Robin Cook, *The Point of Departure*, pp. 189–90.

3   *Taming the Prerogative: Strengthening Ministerial Accountability to Parliament.*

4   HC Liaison Committee, Oral Evidence, 21 January 2003.

5   Farber, *Lincoln's Constitution*, pp. 152, 156–7.

6   Lyndon Baines Johnson, *The Vantage Point: Perspectives of the Presidency, 1963–1969* (Weidenfeld and Nicolson, London, 1971), p. 115.

7   James M. Lindsay, *Congress and the Politics of U.S. Foreign Policy* (Johns Hopkins University Press, Baltimore and London, 1994), pp. 148–50.

8   Cassar, *Asquith as War Leader*, pp. 200–1.

9   For details of the following discussion, see: HC Liaison Committee, 'Scrutiny of Government: Select Committees after Hutton', Note by the Clerks, 8 January 2004; HC Liaison Committee, *Annual Report for 2003*, HC 446 (Stationery Office, London, 2004).

10 Cabinet Office, *Departmental Evidence and Response to Select Committees.*

11 FAC, *Implications for the Work of the House and its Committees of the Government's Lack of Co-operation with the Foreign Affairs Committee's Inquiry into The Decision to go to War in Iraq*, HC 440 (Stationery Office, London, 2004).

12 'Statement by Lord Hutton on 28 January 2004', http://www.the-hutton-inquiry.org.uk/content/rulings/statement280104.htm

13 PASC, Oral Evidence, 13 May 2004.

14 Uncorrected transcript, PASC, Oral Evidence, 21 October 2004.

15 HC Debates, 3 February 2004, col. 631.

16 House of Lords (HL) Debates, 7 September 2004, col. 462.

17 According to the Butler Review website, including privy counsellorships and peerages, excluding honours at different levels within the same order.

18 HC Liaison Committee, 'Scrutiny of Government: Select Committees after Hutton'.

19 Hutton Inquiry, Hearing Transcripts, 28 August 2003, morning.

20 HC Home Affairs Select Committee, *The Accountability of the Security Services*, HC 291 (Stationery Office, London, 1999).

21 Intelligence and Security Committee, *Annual Report 2003–2004*, Cm. 6240 (Stationery Office, London, 2004).

22 Corwin, *The President: Office and Powers, 1787–1984*, p. 128.

23 *Ministerial Code.*

24 HC Written Answers, 14 March 2003, col. 482.

25 'The Royal Prerogative', Memorandum from the Treasury Solicitor's

Department to PASC.

26 Terence Ingman, *The English Legal Process* (Oxford University Press, Oxford, 2002), pp. 512–3.

27 Corwin, *The President*, pp. 271, 266, 271, 283–4, 288.

28 Ingrid Detter, *The Law of War*, second edition (Cambridge University Press, Cambridge, 2000), pp. 10, 14, 431.

29 HC Debates, 26 March 2004, col. 1235.

30 Ibid.

31 'War would be illegal', *Guardian*, 7 March 2003.

4 War, the State and society

1 Peter Hennessy, *Never Again: Britain, 1945–1951* (Vintage, London, 1993), p. 40.

2 Corwin, *The President*, pp. 263–9, 270–1.

3 Ibid, pp. 274–9; 281–2.

4 Daphna Sharfman, *Living Without a Constitution* (M. E. Sharpe, Armonk, London, 1993), pp. 45–6, 50–4, 113–4, 120–3.

5 *Counter-Terrorism Powers: Reconciling Security and Liberty in an Open Society*, Cm. 6147 (Stationery Office, London, 2004).

6 *Anti-terrorism, Crime and Security Act 2001 Review: Report*, HC 100 (Stationery Office, London, 2003).

7 *Counter-Terrorism Powers.*

8 *Anti-terrorism, Crime and Security Act 2001 Review.*

9 John Major, *The Autobiography*, p. 222.

10 *Anti-terrorism, Crime and Security Act 2001 Review.*

11 A. W. Brian Simpson, *In the Highest Degree Odious* (Clarendon Press, Oxford, 1992), pp. 163, 189–90, 1.

12 Diana Mosley, 'The hard lessons from class 18B', *Evening Standard*, 17 December 1992.

13 David Cannadine, 'Bitter part of valour', *Observer*, 14 February 1993.

14 David Pannick QC, 'Human rights become first casualty of war', *The Times*, 4 December 2001.

15 Farber, *Lincoln's Constitution*, pp. 144, 19, 164–5.

16 Erica Harth (ed.), *Last Witnesses: reflections on the wartime internment of Japanese Americans* (Palgrave, Basingstoke, 2001), p. 283.

17 HC Home Affairs Committee, *Identity Cards*, Vol. 1, HC 130–1 (Stationery

Office, London, 2004).

18 Michael Burleigh, *The Third Reich: A New History* (Macmillan, London, 2000), pp. 43–4, 151–2.

19 Geoffery Lean, 'UK civil defence no longer exists', *Independent on Sunday*, 8 December 2002.

20 For details of the following discussion, see: http://www.ukresilience.info/ccact/index.htm

21 Margaret Thatcher, *The Downing Street Years*, p. 412.

22 James Joll, *The Anarchists* (Methuen, London, 1979), p. 110.

23 See: leaders, *The Times*, 17 and 20 February 1894.

24 Thatcher, *The Downing Street Years*, pp. 406–7.

25 Chester Stern and Sarah Oliver, 'The British ex-wife of Abu Hamza talks for the first time of her anguish', *Mail on Sunday*, 1 August 1999.

26 Gordon Thomas and Gareth Crickmer, 'Asylum seeker bomb alert', *Sunday Express*, 9 September 2001.

27 David Leppard, 'MI5 hunts two Al-Qaeda cells in Britain', *Sunday Times*, 23 November 2003.

28 *The Times*, news, 7 April 1883.

29 *The Times*, editorials, 10 April 1883.

30 Roy Jenkins, *The Chancellors* (Macmillan, London, 1998), pp. 53–4.

31 Roy Jenkins, *A Life at the Centre*, (Macmillan, London, 1991) pp. 393–4.

32 *Counter-Terrorism Powers*.

33 Amnesty International USA, *Threat and Humiliation: Racial Profiling, National Security, and Human Rights in the United States*, 14 September 2004.

34 *Counter-Terrorism Powers*.

35 Frances Gibb, 'Judges rule that terror suspects are being imprisoned illegally', *The Times*, 17 December 2004.

36 *The 9/11 Commission Report*, Final Report of the National Commission on Terrorist Attacks Upon the United States.

37 Thomas Balogh, 'The Apotheosis of the Dilettante', in Hugh Thomas (ed.), *The Establishment: A Symposium* (Anthony Blond, London, 1959), p. 87.

38 Corwin, *The President*, pp. 274–9.

39 Douglas Porch, *The French Secret Services: From the Dreyfus Affair to the Gulf War* (Macmillan, London, 1995), pp. 159–63.

40 Miller, *Plain Speaking*, p. 391.

41 House of Lords, House of Commons Joint Committee on Human Rights,

Review of Counter-terrorism Powers, HL 158/ HC 713 (Stationery Office, London, 2004).

42 For a discussion of the subject, see, for example: Richard Norton-Taylor, 'A weapon against ourselves', *Guardian*, 30 November 2004.

43 Peter Hennessy, 'The Lightning Flash on the Road to Baghdad', p. 77.

44 Boris Johnson, 'How not to run a country'.

45 Porch, *The French Secret Services*, pp. 31, 4–5.

46 Miller, *Plain Speaking*, pp. 391–2.

47 Graubard, *The Presidents*, pp. 415–8.

48 'Statement from Elizabeth Wilmshurst', Chatham House Press Notice, 27 February 2004.

49 Intelligence and Security Committee, *Annual Report 2003–2004*.

50 See: Andrew Blick, *People who live in the dark: the history of the special adviser in British politics* (Politico's, London, 2004).

51 Johnson, 'How not to run a country'.

5 Justification and Dissent

1 'The Prime Minister responds', *The Times*, 12 September 2001.

2 HC Debates, 18 March 2003, col. 768.

3 Harry S. Truman, *Years of Trial and Hope: 1946–1953* (Hodder and Stoughton, London, 1956), pp. 111–12.

4 Graubard, *The Presidents*, p. 140.

5 HC Debates, 14 July 2004, col. 1432.

6 Theodore Roosevelt, *An Autobiography* (Macmillan, New York, 1913), pp. 567, 569–70.

7 Cassar, *Asquith as War Leader*, p.33.

8 Harold Nicolson, *Diaries and Letters: 1939–1945* (Collins, London, 1967), diary entry for 3 August 1940, pp. 104–5.

9 Kampfner, *Blair's Wars*, pp. 383–4.

10 Nicolson, *Diaries and Letters: 1939–1945*, diary entry for 10 June 1941, p. 171; diary entry for 3 August 1940, pp. 104–5.

11 'The tyrant will soon be gone', *Sun*, 18 March 2003.

12 PASC Oral Evidence 11 May 2004.

13 Lyndon Baines Johnson, *The Vantage Point*, p. 384.

14 Ibid., pp. 384, 383.

15 PASC, Oral Evidence, 25 March 2004.

16 Bernard Ingham, *Kill the Messenger . . . Again* (Politico's, London, 2003), pp. 353, 296.

17 Hutton Inquiry, Hearing Transcripts, 28 August 2003, morning.

18 David Aaronovitch, 'We're not all peaceniks – but you wouldn't know it', *Guardian*, 18 March 2003.

19 Hutton Inquiry, Written Evidence, BBC/4/0131, Alastair Campbell, Prime Minister's Director of Communications and Strategy to Richard Sambrook, Director of News, British Broadcasting Corporation, 19 March 2003.

20 Alice Thomson, 'Why I point the finger at Campbell', *Daily Telegraph*, 18 March 2003.

21 Michael Meacher, 'This war on terrorism is bogus', *Guardian*, 6 September 2003.

22 David Aaronovitch, 'Has Meacher completely lost the plot?', *Guardian*, 9 September 2003.

23 Mick Hume, 'The conspiracy-theory cynics only confirm their political ignorance', *The Times*, 8 September 2003.

24 Michael Meacher, 'Cock-up not conspiracy', *Guardian*, 13 September 2003.

25 John Pilger, 'What Now?', *New Statesman*, 17 March 2003.

26 Richard J. Walton, *Henry Wallace, Harry Truman, and the Cold War* (Viking Press, New York, 1976), pp. 181, 250.

27 Mark Seddon, 'Iraq war is illegal, immoral and unnecessary', *Tribune*, 3 April 2003.

28 *Mirror*, 'Voice of the Daily Mirror', 18 March 2003.

29 'The text of the letters exchanged between Robin Cook and Tony Blair', *The Times*, 18 March 2003.

30 HC Debates, 17 March 2003, cols 726–8.

31 Philip Webster, 'Labour mutiny leaves Blair out on a limb', *The Times*, 27 February 2003.

32 'Size of a Labour rebellion', *Guardian*, 18 March 2003.

33 Philip Webster, 'Blair rallies the Commons for war', *The Times*, 19 March 2003.

34 'Beyond Debate', *Daily Telegraph*, 18 March 2003.

35 John Major, *The Autobiography*, pp. 223–4, 232.

36 'Beyond Debate', *Daily Telegraph*, 18 March 2003.

37 George Osborne, 'Could a Tory vote for Kerry?', *Spectator*, 28 February 2004.

38 'Honest politics', *The Times*, 8 March 2004.

39 HC Debates, 14 July 2004, cols 1438–9.

40 Paul Addison, *The Road to 1945* (Pimlico, London, 1994), pp. 159–60.

41 HC Debates, 18 March 2003, col. 787.

42 'The Founding Declaration of Respect – the Unity Coalition', 1 February 2004.

43 Mark Thomas, 'Mark Thomas has had enough of the SWP', *New Statesman*, 19 May 2003.

44 Nick Cohen, 'The lesson the left has never learnt', *New Statesman*, 21 July 2003.

45 Nick Cohen, 'Saddam's very own party', *New Statesman*, 7 June 2004.

46 Andrew Collingwood, letter published in *New Statesman*, 14 June 2004.

47 G. R. Searle, *The Quest for National Efficiency: A Study in British Politics and Political Thought, 1899 – 1914* (Ashfield Press, London, 1971), p. 34.

48 Addison, *The Road to 1945*, p. 13.

49 Neil Clark, 'Why left and right should unite and fight', *New Statesman*, 17 March 2003.

50 Mark Gilbert, 'Pacifist Attitudes to Nazi Germany, 1963–45', *Journal of Contemporary History*, Volume 27, July 1992, p.493.

51 Johnson, *The Vantage Point*, pp. 422, 427, 435.

Conclusion

1 Farber, *Lincoln's Constitution*, pp. 198–200.

2 Colville, *The Fringes of Power*, p. 145.

3 HC Debates, 26 January 2005, cols 305–9.

4 *Anti-terrorism, Crime and Security Act 2001 Review.*

5 See: Chapter 4.

6 Uncorrected Transcript, House of Commons Liaison Committee, Oral Evidence, 8 February 2005.

7 Phillipe Sands, 'How could attorney general support such a weak and dismal argument?', *Guardian*, 23 February 2005.

8 The 'Quadrapartite Committee' – a joint committee of the Defence, Foreign Affairs, International Development, and Trade and Industry committees. *Strategic Export Controls – Annual Report for 2002, Licensing Policy and Parliamentary Scrutiny*, HC 390 (Stationery Office, London, 2004).

Epilogue

1 Hennessy, *The Prime Minister*, pp. 137–8.

Index

Index

House of Commons 21, 29, 48, 71, 132,
138, 183, 185, 191, 209, 211–2, 216, 219
David Lloyd George delegates formal
House duties to Andrew Bonar Law
during WW1 8
debate of Butler Review 193
Defence Committee 68
Environmental Audit Committee 70
Foreign Affairs Committee 174, 49,
68–9
Clare Short appears before 46, 175
David Kelly appears before 71, 174
refused access to intelligence agencies
82
refused copies of 'Lessons Learnt' report
from Commanding Operations in
Iraq 73
Robin Cook appears before 42
Health Committee 70
Home Affairs Committee 68
publishes *The Accountability of the
Secret Services* report 83
International Development Committee
68
Leader of 42, 44
Liaison Committee 72, 80–1
Tony Blair appears before 41, 58
provides majority of members of British
Cabinet 20
rebellion on Iraq vote 56
Science and Technology Committee 68,
71
Speaker of 30
Trade and Industry Committee 68
House of Lords 121, 138
committees in 68
Judicial Committee 209
Law Lords rule against government opt-
out from European Convention on
Human Rights 139
Law Lords rule against government over

detaining terror suspects 209–10
House, 'Colonel' Edward Mandell
relationship with Woodrow Wilson
37–40
influences Wilson to intervene during
WW1 37
parts company with Wilson during
Versailles negotiations 38
Howard, Michael 192–3
Howe, Geoffrey 32
Huerto, General Victoriano 163
Human Rights Act (1998) 91, 121, 135,
209
Hume, Cardinal Basil 189
Hume, Mick 178
Hurd, Douglas (Lord) 58
not informed of Operation Desert Storm
until last moment 7
Hussein, Saddam 151, 175, 177, 181–3,
185, 193–4, 197, 199
Tony Blair indicates increased intoler-
ance towards 60
admission by Tony Blair that Iraq did
not have stockpiles of chemical or
biological weapons ready to deploy
165–6
fall of 191
Hutton, Lord
Hutton Inquiry 2, 69, 73, 158, 174,
176–7, 217
Jonathan Powell appears before 47–8
Tony Blair appears before 82, 172–3
Hutton Report 26, 52, 77, 79, 80

impeachment 60–1
Information Department 144
Ingham, Bernard 72, 175
Intelligence and Security Committee (ISC)
73, 81–3, 149, 151, 155–6, 214–5
Intelligence Services Act (1994) 151
International Criminal Court (ICC) 90–1
International Development Secretary 17, 44

245